IRELAND

JOHN RANELAGH

IRELAND

AN ILLUSTRATED HISTORY

New York
OXFORD UNIVERSITY PRESS
1981

To my mother and father

Frontispiece
Dunbrody Abbey,
Co. Wexford

© Telstore Ltd 1981
First published in Great Britain
by William Collins Sons & Co., Ltd., 1981
First published in the United States by Oxford University
Press, Inc., 1981

ISBN 0-19-520261-9
Library of Congress Catalog Number: 81-82689

Printing (last digit): 9 8 7 6 5 4 3 2 1

Printed in the United States of America

CONTENTS

PREFACE

I think this book was born with my father in January 1902. In many ways, it is, I believe, the book he would have liked to write and it certainly contains much that he observed and reflected upon. In the late 1960s, when I first decided that I would like to find out about Irish history and culture, I felt it was important to seek his permission: I knew that I would be entering his world and, as happened, seek to possess it myself. What I had not expected was that I would come to share many of his views and enthusiasms (although his dislike of W. B. Yeats I never understood). The joy that I experienced as I progressed with my research I will always be grateful to both my parents for, since it came from the voyage of discovery they encouraged me to undertake.

The story of Ireland is fundamentally one of a conquered people, who suffered one of the worst of all possible fates: they were made first to feel and then to believe themselves inferior. Tom Barry, the legendary 1919–23 IRA guerrilla leader, once told me that only about half his men could bring themselves to fire at the British Auxiliaries during his famous ambush at Kilmichael, because, when they actually faced naked British authority, they were frightened by their own temerity.

The native Irish that the Vikings and then the Anglo-Normans fought were a proud and sophisticated race, one of the oldest in Europe, with its origins in the Stone Age. Not until the time of the British Tudor monarchs at the beginning of the seventeenth century was Ireland politically subjugated, and even then the power of Irish Gaelic society was such that the majority of Irish people successfully maintained a separate cultural identity right up to the time of the Great Famine in the 1840s. The famine destroyed Gaelic Ireland. Those who did not die emigrated, and by the end of the nineteenth century not only was Ireland's total population half that of 1841, but also as many Irishmen lived outside Ireland as in it. In the same period, the number of Irish speakers fell by 90 per cent, and the peculiarly Gaelic way of life, which had survived centuries of persecution, was abandoned.

The grand banqueting hall of Cormac MacArt's third-century AD palace at Tara, depicted in the twelfth-century Book of Leinster

7

The generation which provided the rebels of 1916 was the last to have a coherent conception of what being Irish meant. But already, these rebels were an unpopular minority in Ireland, and the IRA in 1919–21 only maintained itself by demonstrating that it was prepared to be as terrifying to those who betrayed it as to those who opposed it. This is not to diminish the achievement of the men of 1916 and immediately afterwards. They fought against enormous odds, often with great courage and compassion, and to the point that it seemed their efforts might be crowned with victory. That they were, by their own lights, beaten was perhaps the fault of their idealistic ambition for a completely free and independent Ireland, and perhaps because (how easy it is to forget this today) they were fighting the forces of the greatest Empire the world has known. They were also opposed by the might of the Roman Catholic Church — excommunicated for opposing what the Church considered the lawful British authority in Ireland.

Throughout this book I have tried to correct widespread misconceptions about the key events in Irish history, believing that a more accurate understanding of what really happened is the most effective way of counteracting the sometimes lethal myths about the past which continue to bedevil the people of Ireland. I have tried to bring out two main themes. First, that Irish history is not one of sectarian conflict: that the Church from the late eighteenth century onwards consistently sided with British government and against Irish nationalists. From time to time, sectarian divisions and religious considerations have been of prime importance, as with Cromwell and, incredibly in our own time, in Northern Ireland today. But this is unusual, and the proper importance belongs to social and economic differences (especially the ownership of land), and to the consistent appeal of an ill-defined national ideal which for some time in the eighteenth and nineteenth centuries was welcomed by all Irishmen, Protestant and Catholic, English-speaking and Irish-speaking. Indeed, in the nineteenth century, the leaders of Irish national movements tended to be northern Irish Protestants.

Secondly, the importance of Ireland's own cultural heritage to Irish history has never been properly appreciated. Gaelic culture — its laws, its social structure, its literature, its beautiful artifacts — has been to the Irish people a source of constant and justifiable pride. And, surviving in various forms for over two thousand years, it provided an argument for and a justification of what Irishmen termed patriotism and their governors called treachery, fraud and cowardice. The strength of this appeal was never understood by the government or the Church. Bishop Moriarty of Kerry said when condemning the Fenians in 1867:

PREFACE

*Fenianism, with all its fraud and falsehood, with all its braggart cowardice,
and with that hatred of religion which marked its every utterance,
found sympathy and raised strange hopes in the Irish poor. And unfortunately,
the Irish poor means the Irish people.*

I have concentrated on the personalities of Irish history rather than the economics, since I am convinced that men, not money, play the single greatest part in events. I have also used popular ballads to highlight historical figures because, in a country where oral tradition is so powerful, songs and ballads have often coloured the Irish people's perceptions of their past and their heroes.

I owe many acknowledgements, only some of which I can mention here. To my mother I am grateful for the strength of her confidence, and her advice on much of the poetry and literature I have used. My sister Bawn, Maire de Paor, Deirdre McMahon, Michael Jones and George Cardona all read my text, making corrections and suggestions not all of which I heeded but for all of which I am deeply grateful. June Leech took on the frustrating burden of photographic research. I should also like to acknowledge with gratitude Michael Shaw's enthusiastic championing of my wish to write this book. Finally and most of all, I must thank my wife Elizabeth. This book could not have been written without her advice, encouragement and forbearance. She listened to my ramblings, making more sense of them than I thought possible, and painstakingly went over the text, making chaos clear.

GRANTCHESTER 1980

9

1

EARLY IRELAND
AND HER PEOPLE

Very few things happen at the right time, and the rest do not happen at all;
the conscientious historian will correct these defects. ·

HERODOTUS, THE HISTORIES

Legend holds that St Patrick banished snakes from Ireland in the fifth century AD. In fact the reason why there are no snakes there is that for ten thousand years Ireland has been an island. It was separated from the land mass of Europe at the end of the last ice age, before a variety of plant and animal life common in Europe could reach it. Even earlier, the shape of Ireland's landscape was laid down. Many of the country's most famous land forms owe their existence to the violence of volcanic action — the mountains of Mourne and other ranges were formed some seventy-five million years ago as molten lava cooled — or to the brutal power of ice which two hundred thousand years ago sculpted drumlins, while glaciers gouged out deep valleys like the Gap of Dunloe.

Between the ice ages, Ireland variously experienced tropical forests, tundra and open vegetation. Animal life flourished. The Irish giant deer, with its antlers spanning over nine feet, elephant-like hairy mammoths, hyenas, wolves and foxes all lived there between about 31000 BC and 8500 BC, just before the final cold spell which lasted five hundred years. Man may also have lived in Ireland at this time, but the evidence is unreliable, depending upon one human skeleton found in a cave in Co. Waterford which seems to date from around 9000 BC. In any event, this individual could not have survived the last bout of freezing cold, although some alpine plants managed to do so on the higher mountains not completely covered by ice. To the present day, mountain avens, mountain sorrell and blue gentians can be seen on Ben Bulben in Co. Sligo and on the hills of the Burren in Co. Clare.

As ice melted, the sea level gradually rose: Ireland lost its land link with Britain and became an island separated from the European continent. Britain's land bridge to Europe lasted much longer, crossing what are now the southern reaches of the North Sea to Belgium, the Netherlands and north-western Germany. Erskine Childers, in his famous novel *The Riddle of the Sands*, used the fact that the North Sea is still especially shallow between East Anglia and the Low Countries. With an eye to the tides and a leap of imagination he suggested that an army could rapidly move across sandbanks and invade England.

Erskine Childers (1870–1922)

Before the rising sea submerged these land connections, the first humans came across them to settle in the British Isles. They spread through England, Wales and Scotland, and the earliest people probably crossed to Ireland on the land bridge from Scotland. When this too had been submerged, around 6700 BC, Ireland was left alone, facing the Atlantic. Her western mountains and plains had braved thousands of years of gales and rain which washed away the soil. The first settlers found a country whose principal geographical characteristics were already formed. An eighth of her twenty million acres were hills and mountains, usually bared to rocky inhospitability by ice, wind and rain. Much of the rest was wooded, but by 3000 BC another eighth had become bog as trees and other vegetation collapsed into lakes and streams. Of the remaining fifteen million acres most was good, productive land, although often mixed with bad. Only in the twentieth century has much more than half of Ireland's acreage been used fully as the peat bogs have been developed, afforestation policies followed, and land improvement and reclamation schemes adopted. But eight and a half thousand years ago, before mass human habitation ravaged what nature had left, Ireland abounded with lakes, trees and rivers, providing sanctuary for animal life and food and shelter for the first Irishmen.

It is not surprising that such a rich land should produce nature poetry unique in Europe. Through the centuries the Irishman has especially delighted in his country's beauty, in its detail of sound and shape and colour, as in the ancient Irish 'Song of Summer':

> *The harp of the forest sounds music,*
> *The sail gathers — perfect peace;*
> *Colour has settled on every height,*
> *Haze on the lake of full waters.*

The peat-bog is as the raven's coat,
The loud cuckoo bids welcome,
The speckled fish leaps —
Strong is the bound of the swift warrior.

A flock of birds settles
In the midst of meadows,
The green field rustles,
Wherein is a brawling white stream.

A wild longing is on you to race horses,
The ranked host is ranged around:
A bright shaft has been shot into the land,
So that the water-flag is gold beneath it.

A timorous, tiny, persistent little fellow
Sings at the top of his voice,
The lark sings clear tidings:
Surpassing summer-time of delicate hues!

The first significant human remains in Ireland, dating from 6600 BC, were found at Mount Sandel, Co. Londonderry. Little is known of these Mesolithic (Middle Stone Age) settlers, but they probably came from Scotland and ultimately from Scandinavia. They were nomadic hunter–gatherers, subsisting on hunting and fishing for over two thousand years before the knowledge of domestication of animals and cultivation of plants became widespread. Many Mesolithic settlements have been found, concentrated in north-eastern Ireland, particularly in Co. Antrim. They are usually sited along the coast or on the banks of rivers and lakes, and findings have mostly consisted of rubbish dumps together with chipped flint and stone implements. Only at Mount Sandel have the remains of Mesolithic buildings been discovered by recent excavations, revealing hearths, pits and the post holes of huts. The huts were round, about twenty feet in diameter, with central fire places, and were probably winter dwellings more substantial than those used at other times of the year. Nothing is known of these first Irishmen's language and social system, and after about two and a half thousand years' undisturbed habitation, they seem to have been assimilated by a second group of immigrants.

In the middle of the fourth millennium BC, Neolithic (Late Stone Age) farmers arrived in Ireland. In comparison to the Mesolithic settlers, these newcomers were sophisticated and technically advanced, using polished stone tools to plant and till crops and keeping herds of cattle, pigs and sheep. They originated in the Middle East and were gradually forced to emigrate as expanding population in their homelands increased the pressure for new farming lands. They had moved through the Balkans around 5000 BC, pushing west along the Mediterranean coast into France and Spain and then northwards to the Low Countries and Britain. They probably sailed to Ireland in skin-covered boats across the eastern Atlantic from Spain, Portugal and Brittany. They brought with them their own livestock and seeds, and the art of pottery, decorating their pots and shaping them with round bottoms for storing food, and heavier flat bottoms for cooking. At Lough Gur in Co. Limerick, archaeologists have discovered a major early Neolithic settlement which reveals a wealth of information about the way of life of the first people who tilled the soil in Ireland. Houses were built with stone foundations, some round, some rectangular, with wooden frame walls filled with earthen turves. Polished stone axes with wooden handles were used to cut trees and hoe the ground as forests and vegetation were cleared away to make fields. Picks were made from the antlers of deer, and bones used to make needles, awls and other domestic implements for spinning wool for clothing and warmth. Flint arrow and spear heads show that these people probably hunted birds as well, and the bone and stone beads and bracelets that have been found show that they were as interested in their appearance as we are today. They even set up factories to produce their stone axes, but the most impressive remains of the Neolithic farmers are the massive stone megaliths and dolmens they raised for their dead.

The Neolithic immigrants had been settled in Ireland for several hundreds of years before they took to building these monuments. Over four thousand megaliths have so far been mapped. The earliest date from about 3000 BC and have a forecourt or central open court with long earth-covered stone galleries leading from it, in which the dead were placed together with various artifacts — presumably their personal property — thus indicating that their religion involved belief in an afterlife. Over three hundred of these court-graves have so far been discovered, mostly in the northern half of the country. Interestingly, court-graves have also been discovered on the Isle of Man and in western Scotland, suggesting that court-grave Irishmen may have emigrated there. Another group of Neolithic Irishmen with a different sort of megalith, the passage-grave, may have reached Wales and Anglesey.

The earliest Irish passage-graves date from about 2800 BC. Over two hundred have been identified. Unlike the court-graves, however, passage-graves are not concentrated in the north of Ireland but along the eastern coast and inland. Similar tombs dating one thousand years earlier have been excavated in Spain, Portugal and Brittany, indicating the route of this group of Neolithic emigrants. In Ireland, they generally built their passage-graves on hilltops, covering them completely with earth. They consist of a long stone passage leading to a circular burial chamber, its walls frequently decorated with elaborate spirals and zig-zags. The dead were cremated, and the bones and ashes placed in the burial chamber as with the court-grave people, together with pottery, beads and tools. The finest passage-grave of all, dating from 2500 BC, is at Newgrange in Co. Meath. The extent and intricacy of its stone carvings suggest that some of the patterns had a religious significance, possibly even depicting highly stylized human faces and figures. Newgrange was designed by its builders so that the sun could enter the chamber only once a year, around Midwinter Day, suggesting that the passage-grave people may have had a knowledge of astronomy and involved the sun in their worship.

From the size and positioning of excavated passage-grave sites, archaeologists have been able to suggest even more about the society of their constructors. Although the graves are grouped in cemeteries and used communally, the larger ones seem to have been the repositories of chieftains and their families. Around large graves, less impressive ones varying in size and shape were placed and there were still smaller burials for folk of the humblest sort. Newgrange, Knowth and other Neolithic sites on the banks of the river Boyne reveal these features of hierarchic social order preserved in death. More than this we do not know. Who these people were, where they originated, how they worshipped and learnt the practised skills required to build their monumental tombs still remain some of the most intriguing questions of Ireland's prehistoric past.

Dolmens were built during the Neolithic era, probably by the court-grave people. They were single-chamber tombs, usually with standing stones acting as a support for a large capstone, which was then covered with earth and rocks to form a mound. Some mounds still remain, but most that survive are now bare of earth and stand revealed as impressive monuments to the engineering skills of the Stone Age: the Browne's Hill dolmen in Co. Carlow has a massive granite capstone weighing approximately 100 tons; raising it into position even today would be a challenging task.

The Neolithic monuments which abound in Ireland naturally lent themselves to later tales and lore, and to the present day in parts of Ireland people believe that fairies and leprechauns inhabit these ancient sites. Indeed in 1958 at Belmullet, Co. Mayo, during a government land improvement scheme, workers refused to level a

*Newgrange, Co.
Meath: the interior of
the burial chamber
dating from around
2500 BC*

PHYSICAL FEATURES AND PREHISTORIC SITES

Mahn Head

Tory Is.

Rathlin Is.
Fair Head

Aran Is.

L.Foyle
Mt. Sandel

Antrim Mts.

Bann

L.Neagh

L.Strangford

Donegal Bay

L.Erne

Sligo Bay
Ben Bulben

Killala Bay

L.Allen

Upper L.Erne

*Mourne
Mts.*

L.Carlingford
Dundalk Bay

Achill Is.

Clew Bay

*Partry
Mts.*

L.Gara

L.Mask

Newgrange

Lambay Is.

L.Corrib

L.Ree

Knowth
Tara

Howth Head
Dublin Bay

Galway Bay

Shannon

*Slieve
Bloom*

*Bog of
Allen*

Liffey

Aran Isles

The Burren

L.Derg

Barrow

*Wicklow
Mts.*

Nore

Browne's Hill

Slaney

Tralee Bay

Galtee Mts.

Suir

Gt. Blasket Is.
Slieve Mish

*Knockmealdown
Mts.*

Dingle Bay

L.Gur

Carnsore Pt.

Valentia Is.

Gap of Dunloe

Lee

Youghal Bay

Old Head of Kinsale

Bantry Bay
Clonakilty Bay

Fastnet Rock

Cape Clear

Eighth-century BC beaten bronze shield found near Lough Gur, Co. Limerick

'fairy' mound and succeeded in maintaining it as part of the improvement scheme. Gaelic storytellers two thousand years earlier described dolmens as the beds of Diarmuid and Grainne, the doomed lovers fleeing from a jealous royal suitor, who provide us with the tragic theme later refined outside Ireland as the tale of Tristan and Isolde.

After the Neolithic people, the next series of immigrants brought the Bronze Age to Ireland. Metal working of copper, gold, silver and lead had been developed in the Near East around 3500 BC, and experimentation with alloys led to the discovery of bronze in the later third millennium BC. The toughness of bronze made complex casting possible and also provided a harder cutting edge for tools and weapons. In the period before 2000 BC new migrations took place in Europe, and the first metal-working migrants reached Ireland as the second millennium BC dawned. A variety of distinctive peoples arrived at this time, distinguished by different burial customs and artifacts, but once again apparently mingling with Neolithic Irishmen and ultimately absorbing them. These newcomers established themselves throughout the country and immediately prospected for metallic ores, finding a plentiful supply. Indeed, in modern times whenever copper deposits have been mined, evidence of prehistoric mining has usually been uncovered. The Bronze Age lasted in Ireland until about 700 BC and gave the country its first hoard of wealth. Bronze Irish axes, some with intricate decorations, were exported to Britain and Scandinavia. Beautiful gold neck ornaments with intricate, geometric decorations — finer than anything yet discovered on the European continent — were produced from gold either imported or panned from the gravels of Wicklow rivers. With some justice, these are regarded as Ireland's first indigenous works of art. Judging by the workmanship and materials of golden brooches, rings and other artifacts excavated from Bronze Age Irish graves, these people had extensive trading connections reaching as far as Egypt and the Baltic.

The burial practices of the Bronze Age men were not as elaborate as their Neolithic predecessors, although they often used the same sites. Instead of the communal megalith burials, the new settlers generally buried their dead separately, sometimes after cremating them. They also built impressive stone circles, though none as big as Stonehenge or as extensive as the stone sentinels of Carnac in Brittany. The Irish stone circles probably varied in purpose, some being for religious and ritualistic use, others perhaps to facilitate astronomical measurements. Single standing stones were also first erected during the Bronze Age, perhaps as territorial markers, and continued to be built into the early Christian era some thirteen hundred years later. Many of these stones still stand, often marked with crosses and

inscriptions, cultural refinements which only arrived in Ireland in the fourth century AD. By then the next wave of settlers were established.

Exactly when the Celts started coming to Ireland and whether they came in peace or as conquerors is not clear. Two groups of Celts populated the British Isles, the Gaels and the Brythoni. The Brythoni settled in Britain and the Gaels occupied Ireland and some of Scotland. Many travelled from Britain as well as directly from the continent of Europe and settled in Ireland in large numbers. They brought with them the Iron Age which had begun some three hundred years earlier in central and eastern Europe. Iron swords were stronger than bronze, and iron ploughs dug deep and were long-lasting. The Bronze Age settlers had never been slow to adopt new metallurgical discoveries, so it is difficult to be certain at which point they were superseded by the Celts' iron culture, but by 500 BC Ireland was probably a completely Celtic country enjoying the widespread use of iron implements.

The Celts themselves seem to have originally come from the lands around the Caspian sea, migrating from there in stages in all directions. Sociologists and linguists today have even detected similarities between the Celtic languages, laws and customs and those of the Hindus in India. In fact, much more is known about the Celts than about any other prehistoric group, and the Gaels provide the richest surviving treasury of this period of cultural activity outside Greece and Rome.

Drombeg stone circle, Co. Cork, has been dated to between 153 BC and 127 AD. When it was excavated in 1957–8 the cremated body of a youth was found. The axis of the circle faces south-west towards sunset at the winter solstice.

The first historical mention of the Celts dates from the sixth century BC when they are recorded as being in France and Spain. The historian Herodotus, writing in the fifth century BC, placed them along the Danube and in the Pyrenees and described the Celts as one of two western European peripheral peoples. To this geographical fact Celtic language and culture owed its survival right up to modern times in Ireland, Brittany and parts of Britain. By coming to live on the European periphery (and especially in Ireland) these Celts managed largely to avoid the assimilation into the Roman Empire that befell the Celts in France, Spain and parts of Germany, and later to escape the ravages of the Huns, Goths and Vandals in the Dark Ages after the fall of Rome. As a result, more of their artifacts and more information about them have survived. Because of the survival of Celtic languages (principally Gaelic), the Celts of Wales, Scotland, Ireland and Brittany have always been aware of their forebears. Gaelic remained the dominant language in Ireland until the beginning of the eighteenth century when English began to take over, and it took the awful experience of the famines of the 1840s and 1850s together with emigration and new educational policies finally to bring the widespread use of the language to an end.

From about the same time as Herodotus was writing his history, the earliest known written evidence of Ireland and its people has come to us from a Carthaginian sailor, Himilco, who went on a voyage of exploration and discovery along the western coast of Europe. Having sailed through the Pillars of Hercules (Straits of Gibraltar), he ventured northwards up the coast of Spain to the Bay of Biscay and beyond. He encountered Celts sailing 'at high speed' in coracles of skins sewn together — from the description given, they were made in almost exactly the same way as Aran islanders still make theirs — and he learnt of 'the Sacred Island (so the ancients called it). This lies amid the waves, abounding in verdure, and the race of the Hierni dwell there widespread.' By the time the Greek geographer Strabo, a contemporary of Julius and Augustus Caesar in the first century BC, wrote about Gaelic Ireland, much more was conjectured — as his unflattering description makes clear. The Gaels, he said, were

> *more savage than the Britons, feed on human flesh and are enormous eaters. They deem it commendable to devour their deceased fathers as well as openly to be connected not only with other women but also with their own mothers and sisters. But we relate these things, perhaps, without having trustworthy authorities . . . The natives are wholly savage and lead a wretched existence because of the cold.*

The Gaelic Celts in fact possessed a highly sophisticated society, and they rapidly made their mark on Ireland, or 'Erin' as they called it. They built massive stone forts around the coast and in the interior on hills, strongly suggesting a warlike, dangerous society. Their forts were imposing circular ditched and walled constructions, some encompassing as much as forty acres, inside which lived whole farming communities. Fields and grazing land were spread all round. Sometimes, as at Tara, Co. Meath, these forts were built around Bronze Age grave mounds, thus indicating that the Gaels accepted and, perhaps, assimilated older religious customs. Another type of settlement was the crannog, an artificial island built up of earth and stone in lakes and marshes, upon which a small defended community or family would live, farming and grazing on fields around the shore. Dating from the Bronze Age, these crannogs were inhabited by native Irishmen into the seventeenth century. A recent excavation of a crannog in Lough Gara, Co. Sligo, provided detailed information about the construction and lifestyle of a succession of early Gaelic families. On the island was built a large circular house made up of wooden

A reconstructed crannog, showing the defensive nature of these settlements which were first developed in Ireland during the Bronze Age and continued in use until the seventeenth century.

poles interwoven with wicker and then mud-plastered, capped by a roof of thatch. The floor was paved with large flat stones covered with a layer of gravel, and in the centre stood an open hearth for the cooking fire. Many iron implements were also found, including knives and pans, bronze cooking pots, and an animal yoke Cattle raising was the principal occupation.

Gaelic society was tribal in organization, linked by a common culture, language and religion, but without any political unity. Only once, a century before the Norman-English first arrived in Ireland, were the different Gaelic tribes united under a High King, Brian Boru, and then only for his lifetime. The Gaels differed from other Celtic tribes in maintaining the system of kingship for so long, but in other respects they were similar in customs and practices to the Gauls — the Celts of France.

Not until the Christian era did Celtic scribes and monks begin to write down their laws, tales and customs, but nevertheless much is known about the Celts from Roman sources. Julius Caesar in his books on the Gallic Wars gives one of the most valuable accounts of Celtic society. According to him, they were divided into three social groups, Druids, Warriors and Farmers. Druids were expected to undergo twenty years of study to learn the oral traditions, laws and religious practices of their people. They were the repositories of Celtic knowledge and wisdom and the teachers of succeeding generations. Caesar wrote:

LEFT]
The Turoe stone, an intricately carved granite boulder, four feet high, dates from the first century AD. It originally stood on the site of a Gaelic fort.

RIGHT]
The Janus-like stone figure from Caldragh graveyard, Boa Island, Co. Fermanagh, is attributed to the Iron Age and was probably inspired by a Gaelic cult's worship of the head — regarded by the Celts as the residence of the soul.

It is said that they commit to memory immense amounts of poetry, and so some of them continue their studies for twenty years. They consider it improper to commit their studies to writing ... They also have much knowledge of the stars and their motion, of the size of the world and of the earth, of natural philosophy, and of the powers and spheres of action of the immortal gods, which they discuss and hand down to their young students.

They were the priests of Celtic religion (to which, Caesar tells us, the Celts were much addicted), conducting human and animal sacrifices and teaching of an afterlife. Celts believed in the immortal soul which, the Druids taught, passed into another body after death. They also believed that the god of the underworld, Dis, was the common father of mankind.

The names of over four hundred different Celtic gods are known from Roman and Greek sources. Most of these can be identified as local deities, but approximately one-quarter of them are more widespread and appear to have been generally worshipped. By all accounts, the Celts were fondest of the god of arts and crafts, the patron of traders and travellers, whose Greek equivalent was Hermes. The Roman poet Lucan stated that the three principal gods worshipped by the Celts were Esus (Hermes), Taranis and Teutates, each of which can still be traced in the Irish language. The Irish forename, Eoghan, means 'son of Esus'. 'Torann', the Irish word for thunder, comes from Taranis, indicating that this was the Celtic Zeus. Teutates was most probably the name given to each tribe's god; it comes from the same linguistic root as 'tuath', the Irish for 'tribe'. In the Gaelic sagas warriors frequently take oaths in which they pledge themselves, swearing 'by the god by whom my tribe swears'. Lug was the name of another important god, probably of harvests and fertility, and has lived on in the place-names Lugudunum, Laon, Leon, Loudon and Lyons in France, Leiden in the Netherlands and Liegnitz in Germany. In Ireland the Gaels celebrated Lug on 1 August, and this observance can be traced to Garland Sunday today.

Wells, streams, rivers and trees were religiously respected by the Celts, and some, like the river Boyne, were even regarded as divine. In common with many of their contemporaries, the Celts also worshipped the earth itself, in female form, as a mother, defender and provider. Certain animals — bulls, bears, boars and horses — enjoyed divine representation, and in the great Gaelic saga of the *Tain* the vestiges of the bull-god can be seen in the supernaturally endowed Brown Bull and White Bull.

For centuries the Celts harassed the legions of Rome, constantly threatening the borders of the Roman Empire in Europe, challenging Roman authority in

France, Spain and Germany. Strabo, writing of the Celts of Gaul, described them as 'madly fond of war, high-spirited and quick to battle, but otherwise straightforward and not of evil character'. Another first century BC Greek historian, Diodorus Siculus, who wrote a history of the world in forty volumes, managed to give detailed descriptions of the Gauls: 'Physically the Gauls are terrifying in appearance with deep-sounding and very harsh voices. In conversation they use few words and speak in riddles ... They are boasters and threateners and given to bombastic self-dramatization, and yet they are quick of mind with good natural ability for learning.' Diodorus' account of Gaullish Celtic warriors in battle is remarkably close to the descriptions of the Gaels in the Irish sagas:

> For their journeys and in battle they use two-horse chariots, the chariot carrying both charioteer and chieftain. When they meet with cavalry in the battle they cast their javelins at the enemy and then, descending from the chariot, do battle with their swords. Some of them so far despise death that they descend to do battle unclothed except for a girdle. They bring into battle as their attendants freemen chosen from among the poorer classes, whom they use as charioteers and shield-bearers in battle. When the armies are drawn up in battle-array they are wont to advance before the battle-line and to challenge the bravest of their opponents to single combat, at the same time brandishing before them their arms so as to terrify their foe. And when someone accepts their challenge to battle, they loudly recite the deeds of valour of their ancestors and proclaim their own valorous quality, at the same time abusing and making little of their opponent and generally attempting to rob him beforehand of his fighting spirit. They cut off the heads of enemies slain in battle and attach them to the necks of their horses ... and they nail up these first fruits upon their houses.

These then were the Celts, the Gaelic tribes of which were to dominate Ireland for over thirteen hundred years until Viking incursions challenged their supremacy. But Gaelic culture and social practices remained widespread right into the eighteenth century, two thousand years after the Gaels first established themselves in Ireland at the end of the Bronze Age.

2

GAELIC IRELAND

I invoke the land of Ireland.
Much-coursed be the fertile sea;
Fertile be the fruit-strewn mountain;
Fruit-strewn be the showery wood;
Showery be the river of waterfalls;
Of waterfalls be the lake of deep pools;
Deep-pooled be the hill-top well;
A well of tribes be the assembly;
An assembly of kings be Tara.

AMERGIN (attr.)

The wealth of Gaelic Ireland has always been a source of profound pleasure and pride to Irishmen, for it was their Gaelic ancestors who made Ireland legendary throughout the world, first as a source of beautiful golden objects and ornaments, and later as a seat of learning and holy men. The Gaels themselves had a strong sense of the past, as is shown in their sagas and by the fact that even after they were converted to Christianity, Gaelic monks were still able to overcome their abhorrence of paganism and set down in writing for the first time the records of their pre-Christian forbears. To these monks scholars owe a debt of eternal gratitude. From their writings we have a clear account of the political and cultural organization of Ireland in the centuries before and during the Dark Ages.

Gaelic society was hierarchic, being divided into three broad groups of aristocrats, freemen and slaves. The aristocratic group included not only tribal kings (*ri*), but also warriors (*flaithi*), judges (*breitheamh* or 'brehons'), druids (*draoi*), poets (*fili*), historians (*seanchaidhe*) and a number of professional advisers (*aos dana*) who shared with the king the duties of organizing feasts and sacred occasions, of looking after the well-being of the tribe (*tuath*) and applying the law. By the fourth century AD there were five leading Gaelic kingdoms roughly corresponding to the provinces of Ulster, Leinster, Munster, Connaught and the counties of Meath and

23

THE GAELIC KINGDOMS

From time to time the number of kingdoms changed with the fluctuating fortunes of the leading clans. Munster was the Eoganachta kingdom; Ulster the O'Neills; Leinster was ruled by the MacMurroghs; Connaught by the O'Connors; and Meath by the southern O'Neill family.

Tara, Co. Meath. An aerial view showing the central Neolithic forts both surrounded by a defensive perimeter wall and ditch

Westmeath, with about 150 lesser ones variously grouped in allegiance beneath them. However, unlike the Roman system where centralized control was exercised by an emperor from his capital, Gaelic kings depended upon their own personal qualities for authority, and even a High King (*Ard ri*) had no rights apart from those of honour and respect outside his own tribal kingdom. Lesser kings and chiefs would follow a particular High King and his successors, would give hostages to him as a token of dependence, and would be bound to provide help in time of war. Later, in the Christian era, some High Kings laid claim to sovereignty over the whole of Ireland, but such claims were unknown during the first thousand years of Gaelic settlement. Of the other two social groups, freemen (*cele*) were the farmers and merchants. They enjoyed a client relationship with their king or one of his nobles, paying rent in return for protection and cattle. The number of cattle a tribe owned was the principal mark of wealth in this society since land was held in common. Slaves (*mug*), of which there seem never to have been very many, were usually those unfortunates captured in war.

The two main centres of Gaelic Ireland were Emain Macha, now Navan Fort near Armagh, and Tara in the valley of the Boyne in Co. Meath. Tara was a fortified hill settlement and burial ground, commanding an expansive view. It was already an ancient religious site by the time the Gaels took it over, and it became the royal seat of the kings of Meath and ultimately of the High King of Ireland. In the third century AD the High King Cormac MacArt built at Tara schools for the study of literature, law and military science, and an enormous palace which the Book of Leinster nine hundred years later described as having a banqueting hall 700 feet long. By the time of St Patrick, two hundred years after Cormac, Tara was principally a religious centre and its hold upon popular Irish imagination was firmly established. In 1798 thousands of Irish rebels spontaneously assembled there as if possessed by some ancestral memory. In 1843 one of the biggest Irish gatherings in history met at Tara to hear Daniel O'Connell, the man who had won Catholic emancipation, hurl fury at the government in his campaign to end the union between Britain and Ireland. Charles Gavan Duffy, an Irish journalist later knighted for his services in Australian politics, was at O'Connell's Tara meeting, and estimated that the number of people there 'is supposed to have reached between 500,000 and 750,000 persons. It was ordinarily spoken of as a million, and was certainly a muster of men such as never before assembled in one place in Ireland in peace or war.' Priests celebrated Mass in the open on hills that had centuries earlier been the sites of Druid rites and sacrifices. The nineteenth-century Irish poet Thomas Moore felt the pull of Tara, seeing it as the once pulsing pride of Ireland:

25

The harp that once through Tara's halls
The soul of music shed,
Now hangs as mute on Tara's walls
As if that soul were fled.
So sleeps the pride of former days,
So glory's thrill is o'er;
And hearts that once beat high for praise
Now feel that pulse no more.

Gaelic society, based as it was on local allegiances, remained a series of tribal monarchies right into the Middle Ages. From time to time the number of leading kingdoms changed as some contracted or expanded with the fluctuating fortunes of the leading dynasties. In the fifth century AD there were eight major kingdoms. Three centuries later there were seven. They were all protected from the misfortune of invading Roman legions and later marauding European tribes by the barrier of the Irish Sea. As a result, uniquely in Ireland was preserved an ancient Iron Age culture removed, museum-like, from the mainstream of European development. But the longevity of Gaelic culture was also due in no small part to their refined social organization encapsulated in the Brehon Laws.

The brehons (judges) held a high social position. They were the interpreters of law and custom, and they spent years of study memorizing Gaelic law. For until St Patrick in 438 AD reputedly ordered that the laws and customs of the pagan Gaels be written down this knowledge was passed on orally from one generation of brehons to the next. The laws applied equally to all: no king, noble or brehon was above them. They regulated every aspect of communal life, civil, military and criminal, enumerating the duties, obligations, rights and privileges of each class of society from the king down to the slave. There were detailed rules governing the management of property and contemporary industries such as building, brewing, bee-keeping, and milling, as well as rules for the relations between fathers and sons, masters and servants, rulers and subjects.

From the Brehon Laws comes our knowledge of the system of fosterage which the Gaels employed as a method of preventing tribal and family conflict. Sometimes foster parents were paid — the amount varying with the social ranks of those involved. But sometimes fostering was an indication of friendship. Boys stayed with their foster parents until the age of seventeen and girls until fourteen. Boys were taught the martial arts, how to ride and to swim, and how to play board games before they returned to their natural parents. Children were bound to support and look after their foster parents in old age, and the ties of fosterage remained close. The system served to help keep peaceful relations within and between tribes. When the legendary Gaelic hero, Cuchulain, in single combat slew his foster-brother Ferdia, the event is one of the tragic climaxes of the saga of the *Tain*.

In matters of crime and injury the laws rarely resorted to capital punishment (an omission which the Elizabethans later considered barbarous), preferring instead an elaborate system of compensation. The purpose of this was to avoid long vendettas and to establish the law as the preferred arbitration procedure. Victims of physical injury were entitled to 'sick maintenance' from the culprit, who had to pay not only a penalty but also the complete costs — lodging, food, and medical — of his victim's cure. In the case of murder, a fine was paid to the dead man's family, double that laid down for manslaughter. Many modifying circumstances had to be taken into account: the reasons for the murder; social rank; provocation etc., so the brehon had to possess not only considerable legal knowledge but also great diplomatic skill. The murderer of a freeman, for example, paid an amount (in cattle) which could be anything between one and thirty head depending on his own social position, plus twenty-one head if the murder was not malicious, and twice this amount if it was. If the culprit did not pay his family were held to be liable, and if they did not want to meet the fine, then they had to hand over the offender to the victim's family. Only then could the offender be executed, but he could also be used or sold as a slave.

Grianan of Aileach, Co. Donegal. A late fifth- to twelfth-century fortress of the Gaelic O'Neills on the site of an Iron Age hill fort

Under the laws divorce was allowed freely, and marriages could be ended by common consent with wives enjoying the same rights as their husbands. But while husbands could take secondary wives, a wife who committed adultery could customarily be burnt alive. In *Cormac's Glossary*, an encyclopaedia of Gaelic history believed to date from the ninth century AD, we learn that when Murni of the Fair Neck ran away and married Cumal who was killed in battle soon afterwards, her father, refusing to recognize the legitimacy of his daughter's marriage, urged his people to burn her. But Murni, who was pregnant, had taken refuge with the hero Conn and no one dared face him. The son that Murni bore was to become one of the great figures of Gaelic literature, Finn MacCool.

Among other noteworthy features of the Brehon Laws, one was the practice of fasting, whereby a plaintiff of lower social standing could secure the right to arbitration from a defendant of higher rank by fasting outside the defendant's door. Another was the method of royal succession. The system of primogeniture did not operate. Instead, kings (and also chiefs) were always elected from among the members of the royal family by the freemen of the tribe. Any freeborn man in the family was eligible — the king's son, brother, cousin, nephew etc. Only two conditions had to be met: the man elected had to be free of all physical and mental blemishes, and his father and grandfather had to have been nobles. As a result, when kings were defeated in battle, they were often blinded with a pin jabbed into their eyes so as to ensure their complete subjection.

The Brehon principles of compensation, honour, broad equality under the law and, within limits, democratic procedures were in our own century to be briefly reattempted by the nationalist Dail courts from 1919 to 1921. But the laws were not the only feature of Gaelic life which later generations in Ireland were to revive and revere. The ancient Gaelic sagas not only inspired Douglas Hyde, Standish O'Grady, W. B. Yeats and the Celtic revivalists of the nineteenth century, but also provided later Irish revolutionaries with examples of native valour which they sought to emulate.

The sagas that have come to us were transmitted orally for centuries before being written down by Christian monks. They provide us with a fascinating picture of the way of life, attitudes, beliefs and assumptions of the Gaels, and together they have often been compared to the Homeric epics of Greece. Indeed, only the classics of Greece and Rome give a more complete account of pre-Christian European societies. Unlike the classics, however, the Gaelic sagas were not invented or collected by any single author, and even in the early texts we can detect several different storytellers and versions of the same tale.

Four great collections of sagas have survived: the Mythological cycle, which gives an account of pre-Christian times; the Ulster or Red Branch cycle, which roughly covers the first two centuries AD; the Fenian cycle, which deals with the third and subsequent centuries; and the King cycle, which contains accounts of the history of Ireland in the first millennium. The earliest manuscripts of the sagas are much later in date: the story of the encounter between Oisin, the last of the Fenians, and St Patrick was not written down until as late as 1750. Naturally enough, much of the original verve and detail of the sagas was lost in their transmission through the pen, but their power is attested by their survival for so long in oral form in Gaelic, the oldest living vernacular in the West.

The Mythological cycle purported to be an accurate account of the origins and career of the Gaelic people. The cycle's tales of magic, fabled races and heroes delighted Matthew Arnold and are thought by some scholars to have inspired the French romances about the Holy Grail. A rich tapestry of wonderment was woven for storytellers and listeners alike as the cycle told of the Fomorians, Firbolgs, Danaans and Milesians. According to the tales, the Fomorians were the first inhabitants of Ireland. The written versions of the cycle placed them as being before the Biblical Flood which they somehow survived. They were regarded as the embodiment of evil, monstrous and hideous, always sinister. In some ways they were like the Titans of Greek mythology. The Giant's Causeway in Co. Antrim was their rocky stairway, and the dark cliffs of Tory Island off the coast of Donegal were their sinister homes. After the Fomorians came twenty-four men and twenty-four women led by Partholon, who found in Ireland only one plain, three lakes and nine rivers. Partholon cleared four more plains and formed seven new lakes, and he also introduced farming. Three hundred years to the day after Partholon and his followers arrived, their five thousand descendants were killed by a mysterious illness. Nevertheless their knowledge and skills did not perish, particularly of how to follow laws and rituals, how to work gold, to brew beer, to make cooking cauldrons and to domesticate cattle. Next the Nemedians came to Ireland, making full use of their predecessors' legacy of knowledge. They cleared twelve more plains and formed four new lakes. But the same sickness that had wiped out the people of Partholon decimated the Nemedians; they became the vassals of the Fomorians who had returned from Tory Island and taken over the country once more. As tribute to their masters, on the first day of November the Nemedians had to deliver two-thirds of their new-born children and two-thirds of the produce of their labours. In a last desperate revolt against these Fomorians the hero Conaan and many of his followers were killed, and the Nemedians left for safer lands in northern Europe.

The Firbolgs were the next to arrive. Soon after landing, their chiefs sought each other out and settled on Tara as a meeting place. Here they divided Ireland into five kingdoms, but lived in peace for only thirty-six years until the Danaans arrived.

The Danaans made an alliance with the Fomorian, Balor of the Evil Eye, whose daughter Ethne married the Danaan Cian and produced a son, Lug. They came from the northern islands of the world, where they learnt magic and collected the four treasures: the Lia Fail, a stone which cried out when each new king was inaugurated; the inexhaustible cauldron of their ancient chief, Dagda; the magical sword of their king, Nuada; and the spear of their god-hero, Lug. In a great fleet of ships the Danaans sailed to Ireland, burned their boats on the shore and, after a series of unsuccessful negotiations, defeated the Firbolgs in a great battle near Cong in Co. Mayo. One account says that the Firbolgs' last stand was at Dun Angus, the prehistoric rocky fortress on the Aran coast. The battle started on Midsummer Day and raged for four days and nights until the Firbolgs, reduced to three hundred and heavily outnumbered, sought to resolve the issue by single combat, in accordance with the universally acknowledged laws of chivalry.

The Danaans under Nuada instead offered peace and the choice of one of Ireland's five provinces to the Firbolgs, who accepted, choosing Connaught. During the battle, Nuada's arm was cut off, and so he was no longer fit to be king. He was succeeded by Bres, who ruled for seven years, during which time the Fomorians became more and more oppressive towards the Danaans until finally Bres realized that his people no longer supported him. Treacherously, he left for the court of Balor and joined him in assembling an army on the northern isles of Scotland. They marched into Ireland across an unbroken bridge of ships stretching from the Hebrides to Co. Antrim. Nuada, now with a wonderful silver arm, was recalled as king and he camped at Tara preparing for battle.

Whenever the Danaans were most in need of help, Lug came to their rescue, and he now rode to Tara. The doorkeeper asked him what art he practised, 'for no-one without an art enters Tara'. 'Question me,' says Lug: 'I am a wright.' The doorkeeper replied, 'We need no wright. We have a wright already, Luchta son of Luachaid.' Lug said 'Question me, doorkeeper, I am a smith.' The doorkeeper answered him: 'We have a smith already, Colum Cuailleinech of the three new processes.' Lug continued, claiming to be a champion, a harper, a warrior, a poet, historian, sorcerer, leech, cupbearer and brazier, all of which the doorkeeper told him the Danaans already had. Finally, Lug said, 'Ask the king whether he has one single man who possesses all these gifts, and if he has I shall not enter Tara.' The doorkeeper obliged and Nuada ordered Lug to be tested in a game of chess which the god won. Hearing this, Nuada cried, 'Let him through the gates for his like has never before come to this fortress.'

The Danaans marched into battle against Bres and the Fomorians on a plain about fifty miles north of Cong, on the last day of October. At first, the fight went badly for the Danaans, and Nuada was killed by Balor of the Evil Eye. Their magic well — into which they threw their dead and wounded who then emerged restored — was discovered and bricked up by the Fomorians. Balor, whose eye was normally kept shut because a glance from it killed anyone in sight, finally faced Lug, and as four of his soldiers propped open Balor's evil eye, Lug slung a stone at it so accurately and forcefully that the eye was carried out through the back of Balor's head, and was so turned upon the Fomorians themselves. The Fomorians fled, leaving Ireland to the Danaans.

A great deal of scholarly speculation has surrounded the Danaans, with some authorities maintaining that they may have been the original Gaels. Certainly, the Danaans are treated well by the sagas, being presented as handsome and honourable while the Fomorians and Firbolgs are depicted as mean and evil. The Firbolgs are described as small, dark and cunning and their contests with the Danaans are painted as being between Light and Darkness. Lug and Dagda later became Gaelic gods — and even later Lug became the prototype of the Arthurian Lancelot — and the Danaans themselves after their defeat by the Milesians were believed to have become fairies and leprechauns, haunting the prehistoric burial mounds (*sidhe*) of the country.

The ancient sagas were not troubled by scholarly concerns, and according to them the Milesians (and not the Danaans) were the last race of invaders to take possession of Ireland. With them we are probably at the dawn of history. The Gaels described them as the people who brought the Bronze Age to Ireland. The tales of the Milesians come from the Red Branch cycle of sagas, which say that they came from Spain in thirty ships. But the Danaans with magic cast an inky mist on the sea, forcing the Milesians to sail around Ireland three times before they could land. Once ashore, they made for Tara. On their way they met three queens, Banba and her sisters Fodla and Eriu, who told the Milesians that each of their names was also a name for the country. Each queen begged that her name be retained should the Milesians succeed in defeating the Danaans, and this the Milesians promised, granting Eriu (the dative case of which is Erin) the chief name forever. (These queens were probably invented by the storytellers to explain the three ancient names of Ireland, Erin, Banba and Fodla.) However, once they arrived at Tara the Milesians chivalrously agreed with the Danaan kings to go back to sea in order to make a

Gort Mag Capel,
Inishmore, Aran
Islands, showing
karst topography:
terraced limestone
pavement bared by
rainwater.

second attempt to take the land by force. Once again the Danaans employed magic in their defence, raising a storm so that many of the invaders were drowned and their ships destroyed. The survivors managed to land and in two great battles defeated the Danaans. With them the Milesians had a great poet, Cir, who went to the northern kingdom, and a great harpist, Cennfinn, who went to the south. In this way the Gaels explained how in later centuries the north of Ireland produced poetry, while the south was famous for its music.

From both the Red Branch and the Mythological cycles we also learn about the Gaelic 'Otherworld' of magic and mystery. After their defeat, some of the Danaans went underground into the mounds and burial grounds of prehistory, while others sailed away to the west to Tir na Og, the land of eternal youth and to Mag Mell, the land of happiness, both sometimes described as islands lying near the setting of the sun. Time ceased to have any meaning in the Golden Age that was life in these mystical places. The eighth-century text of *The Voyage of Bran* from the Red Branch cycle gives a wonderful account of this Elysium (Emain). Bran, the legendary king of Britain, was one day approached by a mysterious woman who sang to him and his host:

There is a distant isle
Around which sea-horses glisten,
A fair course against the white-swelling surge,
Four feet uphold it.

Feet of white bronze under it
Glittering through beautiful ages.
Lovely land throughout the world's age
On which the many blossoms drop.

Unknown is wailing or treachery
In the familiar cultivated land,
There is nothing rough or harsh,
But sweet music striking on the ear.

Without grief, without sorrow, without death,
Without any sickness, without debility,
That is the sign of Emain,
Uncommon, an equal marvel.

ABOVE]
*Bronze Age gold
collar found near
Ross, Co. Westmeath,
and dating from
around 1700 BC.
Over sixty of these
Irish lunulae have
been found.*

BELOW]
*Late Bronze Age gold
dress fastener found
at Clones, Co.
Monaghan, and
dating from around
700 BC. These were
used in the manner of
modern cufflinks to
fasten cloaks.*

Bran travelled there, encountering marvels of magic and the supernatural, but when one of his followers returned home, he was turned to dust the minute he set foot on his homeland: he had thought he had been gone for only a year, but it turned out to have been centuries.

The Red Branch cycle, the second great collection of poems and tales, contains the great epic of the *Tain* — the 'Cattle Raid of Cooley' — in which the epitome of Gaelic heroism, Cuchulain, kills his foster-brother and saves his Ulster people. Cuchulain was endowed with superhuman qualities, and his birth remained mysterious: in one version he is described as the son of Lug; in another as having been born three times. He achieved his name, which means 'The hound of Culann', at the age of seven when he killed the watch-dog of Ulster belonging to Culann, the smith, and in return undertook to protect the kingdom of Ulster and its people himself. As a child he travelled abroad to Alba (Scotland) and Britain, where he was trained in the martial arts by a female warrior. He was invincible in battle, and could turn round in his skin in a moment. When he was angered, his long hair would stand on end, each strand tipped with blood or fire. Fire would also belch from his mouth and a strange, dangerous sign would appear on his forehead. When this happened, the only way he could be calmed down was by being ducked three times in cold water. During his career he made enemies, and one of these, Queen Maeve of Connaught, brought about his downfall.

In bed one night with the King, her husband, Maeve argued with him about which of them was richer. The argument became so heated that they eventually decided to resolve it by piling up their respective goods and valuables and comparing them. The King won the contest; Maeve had nothing to compare with his great White Bull. Not to be outdone, she learned of a great Brown Bull of Cooley, in Co. Louth, which if she owned would make her the winner. But the chieftain of Cooley refused to let Maeve have his bull, so she resolved to get it by force. Secretly she promised her beautiful daughter in marriage to every leader in her army, and so secured the help of all the warriors of Ireland outside Ulster. Together, with Maeve at their head, they crossed the Shannon at Athlone and marched to Kells, on the border of the Ulster kingdom, where they pitched camp. Cuchulain, always staying out of sight, now began to harry Maeve's troops, slaying one hundred of them every night with his sling. Maeve sought an interview with the Ulsterman and, amazed to find him a mere boy, offered him gold and great rewards if he would desist. Cuchulain refused, but Maeve secured his agreement to fight one of her heroes each day at the ford that lay between them, reckoning this was better than losing one hundred every night. Day after day Cuchulain fought Maeve's warriors, overcoming Morrigu, the water-goddess, during his fight with the hero Loich whom he still managed to wound mortally. Loich, dying, begged Cuchulain,

'By your love of generosity I crave a boon.'
'What boon is that?' asked Cuchulain.
'It is not to spare me I ask', said Loich, 'but let me fall forwards to the east
and not backward to the west, that none of the men of Erin may say that
I fell in panic or in flight before you.'
'I grant it', said Cuchulain, 'for surely it is a warrior's request.'

After more such combats and deceitful ploys by Maeve, Cuchulain mounted his war chariot and hurled himself against the men of Erin. He 'gave his chariot a wrenching turn so that the iron wheels sank into the ground, so that the track of the wheels was a sufficient fortification, for like a fortification the stones and pillars and flags and sands of the earth rose back high on every side round the wheels'. Maeve, with her forces sorely depleted, resorted once again to single combat. She finally forced Cuchulain's foster-brother, Ferdia, to face the Ulsterman, by threatening him with the spells of her Druids. Ferdia capitulated 'because he thought it easier to fall by valour and championship and weapons than to fall by Druids' wisdom and by reproach'. After a great fight in which Ferdia proved almost a match for him, Cuchulain, badly wounded, emerged as the tragic victor. While he recovered from his wounds, the men of Ulster (who all the while had been laid low by a mysterious illness) began to collect themselves, and the two armies faced each other on the plains of Meath.

While this great battle of the *Tain* was raging Maeve managed to capture the Brown Bull of Cooley, which she sent back to Connaught under escort. Eventually, through the intervention of Cuchulain, the Ulster army defeated Maeve's followers, and they fled back to Cruachan (Rathcroghan in Co. Roscommon), from whence they had originally set out. The two bulls, upon meeting, also fought, crossing most of Ireland during their fight. The Brown Bull won and, while making its way home to Cooley, stopped to drink from the Shannon where one of his enemy's loins impaled on his horn fell off, thus naming the place Athlone, the Ford of the Loin. Back home at Cooley the Brown Bull bellowed so much in victory that his heart burst, and so ended the saga of the *Tain*.

Cuchulain lived on after his incredible feats of prowess in the *Tain*, but not for long. The account of his death is told in the twelfth-century Book of Leinster. Maeve, having bided her time, once again brought an army together to seek revenge from Cuchulain. She had no trouble in assembling a great number of warriors

because there was scarcely one who had not had a relative slain by the Ulster hero. But it was only by magic that Cuchulain was eventually pierced by his own spear. With great difficulty, holding in his own entrails, Cuchulain tied himself to a high stone by a lake, because as a Gaelic hero 'he did not wish to die either sitting or lying: it was standing that he wished to meet his death'. His faithful horse protected him as he died, and it was only when a raven alighted on his shoulder that his enemies knew he was dead. This is the scene which the Irish artist, Oliver Sheppard, used in 1936 for his statue in Dublin's General Post Office to commemorate the Irish Rising of 1916.

In the tales of Cuchulain we can see the Gaelic ideal of a warrior aristocracy with their attributes of bravery, honesty, learning and fighting skill. In the Fenian cycle where Finn MacCool and his followers, the Fenians, perform more heroic deeds and experience magical mysteries, we can see the Gaels' respect for the arts. Poetry is emphasized: Oisin, Finn's son, is the supposed author of many of the poems of the cycle. To become a Fenian, a warrior had to know the laws of poetry and had to agree to observe four rules: always to choose a wife on the grounds of her

Dun Chonchuir, Inishmaan, Aran Islands, still shows the way in which a Neolithic fort related to the surrounding countryside and stone-walled fields. The fort's walls are eighteen feet thick and twenty feet high.

37

good manners and virtue rather than because of her wealth; never to be violent towards a woman; always to accede to requests for help; and never to flee from fewer than ten champions. His family and his tribe had also to agree never to seek revenge should he be killed.

The Gaels' concern for history (as well as drama) is also clearly demonstrated in the Fenian cycle, where historical figures are often mentioned. The seventeenth-century priest and historian, Geoffrey Keating, compiled his *History of Ireland* using the Fenian cycle stories as if they were factual, and many other writers have followed suit. But none of the sagas — not even the later King cycle — is reliable as history: they only help to give us a window on the Gaelic world.

Just as the war between Ulster and Connaught is the hinge of so many of the Red Branch sagas, so the developing enmity between the different High Kings of Ireland dominates the Fenian cycle. The climax of the cycle is the battle of Gabhra, the fall of the High Kings, and the destruction of the warrior band of the Fenians led by Finn MacCool. But many of the tales are concerned with less warlike matters. The longest Fenian saga is preserved in the thirteenth-century Book of Lismore and concerns Oisin and Cailte, the poet. According to a version written down between 1512 and 1526, they were almost the sole survivors of the Fenians after the battle of Gabhra. In very old age — 150 years after the death of Finn — they met St Patrick, who questioned them closely about the legends and customs of their people. St Patrick's scribe, Brogan, took down the stories Oisin and Cailte told, so committing them to writing for posterity.

In the course of his conversations with St Patrick, Oisin complained about the Christian's humble food in contrast to the great Fenian feasts and deplored the ringing of bells and singing of hymns in contrast to the music of the kings. Most of all, however, he rejected St Patrick's beliefs, refusing to accept that a man like Finn MacCool was not in heaven. Oisin, aged, blind, starved and wholly at St Patrick's mercy, roundly defended his dead chief:

ST PATRICK *Let us cease disputing on both sides, you withered old man, devoid of sense. Understand that God dwells in heaven of the orders, and Finn and his hosts are all in pain.*

OISIN *Great then would be the shame for God not to release Finn from the shackles of pain; for if God himself were in bonds my chief would fight in his behalf ... Oh, Patrick of the crooked crozier ... how could it be that God and his clerics could be better men than Finn, the chief king of the Fenians, the generous one who was without blemish?*

One of the most popular tales of the cycle, later given renewed popularity by Yeats in his poem 'The wanderings of Oisin', was the tale of 'Oisin in the Land of Youth', which describes the hero's travels to Tir na Og. One day, soon after the battle of Gabhra, a woman came riding on a beautiful white horse over the waves from the west. Her name was Niam; she told Oisin that she had given her love to him and begged him to return with her to the Land of Youth. Although sorry to leave his father, Oisin agreed to go with Niam. He jumped on her horse with her and disappeared out to sea. Years beyond count later, Oisin decided to return home, homesick for his father and his friends. Niam tried to warn him of the danger he faced, since she knew that mortals returning from the Land of Youth would age immediately they touched earth. She begged Oisin not to get down from his horse once he returned, or he would never be able to come back to her. But despite his promise, Oisin alighted and became a withered old man at once. One version says he saw the great stone trough of the Fenians and got down off his horse to let it drink; another version says that his saddle-girth slipped as he reached to help some men lift a stone.

One of the great love stories of early European literature, 'The pursuit of Diarmuid and Grainne', is also part of the Fenian cycle. Diarmuid of the Love-spot unwittingly caused the fair Grainne, daughter of the High King, Cormac MacArt, to fall in love with him on the eve of her wedding to Diarmuid's leader, Finn MacCool. Grainne persuaded the reluctant Diarmuid to elope with her, and the two young lovers were then pursued round Ireland by Finn, who eventually succeeded in having Diarmuid killed by a wild boar. Grainne hated the very sight of Finn after her lover's death, but the Fenian leader wooed her with gentle passion until 'the heart of woman that changes like water' capitulated and she became his wife.

The fourth collection of sagas, the King cycle, are different from the others in that they are more concerned about matters of importance to the community, the background of tribes and families, and battles and events of historical significance. While it contains many examples of the storytelling and the respect for human qualities like valour, honesty and generosity which characterize the other saga cycles, the King cycle is more properly regarded as primitive history rather than literature. At the same time, while these accounts (like the Fenian cycle) deal with people who actually lived, and describe the arrival of the Vikings and the early Norse settlements in Dublin, it cannot be assumed that they are historically correct.

The most famous tales of the King cycle concern Niall of the Nine Hostages. Niall, an historical figure, actually ruled the united kingdom of Meath and Connaught from 380 to 405. He was the greatest king between Cormac MacArt and the coming of St Patrick, and the founder of one of the great Irish dynasties: his descendants ruled at Tara for six hundred years. The sagas tell us that his father, Eochu Mugmedon, was a High King of the fourth century, and that his mother was the daughter of a British king. As a boy, Niall proved himself worthier than his elder brothers as their father's successor:

> *Eochu Mugmedon was king of Ireland. Aed asked him which of his sons would be king. 'I do not know', said Eochu, 'until a smithy be burnt over their heads.' Thereupon a smithy was burnt. Brion, the eldest son, seized the chariot and all its harness. Fiachra seized the wine vat. Ailill seized all the weapons. Fergus Caechan seized the pile of dry wood. Niall seized all the smith's implements, including the bellows, the hammers, the block and anvil. 'Truly,' said Eochu, 'Niall shall be their king, and his brothers shall serve him.'*

Historically, Niall led several expeditions abroad to Britain, where he defeated the Picts and harried the Romans as they retreated south, ultimately withdrawing from Britain completely in 407. In the fifth and sixth centuries Irish Gaels conquered Scotland, Wales and a large part of western Britain, and the Roman poet, Claudian, wrote about 'when Scots came thundering from Irish shores' to pillage Roman Britain. After Niall's death his sons succeeded to other kingships in Ireland, Eogan becoming the founder of the royal O'Neill family of Tyrone, and Conal Gulban the founder of the royal O'Donnell's of Donegal. The O'Neill's remained the dominant family in Ulster until the Flight of the Earls in 1607. Niall's nephew, Dathi, succeeded him at Tara and, according to the tales, died in the foothills of the Alps. In the eighteenth century the Abbé MacGeoghegan, chaplain to the Irish Brigade in the service of France, noted that in Piedmont there was still a tradition of an invading Irish king in the fifth century.

However, much of the history and mythology of the Gaels was forgotten with the coming of Christianity. Some of the legendary figures stayed alive in popular imagination, particularly the Fenians, but the great hero Cuchulain was forgotten until his story was revived at the end of the nineteenth century. In large part this was because the gods and customs of the Gaels became the devils and demons of Christianity. One monk who helped write down the saga of the *Tain* penned at the end, 'I who have written this history, or rather fable, am doubtful about many things ... For some of them are figments of demons, some are poetic imaginings, some true, some not, and some for the delight of fools.'

The sagas owed their revival in the nineteenth century to the need of Irish nationalists to develop again a separate Irish identity after centuries of British rule.

The revolutionary Irish Republican Brotherhood in the 1860s took on the name 'Fenian' in a successful attempt to stir up popular sympathy and support in Ireland. Even John Fitzgerald Kennedy remembered as a child in Boston being taught to revere the memory of the Fenians. Patrick Pearse, one of the leaders of the 1916 Irish Rising, used to teach the boys at his school to cherish the memory of Cuchulain, whom he saw, not as a blood-flecked warrior, but as a Christ-like boyish figure, 'small, dark, sad boy, comeliest of the boys of Eire', who would re-inspire Irish youth. At the end of his school's first year, Pearse staged a Gaelic pageant with his pupils, and wrote, 'We are anxious to crown our first year's work with something worthy and symbolic; anxious to send our boys home with the knightly image of Cuchulain in their hearts and his knightly words ringing in their ears.' George Russell, known by his pseudonym 'AE', also took up Cuchulain, who he said represented 'as much as Prometheus the heroic spirit of the redeemer in man'. Slieve Gullion in Armagh, where Cuchulain was said to have made his last stand, AE felt, should be as holy to the Irish as Mount Sinai was to the Jews.

After the 1916 Rising Yeats was able to link with no sense of incongruity the devoutly Catholic Pearse and the pagan Cuchulain:

Oliver Sheppard's statue of Cuchulain stands in the main hall of Dublin's General Post Office.

> *When Pearse summoned Cuchulain to his side*
> *What stalked through the Post Office? What intellect,*
> *What calculation, number, measurement, replied?*
> *We Irish, born into that ancient sect*
> *But thrown upon this filthy modern tide*
> *And by its formless spawning fury wrecked,*
> *Climb to our proper dark, that we may trace*
> *The lineaments of a plummet-measured face.*

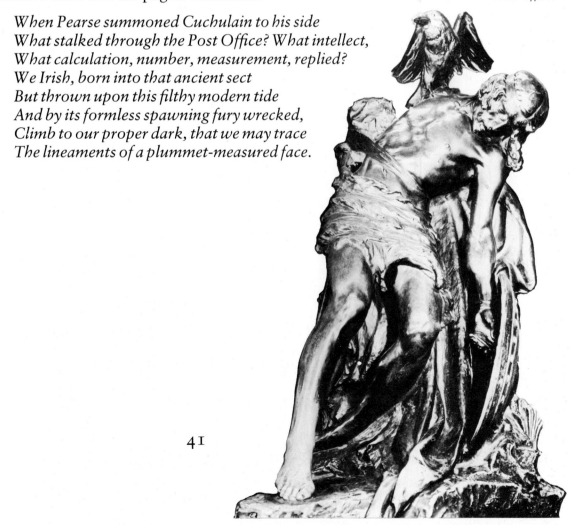

41

3

THE LAND OF SAINTS AND SCHOLARS

*From the very beginning of its faith, Ireland has been linked
with the Apostolic See of Rome ... On Sunday mornings in Ireland,
no one seeing the great crowds making their way to and from Mass
could have any doubt about Ireland's devotion.*

POPE JOHN PAUL II, Phoenix Park, Dublin, 29 September 1979

St Patrick, the patron saint of Ireland, came there in 432 and stayed until he died in about 461. With him he brought the Latin language and the skill of writing. The year before he arrived, Pope Celestine had sent another evangelist, Palladius, to Ireland at the request of the Church of Gaul (France). The Gaulish Church was the best organized branch of the Church in the west, and had been charged to keep Christian 'the Roman island [Britain] and the pagan island [Ireland]'. Palladius died shortly after arriving, and Patrick was chosen by the Church to replace him. He was consecrated a bishop, sent off and became 'the Apostle of Ireland'. He was not completely successful in his own lifetime in seducing the Irish away from pagan practices, but his successors and followers were. They were to make Ireland the jewel of Christianity and the harbinger of Christian civilization during the Dark Ages.

There is some debate about the dates of St Patrick's life. He wrote an account of his own life, the *Confessions*, preserved in the ninth-century Book of Armagh, which indicates that he was born around 390. But on the other hand, some of his disciples without doubt lived well into the sixth century, suggesting that he arrived in Ireland around 456 and died in 490. This extended timespan may mean that there were, in fact, two Patricks, but it is a problem that remains unresolved.

Patrick was born in Britain in a town which he named as Bannavem Taberniae.

All trace of his birthplace has since been lost, but it was in western Britain, probably near Bristol and the river Severn. In his *Confessions*, Patrick tells us that his father was named Calpurnius and was not only a decurion, a member of the Roman British ruling group, but also a deacon of the Christian Church and a landowner. He, and others like him, suffered at the hands of raiding Irishmen — 'Scots' as the Romans called them — and Patrick himself and his two sisters were taken captive (quite possibly by Niall of the Nine Hostages) in one such raid. From the age of sixteen for six years, Patrick was a slave herdsman in Co. Antrim, which occupation gave him plenty of time for contemplation. When he escaped back home at the age of twenty-two he was a convinced Christian. Still, Patrick would have stayed at home with his family were it not for a vision which he later described vividly:

> *I saw in the night the vision of a man whose name was Victoricus, coming as it were from Ireland, with countless letters. And he gave me one of them and I read the opening words of the letter which were 'The voice of the Irish' and as I read the beginning of the letter, I thought that at the same moment I heard their voice . . . and thus did they cry out as with one mouth: 'We ask thee, boy, come and walk among us once more.'*

The annual bare-footed pilgrimage to the rocky summit of Croagh Patrick, Co. Mayo, dates at least from the thirteenth century and is a powerful testament to Irishmen's veneration for their patron saint.

43

There probably were some Christian settlements in southern Ireland before the arrival of St Patrick in 432: Palladius is recorded as the first Bishop of the Irish in 431. Patrick, however, is justly credited as being chiefly responsible for the conversion of the Irish. By 600, over eight hundred monasteries had been founded, and Armagh – Patrick's own see – advanced claims to the Primacy of all Ireland. In these monasteries were trained the great Irish missionaries who were to re-Christianize Britain and much of Europe, and the scribes who wrote and illuminated the great religious books.

He left home after this and travelled to the south of France, where he received instruction and was ordained a priest. Once in Ireland, Patrick based himself in the north-east, at Armagh. He formally established his episcopal see there, and it is to the present day Ireland's religious centre.

Patrick's *Confessions* is the chief source of information about the saint's life and mission in Ireland. From it we learn that he 'was put in irons', 'lived in daily expectation of murder, treachery or captivity', 'journeyed everywhere in many dangers', 'gave presents to kings', 'baptized thousands' and 'ordained clerics everywhere'. However, in south and south-west Ireland, persistent claims by early Irish saints and by some families that they were the first Irish Christians, being converted some years before Patrick's arrival, might help explain the nature of Patrick's mission. The fact that he was consecrated a bishop at the outset suggests that there may have been a sufficient number of converts in Ireland before his arrival to warrant the appointment of such an exalted Churchman. The religious establishments which later claimed St Patrick as their founder are concentrated in the provinces of Ulster, Leinster and Connaught, indicating that this was the area of his greatest activity — perhaps because there was less need of his services in Munster.

Patrick came to Ireland with hopes of introducing the system of archbishops and bishops that existed in France, but found that Ireland, without roads and towns and without the experience of central political unity, was completely unsuited to his plan. So, instead of having a number of city-based bishop and archbishoprics, Ireland developed a monastic Church more in keeping with Gaelic society. By confining himself to the single purpose of conversion, and by not attempting to interfere with Gaelic laws and social customs, Patrick converted the Irish rapidly but gently. Pagan Gaelic celebrations were tolerated and sometimes — like the Feast of All Saints — adopted by Patrick for Christian purposes. The forts and encampments of Gaelic kings and chieftains were chosen as the sites for churches, abbeys and monasteries, although Tara remained resolutely pagan until the middle of the sixth century.

The traditional anniversary of St Patrick's death, 17 March, has become Ireland's national day. The site of his grave on Downpatrick and the summit of Croagh Patrick in Co. Mayo, where he was said to have vanquished the snakes of Ireland, have remained sites of pilgrimage for Catholic Irishmen ever since. His Purgatory on an island in Lough Derg, Co. Donegal, where he had a vision that anyone coming in penance to the island would be forgiven their sins, has also been a place of pilgrimage at least since the thirteenth century. In 1932 the Eucharistic Congress in Dublin, on the fifteenth centenary of the saint's commencement of his mission to Ireland, witnessed the largest crowds ever assembled in Dublin until Pope John Paul II's visit in 1979. Both events serve as massive reminders of St Patrick's success.

One of the great advantages pagan Gaelic society offered the Christian missionaries was that the Gaels' veneration of learning, and the Gaelic class of learned men — the brehons, poets and druids — found a natural place within the Christian establishment. A century after Patrick's arrival, Irish monks and scholars not only abounded in Ireland but also began evangelizing abroad themselves. St Ninian, an Ulsterman, was the first important missionary and teacher after Patrick. From his monastery of Candida Casa at Whithorn in western Scotland came St Enda, after whom Patrick Pearse named his school in 1908. Enda died in 530 after establishing a monastery and school on the Aran island of Inishmore to which students from all over Ireland came. Already, by the first quarter of the sixth century, Patrick's episcopal organization was succumbing to monasticism, with abbots supplanting bishops as the principal Churchmen in Ireland. One such abbot, St Finnian, established the monastic school at Clonard in Co. Meath, where he emphasized study and scholarship to a group of followers known as the Twelve Apostles of Ireland. Two of them, St Ciaran and St Colmcille (also known as St Columba), were to establish monasticism and scholarship as the hallmarks of the Irish Church. St Ciaran founded the church and monastery of Clonmacnois on the Shannon. St Colmcille founded the monasteries of Derry, Swords, Durrow and Kells before setting sail with twelve followers for the island of Iona on the west coast of Scotland, where he built one of the greatest early Christian monastic schools before he died in 597. *The Annals of Clonmacnois* state that Colmcille wrote three hundred books in his own hand, and by tradition he is held to be the scribe of the *Cathach*, the oldest surviving Irish manuscript. Irish monks from Iona converted Scotland and much of England. The Venerable Bede, the seventh-century English monk and historian, was always anxious to give Colmcille and the monks from Iona the credit for converting and maintaining most of England and Scotland in the Christian faith.

LEFT]
A page from the Cathach, *the earliest surviving Irish manuscript, reputedly written by St Colmcille*

RIGHT]
The voyage of St Brendan: a woodcut from Sankt Brandans Seefahrt, *Augsburg, 1476*

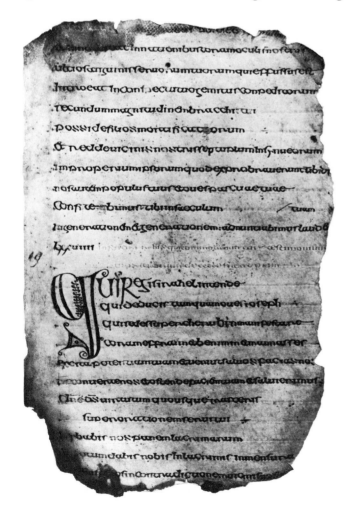

46

Another of St Finnian's 'Twelve Apostles of Ireland' was St Brendan the Navigator, the patron saint of Co. Kerry. While quite possibly owing his tale to the pagan *Voyage of Bran*, St Brendan was reputed to have crossed the Atlantic in a wood and leather coracle-type boat in the middle of the sixth century. The story of his voyage was composed three centuries later and must be treated with caution as history. But we are told that Brendan was convinced of the existence of a paradise over the sea to the west of Ireland, and that he and some companions set out on a seven-year quest for the 'Land Promised to the Saints'. According to the tale, the monks on their voyage encountered demons who flung fire at them, a column of floating crystal, and a sea monster as big as an island. These may have been volcanoes, icebergs and whales. The monks stopped at the Aran Islands, at Iona, and then at an 'Island of Sheep' and a 'Paradise of Birds' (possibly the islands of Streymoy and Mykines in the Faeroes). From there they went on to the 'Island of Smiths', which rained flaming rocks and where they spent a winter: this could be Iceland. They set off again, still sailing westwards, passing a 'crystal column' and going through a 'thick white cloud'. In 1976 a voyage following this course in a replica of Brendan's ship was successfully completed, ending in Newfoundland. It is possible that St Brendan did discover America, but it is also possible that although he definitely lived in the sixth century, and did sail widely, he subsequently became a Christian hero-figure who could be safely credited by Irish monks with the discoveries of pagan predecessors like Bran, and of other Christian and Viking successors for whom there is more evidence.

One of the reasons for voyages such as Brendan may have completed was the constant search by Irish monks for ascetic surroundings for a hermit's life. In 891 the *Anglo-Saxon Chronicle* recounts how 'three Scots came to King Alfred in a boat without any oars from Ireland whence they stole away, because they would be in a state of pilgrimage for the love of God, they recked not where'. Other Irish travellers and missionaries reached Iceland in 795 where, according to the Irish geographer Dicuil, at the summer solstice it was so light that the monks could clearly see to pick the lice out of their habits. In the three hundred years before the ninth century, many Irish monks emigrated and travelled extensively on the European continent, often reintroducing Christianity to areas which had been overrun by the tribes which completed the collapse of the Roman Empire. These monks had a lasting influence on the development of Christianity, notably by replacing the custom of public absolution with the practice of private confession, which is used by the Catholic Church to the present day. The most prominent of these expatriates was St Columbanus, an epitome of Irish learning and asceticism.

Columbanus was born in the province of Leinster around 543 and as a youth entered Bangor monastery in Co. Down. He was there for about twenty-five years before leaving with twelve companions for the continent of Europe to spread the Gospel. He first founded monasteries at Annegray, Luxeuil and Fontaines in the Vosges district of eastern France. In 610 he was forced to leave by King Theodoric II of Burgandy who was angry at the saint's condemnation of the immorality of his court. He travelled to northern Italy, founded the monastery and library of Bobbio in Piedmont and died there in 615. Columbanus' companions also founded monasteries: St Gall in Switzerland; Wurzburg in Germany; Vienna in Austria, possibly even one at Prague in Czechoslovakia. A number of Columbanus' writings have survived, including a full text of the *Rule of St Columbanus*. All monasteries had a set of rules established by the founder, governing behaviour and religious practice, and from those of St Columbanus we can obtain a clear picture of what life must have been like in an Irish monastery.

For the Irish monks who introduced Christianity to western Europe, leaving home was the ultimate sacrifice of asceticism. Colmcille (Columba) and his followers left Ireland in 563 and founded the monastery at Iona in this spirit of mortification. Columbanus, perhaps the greatest of these exiles, not only founded Bobbio and Luxeuil, but also saw monks from his foundations go on to start other monasteries even further afield. Centres of scholarship and piety, these monasteries and Irish monks maintained knowledge of Latin and Greek in the Dark Ages.

IRISH MONASTERIES IN EUROPE

The Gallarus Oratory on the Dingle Peninsula, Co. Kerry, is a perfectly preserved example of an early Irish hermit's dwelling built of stones without mortar – the corbel method of dry-stone construction.

The harsh discipline and frugal nature of these early monks is demonstrated in the first rule of obedience. A monk had to obey the instructions of his superiors without hesitation or answering back, and had to be prepared to die in the pursuit of his faith. 'Thus nothing must be refused in their obedience by Christ's true disciples, however hard and difficult it be, but must be seized with zeal, and even with gladness.' Monks were enjoined to fast, but not excessively, and to feed frugally: 'Let the monks' food be poor and taken in the evening, such as to avoid repletion, and their drink such as to avoid intoxication.' A monk who even thought carnally of a woman was held to have defiled her in his heart and himself in the eyes of God. A host of punishments and penances existed for every conceivable breach of discipline, ranging from corporal punishment and fasting to two hours' silence. In monasteries like Bangor and Bobbio, rules such as these were applied long after their founders' deaths.

When Europe's Dark Ages followed the fall of Rome in the fifth century, the

*Book of Kells, late
eighth century*

light of learning blazed principally in Ireland. Roving bands of Teutonic tribes ravaged the European continent and the Angles and Saxons burned and plundered their way through England. Ireland remained unscathed, and more and more scholars escaped to safety there. By the time of the Emperor Charlemagne in the eighth century, if a man knew Greek it was simply assumed he was Irish.

As Europe recovered after the fall of Rome, Irish monks and scholars emigrated (in complete contrast to the Irish emigrations of the nineteenth and twentieth centuries) to re-educate and evangelize amongst the new kings and princes of the continent. Alcuin, the leading scholar at the court of Charlemagne, and Scotus Eriugena ('Scotus' meaning 'Irish'), Europe's foremost philosopher in the ninth century, both studied at Clonmacnois, where they learnt not only about the Bible and Christian theology, but also about the works of the writers and poets of ancient Greece and Rome. The emperor Charles the Bald in the ninth century was the patron of Sedulius Scotus, a gifted Irish poet and scholar, who wrote *On Christian Rulers* as a guidebook for the emperor. So many Irish monks and scholars went to the continent that Heiric of Auxerre complained in 870, 'Almost all Ireland, disregarding the sea, is migrating to our shores with a flock of philosophers.'

In their monasteries and schools, Ireland's monks also completed the outstanding artistic achievement of the early Christian era: the perfection of illuminated manuscripts. These manuscripts concerned not only Christian subjects, but also the pagan Gaelic sagas and tales which would probably have been lost forever were it not for these monkish scribes. Their workmanship shows influence from Anglo-Saxon Britain as well as from the continent and the Near East, no doubt through scholarly immigrants in the seventh and eighth centuries. The treasure of these manuscripts is the eighth-century copy of the Gospels, the Book of Kells, now the pride of the Library of Trinity College, Dublin. By the time the three scribes who copied the Book of Kells started writing, Viking invaders had already landed in Britain. Indeed, it is likely that the book was begun on Iona and transferred for safety and completion to Kells. The book is not the earliest illustrated manuscript, but it is the finest. The first illustration in it is the earliest representation of the Virgin and Child in a western manuscript. Written in Latin, the language of the Church, the book also has an enormous wealth of birds and beasts, of ornamental letters, unusual full-page pictures and an overall labyrinthine style of decoration which both delights and defeats the reader. In earlier manuscripts, and notably the Book of Durrow, a peculiarly Gaelic script soon developed, permeating the art and the calligraphy of Irish scribes. Indeed, Irish script today is recognizably descended from the script which developed in Ireland in the sixth and seventh centuries. As is

ABOVE]
The eighth-century
Ardagh Chalice,
found in a potato field
near Ardagh, Co.
Limerick in 1868.
Made of gold, silver
and brass, decorated
with rock crystal and
studded with enamel
and glass, it is a classic
example of Gaelic
Christian
craftsmanship.

BELOW]
The Tara Brooch also
dates from the eighth
century. It is made of
bronze, covered at the
front with gold foil
and at the back with
silvered copper, and
studded with glass
and amber.

evident from the great Irish Books, a fantastic amount of painstaking work and skill went into their composition and illustration. For the scribes, it was another way of communing with God.

Together with illumination, the art of metal work flourished in Ireland during the Dark Ages. There was a much longer history of making exquisite metal objects in Ireland than there was of writing or illumination. From the time of the Bronze Age, Irish brooches, clasps, bowls and metal objects of all kinds had become renowned throughout the western world. Christian Irish metal workers were able to draw upon generations of knowledge and skill to make the croziers, chalices, pestles and other religious artifacts which the Vikings prized so much. From the ninth century onwards, as Viking raids increased, the skills of the calligrapher and the metal worker were combined in the third great Irish art form, stone high crosses. While churches and monasteries could have their metal and manuscript treasures plundered and destroyed, the craftsmen of the crosses must have realized that their stone work would not be vulnerable in the same way.

The earliest stone crosses in Ireland date from the eighth century, before the Viking raids, and are of simple design, usually ornamented with carved fret patterns and interlacing. By the ninth century, biblical scenes — usually of the crucifixion and the Disciples and Christ — were incorporated, but the designs were still simple. During the ninth century, however, the art of the high cross developed further. At Moone, Co. Kildare, the high cross is seventeen feet tall, and has on its granite faces intricate carvings of the Twelve Apostles and scenes from the Bible, including Daniel in the Lion's Den and Adam and Eve on the point of eating the apple. Crosses such as this probably stood within religious settlements or on their boundaries.

In the eighth century, stone came to be used instead of wood for the construction of churches and monasteries, and so the earliest surviving Irish buildings date from this period. The Gallarus Oratory on the Dingle peninsula in Co. Kerry is a perfectly preserved example of the sort of church that abounded through Ireland. It is a small boat-shaped building, constructed — without mortar — of stones collected from the fields and hills around, with a doorway facing west and a small window on the eastern side. Its walls are four feet thick, and it measures only twenty-three by sixteen feet externally. Its simple strength secured its survival through Viking raids and centuries of Atlantic winds and weather.

Stone round towers were also built on religious sites by monks from about 900 until 1150. Tall, thin, with doorways some distance from the ground and conical roofs, these probably fulfilled the dual function of bell-towers and places of safety for monks and their valuables during raids. No other buildings are so unmistakably Irish, and only two — both in Scotland — have been discovered outside Ireland.

Between the time of Patrick and the arrival of the Vikings, Irish politics changed considerably. By the ninth century, although there were still many small kingdoms and tribes, the country was dominated by two High Kingdoms. In the north the O'Neills ruled from Tara, while in the south the Eoganachta ruled from the Rock of Cashel. Between them lay a third, small province of Leinster around Dublin. But even before the Vikings came, the Irish political scene was becoming more violent and Irish monasticism was on the decline. The monasteries of Clonmacnois and Birr fought together in 763, and the Eoganachta and O'Neills struggled throughout the ninth century for supremacy, destroying and plundering be-

St Finian's church, Clonmacnois, Co. Offaly, dating from the twelfth century, is unique in having a round tower which is integral to the church: it served as a belfry. One of the earliest and most celebrated of Irish monastic sites, Clonmacnois was finally devastated in 1652 during the reign of Edward VI.

tween them more monasteries, churches and abbeys than ever the Vikings did. As a result, when the Vikings did come, there was no organized Irish resistance. Instead, different Irish kings and chiefs would often make alliances with the invaders against their co-religionists.

The first Viking invaders came from Norway, and their earliest attacks on Irish communities date from 795 when they sacked Iona, desecrating the grave of St Colmcille, and also landed on Lambey Island, off the coast of Dublin. Soon whole fleets of Viking longships with their sleek prows and graceful lines, their colourful sails and fierce, helmeted warriors, descended with increasing frequency on Ireland. In 837 two fleets each of sixty longships sailed up the Boyne and Liffey rivers. Rapidly, the arrival of the Vikings inspired a special terror. One Irish monk wrote thankfully in the margin of his manuscript one stormy night,

> *The wind is fierce tonight*
> *Ploughing the wild white ocean;*
> *I need not dread fierce Vikings*
> *crossing the Irish Sea.*

Moyne Abbey, Co. Mayo, is typical of Norman-Irish monastic building. A Franciscan friary, it was begun in 1460 and burned down in 1590.

55

IRELAND

The Vikings raided not only Ireland, but also Britain and the rest of Europe. Christian civilization, which had with difficulty survived the fall of Rome, once again found itself under severe attack as far afield as Paris, Sicily and Constantinople. For two hundred years the Viking raids lasted, and had it not been for the Scandinavian urge to settle and willingness to adopt Christianity, Christian Gaelic civilization might have been lost completely. Viking kingdoms were founded in Normandy, in the eastern half of England, and in Leinster, where in 841 the Norse king Thurgesius founded Ireland's first city, Dublin, at the mouth of the Liffey.

The Norwegian Vikings were defeated by their Danish kinsmen in 851 at a great naval battle between the rival fleets in Carlingford Lough. But this did not involve any respite from plunder and pillage for the Irish, since the Danes proved just as anxious as their predecessors to relieve the monasteries of their treasures. Monks began to send their manuscripts to Irish foundations on the continent, and to bury for safe-keeping their most valuable chalices and metal objects. But it would be wrong to think of the Vikings as a purely destructive force in Irish history. The name 'Ireland' comes from them: it is the old Gaelic name 'Eire' with the Scandinavian word 'land' added. Vikings soon began to settle, intermarry and trade with the Irish, and during the second half of the ninth century Ireland even enjoyed a period of comparative peace.

Viking spearheads

4

NORSE AND NORMANS

The Irish Sea can be crossed in one short day. William Rufus, the son of King William the Bastard and the second of the Norman Kings in England, penetrated far into Wales in his own day. He looked around him, and from these rocky headlands could just make out Ireland. He is supposed to have said: 'I will collect a fleet together from my own kingdom and with it make a bridge, so that I can conquer that country.' This was reported to Murchard, Prince of Leinster in Ireland. He thought for a while and then asked: 'When the King made this mighty threat, did he add "If God so wills"?' He was told that Rufus had not mentioned God at all when he spoke. Murchard found this very reassuring. He replied: 'Since this man puts all his trust in human agencies and none in the power of God Almighty, I have no reason to fear his coming.'

GIRALDUS CAMBRENSIS, THE JOURNEY THROUGH WALES

The Viking settlers of the ninth century were gradually drawn into Irish affairs as the two great Irish families, the Eoganachta and O'Neills, struggled for the High Kingship of all Ireland. During this struggle, the O'Neills managed to subdue the Viking settlements in the north, and Dublin remained the only strong Norse kingdom. This was partly because the men of Leinster showed themselves willing to ally with the Dubliners against the attempts of both the O'Neills and the Eoganachta to overcome them, and partly because Dubliners enjoyed close personal and trading ties with other Viking settlements in Britain. Viking raids in fact lessened to such an extent that the Eoganachta and O'Neills were able to fight each other in the great battle of Ballaghmoon in 908. The Eoganachta were led by their priest-king Cormac, a learned scholarly man who wrote *Cormac's Glossary*, an attempt to list Irish words in other languages, and organized the *Book of Rights*, describing the rights, duties and relationships of the High Kings and kings of Ireland. Cormac was defeated and killed by the O'Neills, and the power of the Eoganachta never recovered. But before the O'Neills could firmly establish their supremacy, another wave of Viking raids began.

Wooden conduits from the eleventh-century Viking settlement at Wood Quay, Dublin, recently excavated and lost (1980) to commercial development

In 914 a great Viking fleet landed at Waterford. Within six years the Norsemen had established themselves in Dublin and founded towns at Limerick, Cork and Wexford. Ireland's 237 rivers now became highways of invasion, and from this time dates the Irish association of seas and rivers with sorrow. Ireland's experience was in contrast to Britain, where the seas and waterways have traditionally been avenues of expansion eventually bringing imperial success. Over the centuries, starting with the Vikings, different invaders were to find that the Irish inlets and rivers gave them the opportunity to attack widely separated places, often, like Clonmacnois, well inland, within a very short space of time. In 977 King Olaf of the Sandals defeated the O'Neill High King Domnall and extended the Viking kingdom of Dublin to the Shannon, placing the Irish in Meath and Westmeath under an oppression so severe they called it a 'Babylonish captivity'. Bemoaning these new Viking incursions, the Irish chroniclers later still described their extent with great feeling:

The grave of a Viking warrior, buried in traditional style with his sword.

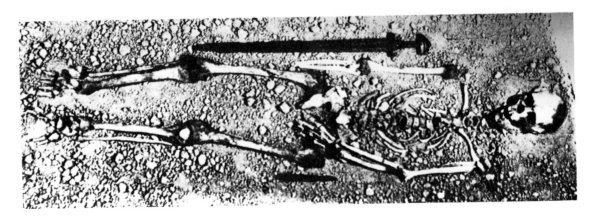

Immense floods and countless sea-vomitings of ships and boats and fleets so that there was not a harbour nor a land port nor a dun nor a fastness in all Munster without floods of Danes and pirates . . . so that they made spoil-land and sword-land and conquered land of her throughout her breadth and generally, and they ravaged her chieftainries and her privileged churches and her sanctuaries, and they rent her shrines and her reliquaries and her books.

However, by the close of the tenth century, two important events had taken place. The Vikings in Ireland had accepted Christianity — King Olaf of Dublin actually died on a pilgrimage to Iona — and Brian Boru had become High King of Munster and the southern half of Ireland.

Brian Boru was one of the greatest Irishmen who ever lived. His achievement puts him on a par with Alfred the Great as a national hero who successfully first united his own people and then defeated the Danes. Brian was born into a Munster

THE VIKING INVASIONS

Unlike the British, for whom seas and rivers have provided historic opportunities and prosperity, for the Irish the seas and rivers have been the allies of invaders and national grief since the years of the Vikings. The Shannon, Barrow and Boyne carried Viking longships into the very heart of Ireland, making vulnerable the glorious wealth of Gaelic Christianity. But the Vikings came to settle too, founding Dublin and other of Ireland's first towns, and ultimately merging with the Gaelic population.

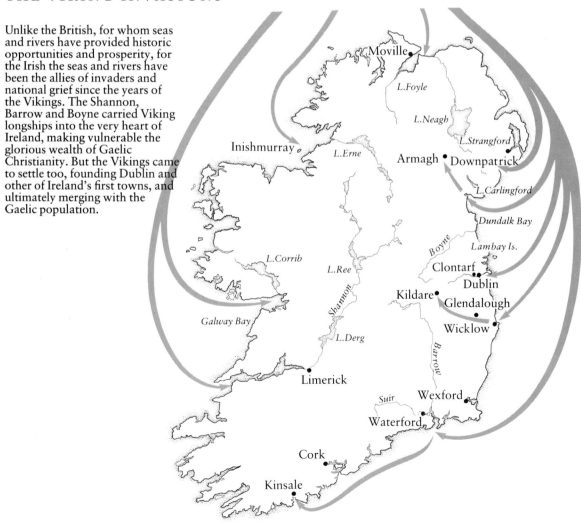

royal family in about 940. He proved himself as a tactician and warrior in countless battles against the Danes around Limerick, culminating in 968 with a victory which regained Cashel. This once again became the seat of the kings of Munster, first of Brian's brother, Mahon, and then, after Mahon was killed by the Danes, of Brian. From 976 until his death in 1014, Brian ruled Munster, and from 1002 he was also acknowledged as the first absolute High King of all Ireland, finally ending the domination of the O'Neills. In 999 he completely defeated the Danes of Dublin, and entered the city in triumph. He restored Armagh, which had been burned and plundered several times by the Danes, and threw his authority behind Armagh's claim to ecclesiastical supremacy in Ireland. In 1004 he completed a grand and triumphant tour of his kingdom, marching northwards from his capital at Kincora, always keeping the sea to his left, through Connaught and Ulster to Armagh, south through Meath to Dublin, and then through Leinster back to Cashel. He was greeted everywhere by local kings and chiefs who recognized him as their overlord.

In Dublin, however, the Danes were reluctant vassals, and they plotted a rebellion against Brian's rule. During the winter of 1013 Brian laid siege to the city, but had to retire for lack of supplies. The defenders formed an alliance with the kings of Leinster and with Sigurd the Stout, Earl of Orkney, who promised two thousand soldiers to them in return for the promise of the High Kingship in the event of success. When the two armies met in Dublin near Clontarf on Good Friday, 23 April 1014, both sides knew the battle would be decisive. The Irish had developed for themselves the warlike skills and weapons of the Vikings, so the contest was even. It lasted for a cold, windy day of fighting at such close quarters that the 'sharp cold wind' from the east blew drops of blood into the faces of Brian's warriors. Eventually, the Danes were driven back to the beach at Clontarf, where an exceptionally high tide drowned hundreds of them before they could reach the safety of their ships.

At the moment of victory, Brian, who now in his seventies had stayed in his tent behind the battle-lines, was killed by a Viking captain named Brodir. According to the Icelandic *Njal's Saga*, Brodir had been a Christian and had been consecrated a deacon but had renounced his faith and instead become 'deeply skilled in magic'. During the battle, Brodir had fled into the woods, from where he pounced on Brian as the king's warriors pursued the other Vikings to their boats. The Irish quickly captured Brodir and, as the saga goes on to tell in gory detail, killed him most horribly in revenge for their High King's death: 'Brodir was taken alive. Ulf Hreda slit open his belly and unwound his intestines from his stomach by leading him round and round an oak tree; and Brodir did not die until they had all been pulled out of him.' The Vikings were forced to admit, as they themselves put it, that 'Brian fell, but won at last.' After Brian's death, no other High King ever attained the complete supremacy he had enjoyed, and for the next 150 years different families jostled for the title.

The battle of Clontarf ended Viking hopes of ruling Ireland. While in England the Danish King Canute established his dominance, the Danes of Dublin settled down to a commercial life. By the tenth century the wine trade was in their hands. Sitric, King of Dublin, married one of Brian Boru's daughters and founded Christ Church Cathedral in the city in 1040. The Danes' connections abroad, however, had two significant results: their trading activities began to concentrate the mass of wealth in Ireland on the east coast, and their ecclesiastical ties with Britain maintained a quality of separateness in the Danish communities of the eastern seaboard. Together, these two elements were to fuel conflicts in Ireland and eventually involve Britain directly in Irish affairs.

Viking pennies

A tenth-century wooden gaming board found at Ballinderry, Co. Westmeath, and probably Danish in origin. The game played on the board has not survived.

Eighth century:
Cross at
Glendalough,
Co. Wicklow

Tenth century:
Muiredach's Cross,
Monasterboice,
Co. Louth

As the Viking threat subsided, Irish art and architecture enjoyed another renaissance. In the monastic schools, scholars and scribes began to turn away from Latin transcriptions of religious texts and instead began to make copies of the old Gaelic poems and sagas in manuscripts like the Book of Leinster and the Book of Armagh. In the eleventh and twelfth centuries, the majority of the lives of saints as well as Irish versions of the Trojan Wars and the Roman Civil War were written. The art of the high cross reached its climax with refined, sophisticated carvings on crosses such as those at Kilfenora and Dysert O'Dea. Metal work attained a new mastery with the extraordinarily fine Cross of Cong, commissioned in about 1123 by Turloch O'Connor, High King of Connaught, to enshrine a relict of the True Cross. Church building was undertaken with new vigour. King Cormac MacCarthy of Munster began building the splendid Hiberno-Romanesque Cormac's Chapel on the Rock of Cashel in 1127, and had it consecrated in 1134 in a ceremony attended by dignitaries from all over Ireland. The rib-vaulting in the roof of the chancel was a technique which the Crusaders had seen in the Near East and brought back with them to Europe, where it was first used in the choir of Durham Cathedral, completed in 1093. The use of the technique at Cashel within forty years was a testimony to the adventurousness and wide-flung contacts of Ireland at this time. Cormac's Chapel influenced many other churches in Ireland, and the Romanesque style rapidly spread throughout the country, culminating in the building of Clonfert Cathedral in Co. Galway, which was completed in 1164.

The building of chapels and cathedrals reflected another change in the Irish Church. Irish monks and abbots, with their rejection of episcopal authority and harsh rules of discipline, were becoming increasingly anomalous. Between 640 and 1080 there was no written correspondence between the Irish Church and the Papacy. No Irish armies took part in the Crusades, and while Irish monks and missionaries still went to the continent to preach and to study, others became lax in their observances, some even ignoring the rules of celibacy.

Reform of ecclesiastical practices had already taken place in the rest of Europe, where the Papacy had successfully insisted upon an episcopal Church hierarchy and upon the recognition of Papal authority in Church affairs. In the programme of 'Unity and Purity' pronounced by Pope Gregory VII (1073–85), Ireland was included, and to carry out Papal wishes the Norman Archbishops of Canterbury revived their claim to be supreme over Ireland. This claim dated from the sixth century, when St Augustine had been appointed to the see at Canterbury with authority over the British Isles as a whole. Soon after their conversion, the Danes in Ireland chose to join Danes in England and recognize Canterbury's ecclesiastical

authority in preference to that of Armagh or local abbots. Patrick, second Bishop of Dublin, who died in 1084, was consecrated by Archbishop Lanfranc at Canterbury and swore allegiance to him. Lanfranc also wrote to Turloch O'Brien, then claiming the High Kingship of Ireland, urging him to help reform the Irish Church. But not until the Synod of Kells in 1152 did the Irish finally accept reforms. These included the proper establishment of an episcopal organization, consisting of thirty-six bishoprics and four archbishoprics at Cashel, Tuam, Dublin and the Primacy at Armagh. In return for placing the Leinster archbishopric at Dublin, the Church there at last accepted Armagh's authority instead of Canterbury's. Such sweeping reform, however, depended upon the support of a powerful, central political authority, and this did not exist. In 1155, by the Papal Bull 'Laudabiliter', Pope Adrian IV granted the lordship of Ireland to King Henry II of England so that he might teach 'the truth of the Christian faith to the ignorant and rude'.

Ireland was certainly not 'ignorant and rude' in the middle of the twelfth century. But the Pope — who was also the only English Pope in history — wanted to

The rock of Cashel, Co. Tipperary. A religious site since the fifth century, with an eleventh-century round tower and late high cross, it fell into disuse in the eighteenth century.

63

*Strongbow
(c. 1130–76).*

secure recognition of his authority and of established Church practices in Ireland as quickly as possible. No doubt he saw in Henry II's desire to expand his power to Ireland an opportunity to secure firm control of the Church there too. The Pope's right to grant such an authority derived from the 'Donation of Constantine', supposedly of 325 but subsequently shown to have been an eighth-century forgery, whereby the Papacy claimed all islands converted to Christianity. Henry II had also promised 'to enter Ireland in order to subdue the people and make them obedient to laws, and that he is willing to pay from every house there one penny to St Peter and to keep and preserve the rights of the churches in that land whole and inviolate'. Controversy has raged as to whether 'Laudabiliter' too was a forgery or a later invention of Norman-English kings to justify their Irish exploits, but unfortunately for the Irish they accepted the Bull without question at the time. No copy of the Bull is in the Vatican Library, and the only existing text comes from Giraldus Cambrensis' untrustworthy *Conquest of Ireland*, written in about 1185. But there is other contemporary evidence for the Bull, and it has been accepted by scholars as genuine.

A year after the Pope had granted Henry II the lordship of Ireland, the High King, Turloch O'Connor, died. The O'Connor dynasty had ruled Connaught for several generations before becoming the dominant family in the twelfth century. After Turloch's death, feuding for the succession raged for six years before King Murcertach of Ulster was acknowledged as High King. In 1166 after Murcertach was killed in battle, Turloch O'Connor's son, Rory, became High King. Before he could firmly establish his suzerainty, however, Henry II, fourteen years after he had been granted them, decided to claim the rights set down in 'Laudabiliter'. He was prompted to do so by the activities of Dermot MacMurrogh, King of Leinster.

In 1152 Dermot MacMurrogh ran off with the wife of his arch-enemy Tiernan O'Rourke, Prince of Breffny. In 1166, O'Rourke gathered the other sub-kings and chieftains of Leinster in his support and succeeded in defeating Dermot, who had broken custom and the Brehon Laws by refusing to pay O'Rourke compensation for his wife. MacMurrogh did not accept his defeat. He travelled to Lismore to consult the Papal representative and, if he did not already know about 'Laudabiliter', he certainly learned about it there. From Lismore Dermot went to Henry's court in Acquitaine, to swear fealty to Henry. In return the King promised his favour to any one who would help Dermot recover his throne.

Dermot next travelled to south-west Wales, where he found an ally in one of Henry's vassals, Richard FitzGilbert de Clare, Earl of Pembroke, known as Strongbow, to whom he promised his daughter in marriage and the succession to his kingdom of Leinster. Men whose surnames are now amongst the most common in

Ireland joined the enterprise. Strongbow's first cousin, Maurice FitzGerald, together with a number of his other knightly relations, agreed to accompany him to Leinster in return for Dermot's promise of bounty. FitzGerald's descendants were to become Earls of Kildare and leaders of later Irish attempts to secure independence from Britain. Dermot also managed to secure the services of a group of Flemish mercenaries led by Richard FitzGodebert de Roche, who accompanied the Irish King when he returned to Ireland in 1167. Thus began the British invasion of Ireland, the consequences of which are with us still today.

For nearly two years after he returned, Dermot pretended to accept the loss of his kingdom. Then, after Strongbow and his relations had prepared for an expedition to Ireland, their first group of five hundred men landed on 1 May 1169 at Bannow in Co. Wexford. Led by Robert FitzStephen, Maurice FitzGerald's half-brother, the Normans first captured Wexford town, using their new longbows and cavalry to great effect. Naturally alarmed by this new invasion which, although small in number, was obviously militarily formidable, the High King Rory O'Connor marched against MacMurrogh. O'Connor was prepared to recognize Dermot as king of south Leinster, and was principally concerned to secure universal recognition for his own claim to the High Kingship. About one-third of the Norman army, led by Maurice Prendergast and convinced of better prospects with the High King, deserted to him, and after a brief skirmish with O'Connor's forces at Ferns in Co. Wexford, Dermot accepted the High King's terms. O'Connor marched away unaware of the strength of the Norman threat.

Dermot immediately wrote to Strongbow to send reinforcements and so brought about the battle which later generations of Irishmen were to regard as crucial. Strongbow sent an advance guard under the command of Raymond Carew, another of FitzGerald's relations, with ten knights and seventy archers. They landed at Baginbun on the Wexford coast and quickly built an earthen rampart on the headland, behind which they sheltered with a herd of cattle. Before MacMurrogh had time to meet them, an Irish army, gathered from among the Danes of Waterford and the Gaels of southern Leinster, attacked Carew and his men. The Normans suddenly stampeded their cattle at their opponents, bringing down many of them, and followed this up with a charge of their own. Seventy Waterford men were captured and, without mercy, first their limbs were broken and then they were thrown over the cliffs. An old verse runs:

At the creek of Baginbun
Ireland was lost and won.

Dermot McMurrogh (c. 1110–71).

65

On 23 August 1170, Strongbow landed at Crook near Waterford with two hundred knights and one thousand soldiers and, joining Carew, two days later laid siege to Waterford. The town held out for a day, but as night fell the Normans stormed in. A fresco in the House of Commons at Westminster depicts what happened next. MacMurrogh joined Strongbow at Waterford where the Norman, with the battle-scarred town as a backdrop, married the Irish King's daughter as promised to him two years earlier in Wales. Within a month, on 21 September, Dermot and Strongbow had captured Dublin, and Leinster, Ireland's richest province, fell completely into their hands.

The superior weaponry of the Normans certainly played a large part in their success, but so did the personal courage and military skill of their leaders. They used to great effect the longbow, which 245 years later was to destroy the flower of French chivalry on the battlefield of Agincourt. The Irish, used to fighting on foot, without armour and with axes, spears and light swords, had no real defence against the arrows and heavy battle-swords of the Normans.

After his success, Strongbow was in a difficult position. Dermot died in May 1171 at Ferns, the home of the Leinster kings, and Strongbow claimed his inheritance. The Leinster Irish, however, were not prepared to accept his right, which flouted the Gaelic law and custom of an elected kingship, and joined with Rory O'Connor in an attempt to vanquish him. At the same time, Henry II, nervous that his vassal might secure sufficient wealth and power in Ireland to challenge his authority, ordered Strongbow to return home. The Earl tactfully replied that he was holding his Irish lands at Henry's disposal, but Henry's action prevented any reinforcements arriving.

Strongbow, in his continued struggle with Rory O'Connor, found himself under such severe pressure during the High King's summer siege of Dublin that he offered to submit to him, 'to become his man and hold Leinster of him'. O'Connor would only agree to the Normans holding the towns of Dublin, Waterford and Wexford, and Strongbow refused to accept these terms. Only by dint of ability, courage and surprise did the Normans raise the siege by routing an attack and following up with a sally which dispersed O'Connor's army. Strongbow and Henry then came to terms in September. Strongbow surrendered the towns to Henry, who in return granted him the rest of Leinster.

On 17 October the British King landed at Waterford with an imposing army calculated to impress the Irish and cow Strongbow by its strength. Almost immediately most of the kings and chieftains of Munster and Leinster, together with Strongbow, paid homage to Henry in Dublin. Finally, in 1175, Rory O'Connor travelled to England where, at the Treaty of Windsor, he swore allegiance to Henry. In return, Henry granted O'Connor the kingdom of Ireland not already in Norman hands.

Neither King was really in a position to promise such a division. O'Connor no longer controlled the native Irish kings and chiefs, and had difficulty in maintaining his own claims in Connaught. Henry, while enjoying the nominal allegiance of his Norman Irish vassals, could not prevent them seizing more land. Hugh de Lacy and his officers, Nugent, Cusack, Fleming, Cruise and Plunkett, divided up the kingdom of Meath between them. John de Courcy in 1177 set out from Dublin with a handful of men and within a few years had conquered most of Ulster. By 1250, less than eighty years after Strongbow first landed in Ireland, three-quarters of the country was under Norman control, with only the rocky outposts of Connaught and west Ulster still not penetrated.

Henry also took steps to justify the claims for religious reform in Ireland which he had advanced to the Pope at the time of 'Laudabiliter'. Towards the end of 1171 the archbishops and bishops of Ireland met at the Synod of Cashel where, with Henry's representative the archdeacon of Llandaff, they accepted Henry's temporal supremacy. Although nothing was said of the claims of Canterbury or Armagh to head the Church in Ireland, among the decrees the Synod published, one stated, 'The divine offices shall be celebrated according to the usage of the Church of England.' Within a generation, most of the leading Churchmen in Ireland were Normans, and the loyalty of the Irish Church to the British crown — even in centuries after the Reformation — was established. In return for royal promises of religious reform and discipline, Popes were to bless British rule. After the Reformation, as the British Empire gradually expanded, the Church recognized the singular advantages of having, through the ever-faithful Catholic Irish, an influence on those who ran the Empire.

In May 1172, seventeen months after the Archbishop of Canterbury, Thomas à Becket, was murdered at his altar by Henry II's agents, the King was reconciled with the Pope, Alexander III, in large part because of his support of reform in the Irish Church. The Pope published three letters to the Irish Church instructing the bishops to assist Henry in keeping possession of Ireland, and he conferred on Henry the title 'Lord of Ireland'. Not until Britain broke with Rome at the Reformation did Henry VIII become the first king to style himself 'King of Ireland' in 1541.

Gerald de Barry, known as Giraldus Cambrensis, one of Strongbow's cousins, chronicled the Norman invasion in 1185 in a work of brilliant propaganda which emphasized Norman attributes and coloured British views of the Irish for centuries afterwards. The Norman invaders were, in fact, a ruthless, cruel and crude group of adventurers intent on the expansion of their own wealth and power which they masked with a show of religiosity. On Strongbow's tomb in Christ Church Cathedral, Dublin, lies in effigy the truncated body of his son, whom according to legend he is said to have hacked in two for cowardice in battle. But for Giraldus Cambrensis such qualities were rather possessed by the Irish:

> *For that we may not omit all mention of the perjury and treachery, the thefts and robberies in which this people with few exceptions so outrageously indulge, nor of their divers vices and most unnatural filthinesses, this nation is the foulest, the most sunk in vice, the most uninstructed in the rudiments of faith of all nations upon earth.*

As with their conquest of England and Wales, the Normans consolidated each gain with a castle. The first castles and fortifications they constructed were of earth and timber, but in a short space of time massive stone towers with crenelated outer walls were built. Carrickfergus Castle in Co. Antrim, dating from between 1180 and 1205, is one of the earliest. Dublin Castle, which was to become the seat of British government in Ireland and a place feared and hated by native Irishmen, was begun in 1204 on the site of the old Norse fort which dominated the city. At Trim in Co. Meath the largest fortress in Ireland was built: over three acres were enclosed within the walls by the time it was completed in about 1200. In 1202 the seat of the episcopal see was moved to Newtown Trim and an Anglo-Norman, Simon de Rochfort, appointed bishop. In 1206 he founded a cathedral there and brought from Paris members of the new religious order, the Augustinians, to staff and serve in it.

The walled towns of Galway, New Ross, Athenry and Drogheda were founded, and other towns were built all over Ireland. Trade with Britain and the continent flourished, and for the first time Ireland came to experience the widespread use of coinage. Also for the first time, in 1297 an Irish parliament was established on the British model, with Norman-Irish representatives coming from every part of the country except the far west of Connaught and Ulster. Three years later, towns and boroughs were also represented, but not until 1922 did an Irish parliament represent the mass of the Irish people.

This first Irish parliament was a parliament of and for the ruling group in Ireland, and one of the first laws it passed prohibited the Norman-Irish from wearing Gaelic dress because it confused relationships between the governors and the governed, and because it led to confusion when it came to killing Gaels. The

native Irish could be killed without penalty: in 1305 the Norman Irish Co. Offaly baron, Piers Bermingham, invited to a feast some neighbouring Gaels, the O'Connors, whose property he coveted, and in the middle of festivities murdered thirty of them. For this, he was rewarded with £100 by the Irish Exchequer for eighteen of their 'rebel' heads. Bermingham sought out the Irish 'as hunter doth the hare', and he and others like him rapidly convinced the Irish that no matter how much Norman-Irishmen might seem to be Irish, they never really would be. In Gaelic literature, the theme of the treachery of foreigners developed with the activities of Normans like Bermingham: 'Woe to the Gael who puts his trust in a king's peace or in foreigners.'

The fragile nature of the Norman conquest was strikingly demonstrated by the invasion of the Bruces of Scotland in 1315. The Norman-Irish population was not large, and it was ultimately dependent upon the political disorganization of the native kings and chiefs. But as the thirteenth century wore on, the native Irish began to cooperate against their new overlords. In 1258 the leading Irish kings united behind Brian O'Neill, the senior member of the great Ulster family, and declared him King of Ireland. This agreement was short-lived, but in 1263 a number of Irish leaders invited King Haakon IV of Norway to lead them against the Normans. When the Scots under Robert the Bruce won their decisive victory against King Edward II of England at Bannockburn in 1314, Norman Ireland seemed an easy last step in the Scottish king's dream of a Celtic kingdom.

Edward Bruce, Robert's brother, landed at Larne in September 1315 and within twelve months controlled most of Ireland north-east of Dublin. He was supported at first by nearly every powerful Irish family, and when Robert landed with a large army to help his brother, the Norman position looked very precarious. But Edward Bruce alienated the Irish by burning and plundering everywhere he went, and when, in 1317, Pope John XXII supported Edward II by excommunicating Bruce's clerical allies, the back of the invasion was broken. Bruce was defeated and killed at Dundalk the following year.

When the Hundred Years' War between France and England broke out in 1337, diverting the English crown from Irish affairs, the Normans in Ireland had little choice but to accept and make the best of their minority position. They had some merits. In their conquest they offered peace and stability to those who submitted to them, in contrast to the feuding which had characterized the relationships between native Irish kings like MacMurrogh and O'Brien. In addition, they recognized the many advantages Gaelic Church and society had to offer. Norman clerics proved anxious to live and work in Ireland, and Norman barons, unlike their

The carved brown sandstone west door of Clonfert Cathedral, Co. Galway, is a fine example of the Irish-Romanesque style. St Brendan the Navigator founded a monastery at Clonfert around 560, but the cathedral dates from 1164.

71

Tudor, Stuart and Cromwellian successors, did not try to rid their lands of Irishmen, but instead encouraged them to stay and continue to farm and herd as before. Only the Gaelic nobility was displaced, because they challenged the Normans' power. But even then, once a Gaelic king or chief accepted Norman superiority, the Normans were prepared to treat him as an equal. Hugh de Lacy married Rory O'Connor's daughter Rose; John de Courcy married a Gaelic princess. William the Marshall, one of the great figures of twelfth-century British history, became the son-in-law of Strongbow by marrying Dermot MacMurrogh's granddaughter.

Intermarriage was not the Normans' only far-sighted practice: they also rapidly adopted Gaelic customs. Just as in previous centuries the Gaels had assimilated Danish and Norwegian invaders, so they came to assimilate the Normans. In an attempt to arrest this process, the government promulgated the Statues of Kilkenny in 1366, which decreed that the two races, Norman and Gaelic, should remain separate and apart. Marriage between the races was made a capital offence, and the Norman-Irish were also forbidden to play the Irish harp or speak Gaelic.

The Statutes remained in force until 1613. The fears underlying them were largely justified and the Statutes themselves were a confession of defeat. They were a last-ditch attempt to rescue the area around Dublin, now coming to be known as the English Pale, from the assimilation that had overtaken the Norman invaders. The

Monea Castle, Co. Fermanagh: an early seventeenth-century Ulster plantation castle with corbelled projections typical of contemporary Scottish fortifications.

Black Death which visited Ireland in 1348 and 1349 had resulted in the death of approximately one-third of the population, forcing the Norman-Irish and Irish even closer in the face of a common calamity. This had been recognized in the preamble to the Kilkenny Statutes:

> *Whereas at the conquest of the land of Ireland and for a long time after the English of the said land used the English language . . . now many English of the said land, forsaking the English language, fashion, mode of riding, laws and usages, live and govern themselves according to the manners, fashion and language of the Irish enemies, and also have made divers marriages and alliances between themselves and the Irish enemies.*

The thirteenth and fourteenth centuries did in fact see a Gaelic revival: many of the greatest books and commentaries date from this period. Gerald FitzMaurice, third Earl of Desmond (1359–98), who in 1366 was appointed Justiciar of Ireland, the chief political and legal officer of the Crown, was known to his contemporaries as 'Gerald the Poet' for his Gaelic compositions, and, as the *Annals of the Four Masters* later declared, he 'excelled all the English and many of the Irish in knowledge of the Irish language, poetry and history'. He even adopted the Gaelic custom of fosterage, sending his own son to the household of an Irish chief.

By the close of the 1300s, the Normans outside the Pale had merged with the native people, becoming more Irish than English. And as resurgent Gaelic chieftains, often with the support of gaelicized Norman families like the Burkes of Connaught, gained control of more and more land, the cost of the Irish colony began to tell heavily on the Royal Exchequer. Art MacMurrogh in 1376 was able to claim the old Irish kingdom of Leinster. This so alarmed King Richard II that, seizing the opportunity of a lull in the Hundred Years' War, he came to Ireland in 1394 with a large army. He was the first British king since Henry II to set foot in Ireland. MacMurrogh prudently submitted, and Richard formally established the Pale to extend from Dundalk to the river Boyne and down the Barrow river to Waterford. No sooner had Richard left, however, than MacMurrogh rebelled again, killing in battle Roger Mortimer, heir to the childless Richard II's throne. Richard returned to Ireland in 1399 to bring MacMurrogh to terms, but instead found his own Crown challenged in England by Henry Bolingbroke, Duke of Lancaster. Richard sailed back to England to meet deposition and death in the Tower of London. From this time throughout the fifteenth century, English rule was in practice confined to the ever-diminishing area of the Pale.

Gaelic chiefs had once again learnt from the invaders, and English armies no longer enjoyed technical superiority. Only by bribery were the inhabitants of the Pale able to keep those they termed Irish enemies and rebels at bay. In 1435 members of the Irish parliament requested King Henry VI to consider

> *How that this land of Ireland is well nigh destroyed and inhabited with his enemies and rebels, in so much as there is not left in the nether parts of the counties of Dublin, Meath, Louth and Kildare that join together, out of the subjection of the said enemies and rebels scarcely thirty miles in length and twenty miles in breadth, thereas a man may surely ride or go in the said counties to answer the king's writ and to do his commandments.*

Outside the Pale, only the Church and the religious orders — the Cistercians, Dominicans, Franciscans and Augustinians — which had arrived around the time of the Norman invasion maintained an awareness separate from that of Gaelic society. However, the Synod of Kells' acceptance of Papal authority was at a time when the Papacy was entering the most sordid period of its history, and this was reflected in Ireland. Religious discipline slipped, and many priests, bishops and archbishops took wives and fathered families. As early as 1221 a visiting French monk noted, 'In the abbeys of this country the severity of Cistercian discipline and order is observed in scarcely anything but the wearing of the habit.' As late as the mid-sixteenth century a bishop of Killaloe married a daughter of the Earl of Thomond. Gaelic customs such as divorce, secular marriage and fosterage remained widespread.

Amongst the laity, two great families of the Norman-Irish (from the fourteenth century onwards known as 'Old English') dominated the scene, the Butlers in their earldom of Ormond, who remained substantially loyal to the Crown and English customs, and the FitzGeralds of Desmond and Kildare who did not. They conducted their affairs like the Irish chieftains around them, according to the Brehon Laws and private agreements between themselves and their neighbours, with a nominal loyalty to the British Crown. The O'Neills and O'Donnells of Ulster with the MacMurroghs of Leinster regained supremacy in their areas, remaining unchallenged until the Reformation. They all built fortified tower houses as easily defensible strongpoints: over two thousand of them still, in ruins, dot the Irish landscape. In contrast to the many-windowed manor houses characteristic of England at this time, the dark fortress-like tower houses stand as stark testimony to the anarchy of fifteenth-century Ireland.

In July 1449 Henry IV appointed Richard, Duke of York, his Deputy in Ireland in an attempt to divert the Duke's ambitions to take Henry's crown. Richard of York was to become the most popular British ruler Ireland ever had, largely because of his personal charm and diplomatic skill. After landing at Howth with a large army, he acknowledged his Irish and Norman-Irish ancestors, among them Brian Boru, and made plain his interest in securing the support of all Irishmen in his inevitable struggle for the British crown. Accordingly he promoted and favoured those who, regardless of ancestry, submitted to him and so soon secured the promised loyalty of Ireland. As one contemporary observer put it, 'ere twelve months come to an end, the wildest Irishman in Ireland shall be sworn English'.

Three months after he arrived, Richard's third son George, afterwards Duke of Clarence, was born and baptized in Dublin. The event was greeted with enthusiasm by the people of Dublin, and it cemented the attachment of nearly all Ireland to the White Rose of York. (In 1487 the impostor Lambert Simnel was crowned King of England in Dublin in the belief that he was George's son.)

When Richard returned to England in September 1450, he left behind a country broadly united in loyalty to him. In 1459, after being defeated at Ludlow, the second major battle of the Wars of the Roses, he fled back to Ireland, and was received with open arms. The Irish parliament, in its attempts to protect the Duke from the English parliament's allegations of treason against him, went so far as to give the first clear statement of the Norman-Irish perceptions of independence which had gradually developed in the previous century and a half:

> *The land of Ireland is, and at all times hath been, corporate of itself by the ancient laws and customs used in the same, freed of the burden of any special law of the realm of England, save only such laws as the lords spiritual and temporal and the commons of the said land had been in great council or Parliament there held admitted, accepted, affirmed and proclaimed.*

Only the personal link of the Crown was now held to connect Ireland with England. Richard left Ireland with an army in 1460, only to be killed at the battle of Wakefield, but the Yorkist cause triumphed and his eldest son was crowned Edward IV of England in March 1461.

Loyalty to York continued in Ireland after the first Tudor, Henry VII, became King of England in 1485. Garret More FitzGerald, eighth Earl of Kildare, was elected Justiciar by the Irish parliament in 1477 and, until his death in 1513, the 'Great Earl', as he was known, fought first for the Yorkist cause and for Norman-Irish freedom. Through marriage he established close ties with the O'Neills of Tyrone and a number of the leading Irish and Old English families. In all but name he became effective ruler of Ireland, enjoying the support and obedience of most of the chiefs and Gaelic nobility. He supported the claims of Lambert Simnel and subsequently in 1491 of Perkin Warbeck to be the Yorkist pretenders to the throne.

Fearing his power, Henry VII sent Sir Edward Poynings to Ireland as his Deputy in 1494 to replace FitzGerald and bring the country to 'whole and perfect obedience'. Poynings was an able soldier and administrator, completely loyal to his monarch, and FitzGerald apparently recognized the danger he presented. He wrote to a northern chieftain, O'Hanlon, 'Do not attempt anything against the Deputy that you would not attempt against me myself, for he is a better man than I am, but enter into peace with him and give him your son as surety.'

Poynings immediately set out to reduce the authority of the Irish parliament. He called an assembly of picked men which met at Drogheda in December 1494 and passed the legislation known as 'Poynings' Law'. This law, which remained in force until repealed in 1782, declared that an Irish parliament could meet only with the King's permission, and could pass only laws previously approved by the King and his English Council. Poynings' purpose was to prevent another Simnel or Warbeck securing the blessing of the Irish legislature, or of another more proper pretender to the throne finding the protection afforded Richard of York in 1459.

Defence of the Pale as the most loyal part of Ireland also concerned Poynings, and the Drogheda parliament voted to pay for a double ditch to be built from the mouth of the Liffey to Kildare, up to Trim and through Meath to Dundalk. The parliament also arrested FitzGerald and sent him to London. But there Henry VII realized that 'since all Ireland cannot rule this man, this man must rule all Ireland', and in 1496 appointed FitzGerald to the position of Deputy to succeed Poynings. He held this office until his death, and was given a completely free hand by Henry.

Poynings' Law even made it easier for the Great Earl to override objections to his rule from the Pale. He spent the revenues raised in Ireland as he wished and, again as the result of Poynings' parliament, appointed all the highest officers of the Church and State except bishops and archbishops, the Chancellor, Treasurer and chief judges. He repaid the King's trust with fair government, which in turn owed a great deal to the general royal policy of non-intervention in Irish affairs characteristic of the Norman settlement. As long as Ireland did not threaten the English Crown, and as long as the expense of Irish government was defrayed from Irish sources, kings of England were prepared to leave Ireland alone. Garret More FitzGerald's career was striking evidence of this. Had not Henry VII's successors decided to intervene actively in Irish affairs, even Poynings' Law, with Deputies like FitzGerald, might have secured a degree of Irish freedom and an acceptance of English claims to Irish lordship which would have averted the strife and bitterness of the next four hundred years.

5

REFORMATION AND REVOLT

*I prefer to rely on my own knowledge, and to point out who it was in actual fact that
first injured the Greeks; then I will proceed with my history, telling the story as I go
along of small cities no less than of great. For most of those which were great once
are small today; and those which used to be small were great in my own time.
Knowing, therefore, that human prosperity never abides long in the same place,
I shall pay attention to both alike.*

HERODOTUS, THE HISTORIES

The Tudors in England ushered out the
Middle Ages and hurried in the Modern Age with ruthless determination. To Henry
VIII and his Chancellor, Cardinal Wolsey, Ireland seemed full of 'the King's
decayed rents and embezzled lands', with powerful and unruly lords speaking a
heathen language and a Church which bore little relation to theirs. Certainly,
outside the Pale, Gaelic cultural and social traditions dominated life, and high
chieftains and kings ran their own affairs with no reference to English authority.
John Kite, one of Wolsey's officials, who became archbishop of Armagh, complained regularly to his master about the 'barbarity' of the Irish. The Earl of Surrey,
whom Henry appointed Deputy in 1519, was recalled two years later after report-
ing that he would need an army of more than five thousand with matching supplies
and munitions in order to bring Ireland firmly under royal control. From 1515 the
Pale-dominated Council of Ireland sent regular reports to Henry complaining about
Surrey's predecessor, the ninth Earl of Kildare, accusing him of attempting to make
the whole island Gaelic once again, and pointing out that the loyal Pale was rapidly
shrinking. By 1537 the Pale was smaller than ever before, 'cramperned and
crouched into an odd corner of the country named Fingal, with a parcel of the
King's land of Meath and the counties of Kildare and Louth'.

When Henry came to the throne in 1509, Garret More FitzGerald's power was

These are the families – both Gaelic and Norman – which to the present day dominate their respective parts of Ireland. In Gaelic times, many of these were the families of the major clans – notably the O'Neills of Ulster – but some Norman families, like the Fitzgeralds, Burkes and Berminghams, came to rival the local influence of their Gaelic neighbours. The Fitzgeralds indeed in many ways became successors to the Gaelic O'Neills, providing in the fifteenth and sixteenth centuries the leaders of Ireland much as the O'Neills had done in the centuries preceding the Norman invasion.

O'Doherty · MacSweeney · O'Cahan · MacDonnell · MacSweeney · O'Donnell · O'Neill · O'Neill Clanaboy · McGuinness · O'Rourke · MacMahon · Barret · O'Dowd · O'Hara · Maguire · O'Reilly · Plunket · MacDonagh · Preston · O'Malley · O'Gara · Macdermot · O'Farrell · Barnewall · Costello · O'Connor · St Laurence · O'Flaherty · Don · O'Connor · Bermingham · O'Madden · O'Molloy · Blake · Burke · O'Carroll · O'Dunn · O'More · O'Toole · Fitzgerald · O'Byrne · O'Brien · O'Kennedy · MacMahon · MacNamara · Butler of Ormond · MacMurrogh · Burke · Fitzmaurice · Fitzgerald · Roche · Fitzgerald · Power · MacCarthy · Mor · Barry · O'Sullivan · O'Sullivan · MacCarthy · O'Driscoll

firmly established in Ireland. Upon the Great Earl's death four years later his son the ninth Earl, Garret Og, was confirmed as Deputy by the King. The new Deputy proved himself as skilful and popular as his father, and further strengthened the power of his family by a series of marriage alliances with the leading Irish and Old English families. Henry, it seemed, was willing to continue his father's policy of giving power to the FitzGerald's in return for calm and loyalty. But Henry was also determined to root out 'overmighty subjects' and men of independent thought who would oppose him, and Garret Og was both. He was called to London three times — in 1519, 1527 and 1534 — to answer treasonable charges, and he died under arrest in the Tower of London in 1534. Before he left for the last time, the Earl appointed as his deputy his eldest son 'Silken' Thomas, Lord Offaly, a young man of twenty-one, 'of stature tall and personable; in countenance amiable; a white face

78

and withal somewhat ruddy, delicately in each limb featured . . . easily with submission appeased, hardly with stubbornness weighed; in matters of importance a headlong hotspur'. Well aware of his son's character the Earl warned Thomas to be guided by the advice of the Irish Council (the small group of Old English nobles who ruled Ireland in consultation with the Deputy). But, upon hearing a rumour that his father had been executed in the Tower, Silken Thomas declared himself in revolt against the King, sending for aid to Pope Paul III at the very moment when Henry had renounced the Pope's authority.

Thomas quickly gained control of most of Leinster and the Pale. He laid siege to Dublin, and for a short while it looked as if he might have Ireland at his feet. However, a royal army equipped with the new siege cannons and artillery defeated the young lord before any foreign help arrived, and Silken Thomas surrendered in 1535. The following year five of his uncles were arrested on trumped-up charges and in February 1537, together with Thomas, they were all executed at Tyburn. In the Beauchamp Tower in the Tower of London where Silken Thomas was kept, one may still see his unfinished lettering on the wall of a cell, 'Thomas FitzG', cut short no doubt by the headsman's axe.

Henry VIII
(1491–1547)

The FitzGerald revolt of 1534 had not been inspired by opposition to Henry VIII's break with the Papacy. Silken Thomas had sought only to take advantage of the schism for immediate political purposes. Later Irish rebels perceived the Old English and the FitzGerald revolt as inspired not by nationalism but by selfish interests of the originally English ruling group faced with the prospect of losing their power and wealth. Nevertheless, by his appeal to foreign power and the Pope, Silken Thomas established what was to become the traditional pattern of Irish nationalism. England's difficulty was henceforth seen as Ireland's opportunity; Britain's enemies were to become Ireland's friends. And while Catholicism was certainly a common denominator between Ireland and many of Britain's enemies, it was always the national appeal, not the religious, which motivated Irishmen: in 1919 Irish Nationalists despatched an envoy to the new avowedly anti-Catholic communist government of Russia to request 'sympathetic recognition for Ireland as a sister state', simply because Britain was supporting that government's opponents.

Henry VIII played a major part in the development of this international element in Irish nationalism by instituting the Anglican Church. The Henrician Reformation was also to be the single most revolutionary event in the relations between Britain and Ireland. By the end of the sixteenth century Ireland was to represent a persistent threat to the security of the British government because Irish Catholicism provided a natural opening to Britain's Catholic European enemies;

and Irish hostility to British rule could always be fuelled by religious antagonism. As naval developments progressed, this threat became ever more real, and Ireland assumed greater strategic importance. In 1579 Pope Gregory III and Philip II of Spain financed an expedition described as a religious crusade which landed at Dingle, Co. Kerry. The following year a Papal force landed at Smerwick, Co. Kerry. In 1601 over three thousand Spaniards landed at Kinsale to help Hugh O'Neill's rebellion against Elizabeth I. In 1690 King Louis XIV of France sent a French army of seven thousand to Cork which later fought for James II at the Battle of the Boyne. In 1798 over four thousand French soldiers landed in Ireland in support of Wolfe Tone's rebellion. During the Second World War one of the principal fears of the British Admiralty was that German U-boats might find refuge in Irish inlets.

The survival of Catholicism throughout most of Ireland after the Reformation added another factor to those of language, culture and tradition which already separated her from England. The Act of Supremacy, passed by the Westminster parliament in 1534, declared Henry VIII to be the supreme head of the Church in England, and did not extend to Ireland. For the title of 'The only Supreme Head on Earth of the whole Church of Ireland' he had to wait until the Irish Reformation

Ballinderry Middle Church, Co. Antrim, is one of the earliest surviving Protestant churches. It was built by settlers in the seventeenth century.

parliament met in 1536. This was the only change that actually took place: Church services otherwise remained the same. Even then, despite the fact that the parliament consisted principally of loyal supporters of Henry from the Pale, he met opposition to his religious policy, only securing the legislation he wanted in December 1537 after excluding most of the clerical representatives from the parliament. Before the split with Rome, the Catholic Church in Ireland was kept alive largely by the efforts of the Friars. One observer reported in 1515, 'There is no archbishop, no bishop, abbot or prior, parson nor vicar, nor any other person of the Church, high or low, great or small, English or Irish, that is accustomed to preach the word of God, saving the poor friars beggars.' The great age of Irish Christianity was over, and had been for some time. By 1517 the cathedrals of Clonmacnois and Ardagh were in ruins, and beyond the Pale generally religious observance had become a distinctly perfunctory affair. When Henry VIII in 1536 appointed as archbishop of Dublin George Browne, the English Augustinian who had performed the marriage service between the King and his second wife Anne Boleyn, the Irish hierarchy welcomed him. Most Irish bishops also accepted the Reformation and the claims to religious supremacy advanced by Henry. As in England, the monasteries were suppressed, and Irish bishops and local nobles and chieftains proved just as willing as their English counterparts to despoil them. Over four hundred monasteries were leased or sold to laymen during the reigns of Henry VIII and his daughter, Elizabeth. In Ireland — unlike England — there was no Pilgrimage of Grace, no martyrs, no Sir Thomas More. In 1541 when the Irish parliament passed an Act declaring Henry to be King of Ireland, there was no opposition. From this time to the present day, British monarchs were to claim their Irish title as of right endorsed by parliament, and not, as the previous claim to the 'Lordship of Ireland' had been, derived from the Papal grant to Henry II four hundred years before.

The parliament that endorsed the Reformation and the royal title, however, represented only perhaps nine counties and between twenty and thirty boroughs, and only the English ruling group therein. More than seventy years after this, the Irish parliament of James I was told,

> Before the thirty-third year of King Henry VIII we do not find any to have place in parliament but the English of blood or English of birth only; for the mere Irish in those days were never admitted, as well because their countries lying out of the limits of counties, could send no knights and, having neither cities nor boroughs in them, could send no burgesses to the parliament.

Henry VIII did more than introduce Protestantism to Ireland. He also set about firmly establishing British government in his new kingdom. One of the earliest official Irish documents of his reign, the 1515 'State of Ireland and Plan for its Reformation', indicates the extent to which Henry realized the true nature of his authority there:

And first of all to make his Grace understand that there may be more than sixty countries, called regions in Ireland, inhabited with the King's Irish enemies; some regions as big as a shire, some more, some less, unto a little; some as big as half a shire and some a little less; where reigneth more than sixty chief captains wherein some call themselves Kings, some Princes, some Dukes, some Archdukes, that liveth only by the sword and obeyeth to no other temporal persons, but only to himself that is strong, and every of the said captains maketh war and peace for himself . . . Also there be thirty great captains of the English folk that follow the same Irish order . . . and every of them maketh war and peace for himself without any licence of the King.

In order to rectify this state of affairs, as well as to extend royal authority, the Irish parliament in 1541 enacted the Surrender and Regrant legislation, which had drastic consequences for the old Gaelic chieftains and their people. From 1541 onwards, all land in Ireland was deemed to be theoretically surrendered to the King, who regranted it to those who were prepared to recognize his supremacy. No longer would the customs of Brehon Law and the common ownership of property which marked Gaelic society determine land and property inheritance. Most signally, in applying the new law to Gaelic, Old English (Norman) and English Irishmen fairly, and in encouraging Irish chiefs to surrender in return for the regranting of their tribal lands to them personally, Henry and his Tudor successors took the first major step in subverting Gaelic Ireland. The chief of the Ulster O'Neills, Con, submitted on this basis in December 1541, taking the title of Earl of Tyrone and having his eldest son recognized as his successor rather than his other son, Shane, or his nephews, who had traditional Gaelic claims to be considered as successors. Con's grandson, Hugh, was to find that after a failed rebellion his rights to his lands and his power within them were at the disposal of the King as a result of Surrender and Regrant. In the following centuries, Irish peasants who, in Gaelic society, benefited from the common wealth of their tribe, were to suffer in poverty and starvation from the concentration of ownership in the hands of a few under the Tudors.

Under Henry VIII's son, Edward VI, royal government in Ireland was extended from the Pale by military campaigns against the chiefs of Leix and Offaly

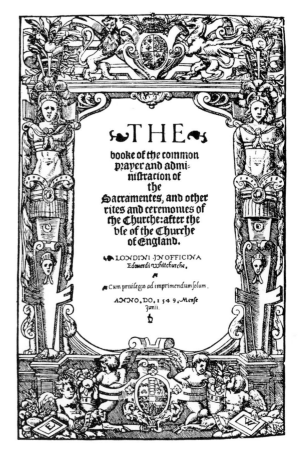

who resisted the policy of Surrender and Regrant. Castles and the first forts were constructed, at Maryborough (now Portlaoise), Co. Leix, and Philipstown (now Daingean), Co. Offaly. They were to become the centres of a dramatic new Tudor policy: plantation.

It was the Earl of Surrey, while he was still Deputy in 1521, who first suggested that the best way of subduing Ireland was to evict the native Irish from the land and replace them with loyal English immigrants. Mid-way through Edward VI's reign, in June 1550, the English Privy Council agreed 'that Leix and Offaly, being the countries late of the O'Connors and O'Mores, should be let out to the King's subjects at convenient rents, to the intent it may both be inhabited and also a more strength for the King's Majesty'. But the first attempts to implement the policy met with resistance from the Deputy, Sir Anthony St Leger, on the grounds that the

Main Street, Youghal, Co. Cork: one of the very few surviving Tudor stone houses in Ireland

The title page of the first Anglican Book of Common Prayer. *There was no Irish language edition and so the new Protestant religion did not easily gain Irish adherents.*

policy was unfair to those supplanted and that it would require too great a military presence to sustain it. The first planters found this to be true as their cattle were driven off and their homes burned by the original occupiers of the land. Ironically, in view of Ireland's later claims to steadfast Catholicity, it was during the reign of the devoutly Catholic Mary Tudor (1553–8) that the first effective plantations took place.

By the time Mary came to the throne, Protestantism was already waning in Ireland. There were few towns and no strong middle class, which elsewhere in Europe provided the basic congregation of Protestantism. But these factors were by no means crucial. It was a combination of shortsightedness and insensitivity that doomed the Reformation to failure from the start. The Irish Reformation Parliament in 1536, while enacting religious changes, also passed a law to promote 'English Order, Habit and Language'. In many ways, this piece of legislation was a reaffirmation of the Statutes of Kilkenny of 1366. The Gaelic language was prohibited throughout Ireland, as was the Gaelic form of dress — saffron-dyed clothing, moustaches, long hair and forelocks. The brehons and Gaelic poets and harpists were banned and persecuted. Intermarriage between native Irishmen and those of English blood was again forbidden, and was made treasonable in certain circumstances. In 1549, under Edward VI, the Mass was banned without even the Irish parliament being consulted, let alone the officials of the Irish administration who might have given other advice. The English-language *Book of Common Prayer*, drawn up by the Protestant Archbishop of Canterbury, Thomas Cranmer, was foisted upon the Irish Church, the vast majority of whose members spoke nothing but Irish.

Still, there was no revolt. Nor, for that matter, was there much rejoicing when the Catholic Mary came to the throne, and when she carried out the plantations of Leix and Offaly, renamed King's and Queen's Counties, it must have been clear to most Irishmen that Tudor government took no account of religious distinctions in its search for power. Dowdall, the Catholic Archbishop of Armagh appointed by Mary, was one of the principal supporters of the plantation policy, writing to the Queen that the solution to the problem of the rebellious Irish — his own flock! — was to drive out or kill them, settling their lands with Englishmen instead. The consequence was that during the next century the native Irish and the descendants of pre-Reformation settlers were to come together as one nation in defence of their old religion and in defiance of the discrimination practised in the growing British Empire. Colonists in Ireland, just as in America, found that the interests of English landlords and taxpayers, of Bristol and London merchants, were consistently placed ahead of theirs.

One of the by-products of the Reformation was Ireland's first university, Trinity College, Dublin, established in 1592 by Queen Elizabeth I. The seventh Earl of Desmond, who was chief governor of Ireland for four years from 1463, had tried to create a centre of higher education in the country. Irish undergraduates at Oxford and Cambridge were not popular — parliament had even legislated against 'wild Irishmen' at Oxford in 1422 — and they faced many restrictions during their residence. Desmond tried to set up a university at Drogheda 'in which may be made bachelors, masters and doctors in all sciences, as at Oxford', and in 1464 he did manage to found a college at Youghal. Elizabeth's decision to set up Trinity College, however, was part of an attempt to counteract the growing tendency for young Irishmen to journey to universities in Catholic Europe where they could learn seditious ways. For the first thirty years of its existence, the College, although Protestant, freely accepted Catholics. The study of Irish language and literature was also first instituted at Trinity.

The only distinctly Catholic attempts to overthrow English rule in Ireland were inspired from abroad. The first was in 1579 when six hundred soldiers armed by Spain landed at Dingle, Co. Kerry, under the command of Sir James Fitzmaurice, but this attempt fizzled out quickly after Sir James's death in a skirmish. The next year Pope Gregory XIII granted a plenary indulgence to all who took up arms against Queen Elizabeth I, and another Spanish-supported invasion force landed in Kerry, but after a hard fight it was defeated and every survivor was put to the sword

A page from a primer of the Irish language prepared for Elizabeth by Sir Christopher Nugent, Baron of Delvin in the County of Westmeath. 'Among the manyfold actions (moste gratious and vertuous soveraigne) that beare testymonie to the world of your majestyes greate affection, tending to the refformation of Ireland, there is noe one (in my opinion) that more evydent shewithe the same, than the desyer your Highness hath to understande the language of your people theare...' signed: C. Delvin

Elizabeth I (1533–1603)

Iryſhe. Latten. Engliſhe.

Iryſhe	Latten	Engliſhe
Coneſ za zu.	Quomodo habes.	How doe you.
Caim ʒo maih.	Bene ſum.	I am well,
ʒo ſio maih aʒai,	Habeo gratias.	I thancke you,
In eol oyz ʒealaʒ do lauaiſio.	Poſſis ne — hibernice loqui	Cann you — speake Fryſhe
A baiſ laooen.	Dic latine.	Speake Latten
Dia leſiuean ʒ ſaſoma	Deus adiuat — ʒ Reginã Angliæ	God saue the Queene off Englande.

*Map of Ireland by
John Goghe, c. 1587*

by one of the English commanders, Sir Walter Raleigh. In 1583 the fourteenth Earl of Desmond, the nominal leader of these attempted insurgencies, was captured and his head sent to Queen Elizabeth as 'a goodly gift', ending up in an iron cage on the Tower of London while his truncated body was spread across the walls of Cork. What was to become the all too familiar pattern of governmental suppression of Irish rebellion was bluntly stated by Raleigh's half-brother Sir Humphrey Gilbert:

I slew all those from time to time that did belong to, feed, accompany or maintain any outlaws or traitors; and after my first summoning of a castle or fort, if they would not presently yield it, I would not take it afterwards of their gift, but won it perforce — how many lives soever it cost; putting man, woman and child to the sword.

After what became known as the Desmond Rebellion was over, several of the English soldiers wrote about the campaign. Sir Peter Carew, a Devonshire knight, described the capture of an Irish camp: 'found none but hurt and sick men whose pains and lives they soon terminated ... Those whom the sword could not reach were deliberately given a prey to famine.' Sir William Pelham, having marched from Dublin to Limerick in 1580, wrote that he had 'passed through the rebel countries, consuming with fire all habitations and executing the people wherever we found them'. The poet Edmund Spenser, author of *The Faerie Queen*, who had come to Ireland in 1580 as secretary to the Deputy, left a graphic description of the state of Munster after the rebellion:

Out of every corner of the woods and glens they came creeping forth upon their hands, for their legs would not bear them. They looked like anatomies of death; they spake like ghosts crying out of their graves; they did eat of the dead carrions, happy were they if they could find them, yea, and one after another soon after, insomuch as the very carcasses they spared not to scrape out of their graves. And if they found a plot of watercresses or shamrocks, they flocked there as if to a feast.

Real and enduring hatred of British rule stemmed from these times.

A year after Desmond's death, his whole territory — over half a million acres in Munster — was confiscated by the Crown and regranted to 'undertakers' who agreed to repopulate their new lands with English settlers. Raleigh was given forty thousand acres, Spenser, four thousand. However, less than half the Desmond lands were planted, and the Munster plantation was judged a failure by Elizabeth, who did not encourage its repetition. In 1591 when The MacMahon of Monaghan was

charged with treason and his lands confiscated, Elizabeth rejected plantation and preferred to divide the lands amongst the chieftain's neighbours and competitors.

One of the most stirring escape stories in Irish history sparked off the next and most dangerous rebellion. Red Hugh O'Donnell, son of the chief of the Tyrconnell O'Donnells, was kidnapped in 1587 as a hostage by the Deputy, Sir John Perrott, who feared the family's power. An innocent-looking merchant ship carrying Spanish wine was sent to Lough Swilly, where the sixteen-year-old Hugh was being fostered by MacSwiney, Lord of Fanat. MacSwiney and his retinue, including his foster-son, were invited aboard the ship where, while tasting wines, they were surrounded by soldiers who had been hidden in the hold. MacSwiney and all but O'Donnell and two companions were released, and the boat sailed with them to Dublin, where they were imprisoned in the Birmingham Tower of Dublin Castle.

Three years later O'Donnell escaped, but was recaptured after a few days in the Wicklow mountains where he had been searching for Fiach MacHugh O'Byrne, one of the leading Irish chiefs resisting Tudor rule. A year later, on Christmas night 1591, Red Hugh escaped again, this time with two other prisoners, Henry and Art O'Neill, whose father, Shane, had been chief of the O'Donnell's Ulster neighbours. It was freezing and snowing as the young men slipped away. Henry O'Neill made his own way back to Ulster, but his brother and Red Hugh struggled through the bitterly cold Wicklow mountains towards Glenmalure, where Fiach MacHugh O'Byrne's encampment lay. They took refuge in a shallow cave near Glendalough, and two days later Fiach found them wrapped in each other's arms, covered in snow. Art was dead. Hugh recovered, and with Fiach's help made his way to his father's castle at Ballyshannon, Co. Donegal, where physicians had to amputate his two big toes as a result of his ordeal.

Meanwhile in Ulster, Hugh O'Neill, cousin of the escaped brothers, was contemplating revolt. He had organized Red Hugh's escape from Dublin Castle, and in 1588 he had given help to survivors of the Spanish Armada wrecked on the Donegal coast. His rebellion was unexpected, since as a boy of nine he had been taken to England by Sir Henry Sidney and brought up at his castle at Ludlow, at Penshurst Place in Kent, and in London. By the time Hugh returned to Ireland aged eighteen in 1568, he was to all appearances a Protestant English gentleman. In 1569 he led a troop of horse in the Queen's pay, helping to suppress a Munster rising; and in 1575, when Sir Henry Sidney was appointed Deputy, Hugh fully supported his patron's attempts to extend the power of the Crown in Ireland. In 1582 he was rewarded by Elizabeth with the earldom of Tyrone and the grant of the O'Neill lands, and for the next ten years he concentrated on establishing his supremacy over

Sir Thomas Lee, the English Captain-General of the Kern (foot soldiers of Ireland), dressed in the garb of an Irish gentleman. Painting by Marcus Gheevaerts, 1594. Lee married an Irish woman who acted as his interpreter. He was executed for treason in 1601.

While Henry VIII and Elizabeth I were content merely to confiscate land, it was, ironically, the Catholic Queen Mary who in 1556 instituted the first plantation of the counties of Leix and Offaly (then renamed King's and Queen's Counties) with loyal families from the Pale and England.

After the Flight of the Earls in 1607 their six counties of Armagh, Coleraine (later Londonderry), Donegal, Tyrone, Fermanagh and Cavan were confiscated by the Crown. By the time of James I's death in 1625 over fifty thousand Scottish Protestant immigrants had settled in Ireland.

By 1660 the extent of Cromwell's confiscations and the English government's reservations meant that Ireland was mostly owned by Protestants: the numbers on the map indicate the percentage of each county confiscated.

The native Catholic Irish were assigned an area in the west of the country, but they were not allowed to settle in towns, on islands, or within a mile of the Shannon or the sea.

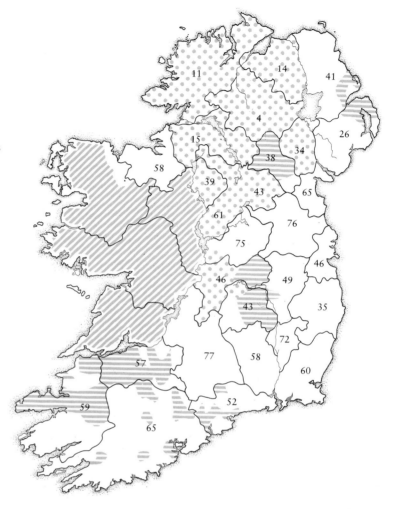

the other lords and chiefs of Ulster. In this personal endeavour O'Neill saw the opportunity to found an Irish national movement in defence of traditional Irish ways, and his part in engineering Red Hugh O'Donnell's escape was his first tentative step towards disloyalty.

In 1592, some weeks after the escape, Red Hugh stayed with O'Neill at Dungannon, and the two men agreed to an alliance ending the feuds that had plagued relations between the O'Donnells and O'Neills in previous years. In May 1593, Red Hugh brought together a Confederation of Irish chiefs in revolt, sending the Archbishop of Tuam to Spain for help. Hugh O'Neill stood apart at first, still uncertain that British rule could be successfully challenged. Then in 1595 he made his choice. He decided to lead the Confederacy, and immediately made an appeal to national and religious sentiment in Ireland for support. He adopted the role of champion of 'Christ's Catholic religion' and called on the Munster Irish to make war with him. This was one of the watersheds of Irish history. Not only was there a sense of religious solidarity, but also and most importantly, for the first time since Rory O'Connor had attempted to expel the Normans, the glimmerings of an Irish national resistance emerged.

Philip II of Spain offered O'Neill help in his war, which Philip chose to see as in defence of the Catholic religion. O'Neill in negotiations with British commanders and the government did ask for freedom of conscience, but he was more concerned about the restoration of lands to himself and his allies. In this he secured the support not only of the Munster lords, but also of the O'Byrnes of Wicklow and most of the leading Irish families beyond the Pale. With his experience of soldiering in the service of the Queen, O'Neill trained a professional army, changing the kernes and gallowglasses who had typified previous Irish forces into musketeers and pikemen. All he lacked in armaments was cannon, and so he adopted the tactics of guerrilla warfare, never seeking a pitched battle. Then, in the winter of 1598 at Yellow Ford on the Blackwater river in Armagh, O'Neill ambushed and defeated a force of over four thousand, killing more than half the number including its commander. The

A 1521 engraving by Albrecht Dürer of Irish warriors and peasants armed for war

victory was seen as a major one, and O'Neill began to be spoken of as the 'Prince of Ireland', a harking back to his family's claims to the Gaelic High Kingship.

Seriously alarmed, Elizabeth sent over her favourite, Robert Devereux, second Earl of Essex, with viceregal powers and the largest army Ireland had yet seen, over sixteen thousand strong. But instead of planning a concerted and powerful campaign, Essex agreed a truce with O'Neill and returned to London where, in consequence, he was disgraced and executed.

Essex's successor as Deputy was Charles Blount, Lord Mountjoy, who arrived in February 1600. He proposed to defeat O'Neill by surrounding Ulster with forts and to use famine 'as the chief instrument of reducing this kingdom'. O'Neill once again stressed the religious aspect of his struggle, pressing for Spanish aid and sending for papal recognition of his war as a Catholic crusade. In the winter of 1599–1600 he made a royal progress through Munster, and his confidence grew.

At last in September 1601 about three and a half thousand Spaniards landed unopposed at Kinsale, and took over the town. O'Neill had wanted the force to land further north, closer to him in Ulster, because Mountjoy's forces were slowly gathering strength on his borders and in places had even penetrated O'Donnell lands. In November, O'Neill and O'Donnell began the march south to join the Spanish army, managing in a series of brilliant manoeuvres to avoid Mountjoy, and O'Neill even launched an attack on the Pale on his way. Then, outside Kinsale on Christmas Eve, the Irish army met Mountjoy as he besieged the town. Within hours the battle was over, and O'Neill's army was broken, beaten by superior discipline and cavalry before they could join up with their Spanish allies. The battle marked the end of the war and the beginning of the end of Gaelic Ireland. Red Hugh went to Spain in another attempt to obtain help, but died there on 10 September 1602, probably as the result of poisoning by one James Blake of Galway, an agent of Mountjoy. O'Neill returned to Ulster where, in a desultory manner, he remained in rebellion until 1603, when Mountjoy accepted his submission on 23 March, one day before Queen Elizabeth died.

With O'Neill's surrender the last unconquered province of Ireland, Ulster, was subjected to direct British rule and law. At her death, Elizabeth was the first British monarch who could properly claim control of most of the Crown's second kingdom. However, the legacy of Elizabeth's Irish wars was a memory of bitterness and hatred etched deeply in Irish consciousness. After submitting to Mountjoy, O'Neill journeyed to London where he was received ceremoniously by the new Scottish Stuart King, James I. Sir John Harington, who had spent years fighting the Irish Earl, spoke for many after seeing O'Neill's reception. 'How did I labour after that

Conscientia mille testes

Tyrones false Submission afterwards rebelling.

A contemporary woodcut of Hugh O'Neill, Earl of Tyrone, submitting his fealty to Lord Deputy Essex before he launched the last campaign of his great rebellion

knave's destruction. I adventured perils by land and sea, was near starving, ate horse flesh in Munster, and all to quell that man who now smileth in peace with those what did hazard their lives to destroy him.'

For four more years O'Neill withstood in silence and in peace the encroachments of British administrators and settlers. James I and Mountjoy were well-disposed towards the defeated Earl, and both men tried to implement a liberal policy in Ireland, including religious toleration. As James said some years later, 'though he would much rejoice if the Irish Catholics would conform themselves to his religion, yet he would not force them to forsake their own'. In 1604 the King ordered a survey which clearly revealed that the Protestant presence in Ireland was purely nominal. Sadly, in 1605, with the fears of a Catholic coup generated by Guy Fawkes and the Gunpowder Plot, the pressures upon James at home to prove that he was not a closet Catholic himself forced a tougher line, and he acceded to the Irish Council's requests for a vigorous anti-Catholic policy. Sir Arthur Chichester was

93

appointed Deputy, and using the powers of Surrender and Regrant together with religious persecution, he began whittling away the O'Donnell and O'Neill lands.

O'Neill determined to argue his case in London; but before he could do so, Red Hugh's younger brother Rory O'Donnell, Earl of Tyrconnell, pre-empted his decision by plotting a secret flight to France. O'Neill, convinced that Chichester and the government would interpret O'Donnell's action as meaning that the Ulster lords were once more planning war, quickly joined the flight. On 4 September 1607 the two Earls with ninety-nine followers set sail in a French ship from Rathmullan, Co. Donegal, never to return. Nearly thirty years later the *Annals of the Four Masters* mourned their departure:

> *It is certain that the sea has not borne and the wind has not wafted in modern times a number of persons in one ship more eminent, illustrious, noble in point of genealogy, heroic deeds, valour, feats of arms, and brave achievements than they. Would God had permitted them to remain in their inheritance.*

Once on the continent, the Earls journeyed through France to Spanish Flanders and thence to Rome where, in 1608, they were received by the Pope and given papal pensions. O'Donnell died in July that year and was buried in the Franciscan church of San Pietro di Montorio on the Janiculum hill in Rome. Eight years later O'Neill was laid to rest beside him with royal honours. British agents who kept an eye on him during his last years reported that the Great Earl, in the evenings after dinner, had only one subject of conversation: 'his face would glow, he would strike the

*Charles Blount,
Lord Mountjoy
(1563–1606)*

*A sixteenth-century
Irish chieftain's feast
unflatteringly
portrayed in this
contemporary
woodcut by John
Derricke in his book*
The Image of Irelande
(1581)

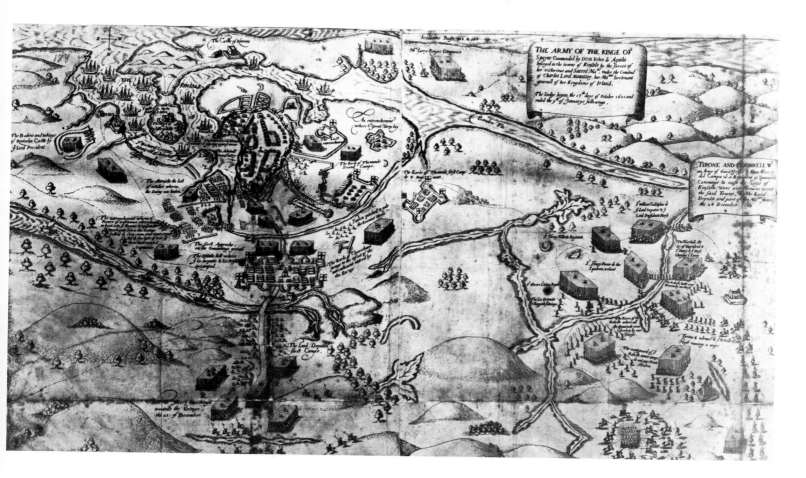

table, he would say that they would yet have a good day in Ireland'. Sean O'Faolain has summed up O'Neill's Roman years as 'habituated to melancholy and homelessness and the routine of idle days'.

    After the 'Flight of the Earls', as Irish history soon called it, the O'Neill and O'Donnell lands were declared forfeit to the Crown. Advantage was also taken of the Flight to abandon the slow process of anglicizing the native population through law and practice in favour of a return to the policy of plantation. Sir John Davies, the Irish Attorney General, who had long coveted land in Ulster, could not conceal his jubilation:

> *As for us that are here, we are glad to see the day wherein the countenance and majesty of the civil law and government hath banished Tyrone out of Ireland, which the best army in Europe and the expense of two millions of sterling pounds did not bring to pass. And we hope His Majesty's Government will work a greater miracle in this kingdom than ever St Patrick did; for St Patrick did only banish the poisonous worms, but suffered the men full of poison to inhabit the land still; but His Majesty's blessed genius will banish all those generations of vipers out of it, and make it, ere it be long, a right fortunate island.*

A contemporary map of the Battle of Kinsale (1601), which marked the beginning of the end of Gaelic Ireland

95

6

NO SURRENDER!

*Religion is a great force — the only real motive force
in the world; but what you fellows don't understand is
that you must get at a man through his own religion
and not through yours.*

GEORGE BERNARD SHAW, GETTING MARRIED

The plantation of Ulster was one of the most thoroughgoing relocations of population in British history. Never before were so many people moved in such a short period of time. By 1700 about 170,000 planters — 150,000 of them from lowland Scotland — had settled. The first step was formally taken in 1608 when the O'Neill and O'Donnell lands, now designated the new counties of Armagh, Cavan, Coleraine (later renamed Londonderry), Donegal, Fermanagh and Tyrone, were declared to be in the King's hands. A committee was appointed in London to prepare a detailed scheme of plantation, and in January 1609 it reported back recommending that the planters should outnumber the native Irish. The following year its proposals were put into effect. As in the earlier Munster plantation, English and Scottish 'undertakers' were granted parcels of land which they in turn had to populate with imported tenants. Complete separation of the imported and native populations was also established, with the new settlers taking lands which had been almost completely cleared of their previous inhabitants. Those who had been evicted were allowed to live only on lands specially allocated to favoured Irishmen, the Church, or to 'servitors' — military officers who had served against O'Neill. Twenty-three new towns were planned, each with a grid pattern surrounding a central square or diamond such as

'The Diamond' of Londonderry today. Before this there were only two towns in Ulster of any size, Carrickfergus and Newry. The Guilds of the City of London were granted the towns of Derry and Coleraine and much of the countryside in between, and by September 1610 the reorganization was virtually complete. Three years later, most of the new settlers had arrived. Calculations based on a survey conducted in 1622, and on related evidence, indicate that in the previous fourteen years about 3700 English and Scottish families — about 13,000 people — had been brought as planters over to the six escheated counties. Down and Antrim, which had been settled privately and for the most part before the Ulster plantation, had an adult British population of about 7500 in the early 1620s.

Still, the plantation was not successful, largely because not enough settlers could be found to make ownership of the lands a viable financial proposition without native labour and therefore tenants. Also, prospective settlers were naturally frightened of the brooding resentment of native Ulstermen faced with the wholesale loss of their ancestral homes. 'Although there be no apparent enemy,' a contemporary observer wrote in 1610, 'nor any visible main force, yet the woodkern and many other (who have now put on the smiling countenance of contentment) do threaten every house, if opportunity of time and place doth serve.' In the town of Derry, renamed Londonderry after the City Guilds' investment there (the use of the older 'Derry' still signifies nationalist sentiment, opposed to London's 'theft' of their town), settlers worked 'as it were with the sword in one hand and the axe in the other'. As a result, two developments followed swiftly upon the plantation: many of the 'undertakers' defaulted in their payments to the Exchequer because their expected rents were not forthcoming as the settlement fell below its planned numerical strength; and many of the native Irish quickly crept back and were accepted by desperate landlords as tenants and workers on lands they once had owned. In 1628 the government was forced to recognize the facts of the plantation and allow Irish tenants to live on one-quarter of the lands previously allocated to planters on payment of fines and double rents.

From the Irish point of view, the plantations, the savage wars and the rigours of Tudor government were confirmation that Albion was, indeed, perfidious. The concentrated attack on Gaelic culture and law was seen as fundamentally incomprehensible, with only racist terms going some way to explain the slaughters of women and children during the Desmond Rebellion in Munster, and the loss of lands and property throughout the centuries. An anonymous seventeenth-century Irish poet observed without hope:

Men smile at childhood's play no more,
Music and song, their day is o'er;
At wine, at Mass the kingdom's heirs
Are seen no more; changed hearts are theirs.

No praise in builded song expressed
They hear, no tales before they rest;
None care for books and none take glee
To hear the long-traced pedigree.

The packs are silent, there's no sound
Of the old strain on Bregian ground.
A foreign flood holds all the shore,
And the great wolf-dog barks no more.

Woe to the Gael in this sore plight!
Henceforth they shall not know delight.
No tidings now their woe relieves,
Too close the gnawing sorrow cleaves.

For the Tudors and their agents, however, a different view was taken. They claimed the right to govern Ireland as a result of conquest, and Irishmen who refused to accept this were seen simply as traitors. As more and more Irishmen proved 'treacherous', the Irish as a whole were regarded as unreasonable and as somehow not as good as Englishmen. Edmund Campion, the English Jesuit executed as a spy in 1581 by Queen Elizabeth, wrote in the most scathing terms about his Irish co-religionists' influence on 'the very English of birth, conversant with the brutish sort of that people, become degenerate in short space, and quite altered into the first rank of Irish rogues'. Elizabeth herself saw the Irish as 'vile rebels'. The great nineteenth-century Irish historian, William Lecky, concluded that for Englishmen in the sixteenth and seventeenth centuries, 'the slaughter of Irishmen was looked upon as literally the slaughter of wild beasts'.

At the same time, it should also be remembered that the British attitude towards the Irish was not unusual. The Crown dealt just as harshly with opponents and rebels within Britain. British traitors and heretics had to face the tortures of the Star Chamber. British martyrs (there were few Irish ones) were burnt alive at the stake or, like Campion, hanged, drawn and quartered. Outside the British Isles, the age was possibly even more severe. In South America the Conquistadores indulged in an orgy of plunder and slaughter which make Ireland's experience look like a minor skirmish in comparison. The Roman Catholic Church had instituted the Inquisition in 1229, and in the sixteenth century revived it with vengeance in Europe. In France in 1582 on 24 August, St Bartholomew's Day, thousands of Huguenots were slaughtered by the government. Tudor and Stuart excesses in Ireland have to be seen in this wider context.

Apart from the plantation of Ulster, the government also faced the perceived threat of Catholicism. Without their lands, and without leaders, Irishmen turned to their religion for support and guidance. The Counter Reformation had revived the discipline and fervour of the Catholic clergy, and as Spenser noted,

> *it is great wonder to see the odds between the zeal of Popish priests and the ministers of the Gospel. For they spare not to come out of Spain and from Rome by long toil and dangerous travelling, where they know peril of death awaiteth them and no reward or riches are to be found, only to draw the people unto the Church of Rome: whereas some of our idle ministers, having the livings of the country offered unto them without pains and without peril, will neither for the same nor any love of God nor zeal of religion be drawn forth from their warm nests.*

Gradually, in the face of discrimination and persecution, the cause of Catholicism and the cause of a 'free' Ireland became almost identical. The Catholic Church, by a diplomatic policy of appointing native Irishmen to native and Old English to Old English sees, helped the growth of this identity, and also helped forge a new national consciousness in which calls for religious toleration mirrored simultaneous demands for devolution and economic freedom. The first demonstration of this came in the Irish parliament which assembled, for the first time in more than twenty-five years, in 1613.

The parliament which met in Dublin in May 1613 was different from its Tudor predecessors in several respects. In the first place, it was larger and represented more of Ireland than any previous assembly. Secondly, of the 232 members in the Irish House of Commons, 100 were Catholic. Unlike the Westminster parliament which had banned Catholics, the Irish parliament still accepted them. Most were Old English, although eighteen native Irishmen had seats, and they formed the first distinct opposition group in an Irish parliament. Their opposition, however, was not on religious grounds, but was based on fear for their lands and possessions. The Crown's demonstration of the ability to confiscate and regrant the Ulster lordships was a source of worry to many who saw that their lands also could be forfeit at royal whim. But the parliament, for all its differences, was representative only of the loyal colonists in a hostile land. The Earls of Tyrone and Tyrconnell were formally attainted for treason, thus legalizing the seizure of their lands. The Brehon Laws were declared abolished, and the whole panopoly of English law — juries, assizes, and common law — was introduced in their stead.

Gaelic customs remained, and the Brehon Laws continued to be used by Irishmen remote from central government for generations to come, but as the Irish parliament's legislation was pressed home upon an uncomprehending people, there developed a hidden, secret Ireland which despite the superficial conformity would remain consciously Gaelic. In the eighteenth century the 'hedge schools' thrived, where the successors of the Gaelic brehons, storytellers and harpists surreptitiously taught young Irish boys and girls the history, the traditions and the tales of their forbears. John Millington Synge, in the first decade of the twentieth century, was still able to hear the voices of this hidden world as he lay in lodgings on the Aran Islands and in Wicklow with his ear pressed to the floor or wall listening to the conversations of his hosts. In *The Playboy of the Western World*, *In the Shadow of the Glen*, *The Aran Islands* and *Riders to the Sea*, Synge captured the earthy commonsense, the disrespect for authority and the living memories of an old Irish world. From the perspective of this hidden world, the Playboy is still able to see as foreign the superimposed authority all around him: 'Drink a health to the wonders of the western world, the pirates, preachers, poteen-makers, with the jobbing jockies; parching peelers, and the juries fill their stomachs selling judgements of the English law.'

Under the Stuarts, the practice of government in Ireland was increasingly placed in the hands of men sent from England. The Old English were no longer trusted: they had become too closely identified with the native Irish and their own loyalties to each other, rather than to the Crown's interests. The Irish parliament of 1613, despite its willingness to pass anti-Gaelic Laws, had shown that it was prepared and able to obstruct the government when its members were denied power and the sinecures of office. In July 1633, Thomas Wentworth, Earl of Strafford, arrived in Dublin as the Lord Deputy of the new King, Charles I. He was determined to ensure that his administration would be financially independent, immune to local influence and would be controlled centrally by himself alone as the King's agent.

To effect this he developed a policy of 'Thorough' — efficient (if rapacious) government — which Archbishop Laud was to deploy with disastrous results in England. Strafford treated the Catholic Old English and native Irish alike, promising the King's 'Royal Grace and Bounty' to them in return for money, and then withholding the 'Graces', as they were called, fining and confiscating property on the least excuse. The Earl of Cork was forced to surrender the college of Youghal and was fined £15,000 for not fulfilling the terms of the original grant. The City of London Guilds had to pay a fine of £70,000 and lost their charters in Ulster for similar reasons. Strafford allowed religious toleration to Catholics in return for a payment of £20,000, although in 1634 for the first time Roman Catholic students at Trinity College were asked to take the oath of Supremacy. Those who did not could still attend, but would not receive degrees, fellowships or scholarships. As Charles' wars with Scotland began, Strafford forced Scottish settlers in the north to take the hated 'Black Oath', swearing allegiance to the King. In carrying out his policy, Strafford managed to alienate every influential group in the country, and some — like the London Guilds — in England too. After he was recalled by Charles in November 1639, Catholic Old English and Protestant New English (Elizabethan and Stuart landlords and administrators) in Ireland combined with English Puritans at Westminster in the revolutionary Long Parliament to throw off Strafford's administration. It was only when the Puritans began to press for anti-Catholic measures in 1641 that this strange alliance dissolved.

The storm-clouds of religious persecution, resentment of Strafford's government, and the inability of the Ulster Irish to accept the plantation generated Ireland's greatest popular uprising. Under James I Catholic priests had been banned from Ireland and fines were imposed for non-attendance at Protestant Church of Ireland services; consequently much of the unrest was among priests, who took a leading part in organizing the rebellion. It was widely held in England that Catholics were natural traitors: if they acknowledged the Pope's right to approve or depose rulers they could not be equally loyal to both Pope and King. This view seemed now to be vindicated. But the rebellion was not religious, and the rebels constantly emphasized their loyalty to the Crown. Irishmen now accepted the Crown's right to govern them, but not the Crown's officers. An all-Ireland revolt was planned, only to be betrayed on the very eve of its commencement on 23 October 1641. Nevertheless, it went ahead in Ulster: Dundalk was captured and Drogheda besieged.

The Irish administration was hamstrung by the internal conflict that was developing in England, not knowing whether to seek support from the King or parliament in suppressing the rebellion. The leaders of the rising professed at the start their loyalty to the King, demanding only their lands back, and slowly it became clear after the civil war started in 1642 that Ireland was fundamentally more hostile to the parliamentary Puritans than to the Crown. In 1641 possibly as many as four thousand Scottish and English Ulster planters (mostly Presbyterians)

OVERLEAF]
Anti-Irish Catholic propaganda from Thomason Tracts, 1647, depicting in horrifying detail atrocities suffered by Ulster Protestant settlers at the hands of rebel Irish troops in 1641 during the Confederation of Kilkenny rebellion. Some massacres did take place, but nothing on the scale that contemporary propagandists claimed. Cromwell seems to have believed that horrors such as these really did happen, and later partly explained his slaughters at Drogheda and Wexford as revenge for 1641. To the present day many northern Irish Protestants believe that these massacres were an attempt at genocide.

Owen Macke-onell who discouered the plot of takinge Dublin, had a Pistoll charged with too Bullets, the pane primed with powder & Brimstone twice offered against him tooke not fire, so the Rebells said God will not suffer him to be killed & he will be on our side. I warrant you

Owen Macke-onell leapinge ouer a wall esca: ped & was sent to our Parlament with letters & was rewarded 500 li & 200 per annum.

At one M.r Atkins house 7 Papistes brake in & beate out his braines, then riped vpe his Wife with childe after they had rauished her, & Nero like vewed natu: res bed of conception then tooke they the Childe and sacrificed it in the fire

English Protestantes striped naked & turned into the mountaines in the frost, & snowe, whereof many hundreds are perished to death, & many lyinge dead in diches & Sauages vpbraided them sayinge, now are ye wilde Irish as well as wee.

Multitudes of Herringes driuen into Dublin. 20 a peny.

St Patrike Dunsons Wiffe rauished before him, slew his Seruants, spurned his Children tell they died, bound him with Rowles of match that his eyes bursted out, cut of his eares & nose teared ofe both his Cheekes after cut of his armes & legges, cut out his tongue after run a red hot Iron into him.

Mrs Fordes house rifled, and to make her Confesse where her mony lay, they tooke hot tonges clappinge them to the Soules of her feete & to the Palmes of her handes so tormented her that with the paine thereof shee died.

They haue set men & women on hot Grideorns to make them Confesse Where there money was.

Hauing rauished Virgens & Wifes they take there Children & dase there braines against the walls in sight of there weepinge Parents & after destroyed them likewise.

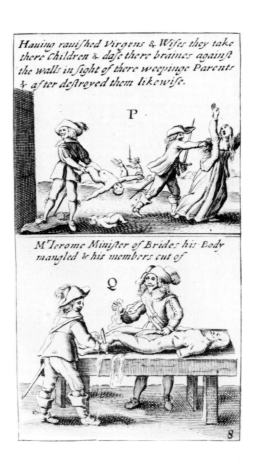

Mr Ierome Minister of Brides his Body mangled & his members cut of

The Preostes & Iesuites anoite the Rebells with there Sacrament of vnction before they go to murther & robe ashuringe them that for there meritorious Seruice if they be killed he shall escape Purgatory & go to heauen immediatly.

They do vsually mangell there dead Carcases lay Wagers who shall cut deepest into there dead flesh with there Skeyns.

they destroy our English Sheepe in detestation of us, although one is better then 4 of theirs, they haue vowed to roote out the name of the English

Driuinge Men Women & children by hund:
reds vpon Briges & casting them into Riuers,
who drowned not were killed with poles &
shot with muskets.

G

M.r Blandry Minister hanged after pulled his
flesh from his bones in his wiffes sight.

H

The Lord Blany forced to ride 14 miles with:
out Brittle or Sadell to saue his life, his Lady
lodged in Straive being allowed 2.d a day
to releue her & her Children, slew a kinsman
of hers and hanged him vp before her face.
2 dayes telling her she must expect the
same to terrifie her the moore.

I

M.r Dauenant and his Wife bound in their
Chaires striped the 2 Eldest Children of 7
yeares old rosted vpon Spittes before their
Parents faces Cutt their throte and after
murdred him.

K

Arthur Robinsons daughter 14 yeares old the
Rebbels bound her armes a broad, deflowered
her one after an other, tell they spoyled her then
pulled the haire from her head and cut out her
tongue that she might not tell of their Cruelty,
but she declared it by writing.

L

A Minister and his wife came to Dublin Ian 30
1641 left behinde him some goods with a supposed frend, sent for them but could not be de.
liuered vnlesse he or his Wife came for them
she came and presently they hanged her vpe.

M

6

Pulling them about the streetes by the haire of
the head, dashing the Childrens braines against
the postes sayinge these were the pigges of
the English Sowes.

T

Drooghedah so bloked vp that a bushell of wheate
was sold for 23 Shill.s & meate scarce to be
had at any rate. Ian 4.   1641

rogheda

V

A Woman mangled in so horred a maner that it
was not possible shee should be knowne &
after the Villaine washed his handes in her
bloode, was taken by the Troopers adiuged
to be hanged leaped of the lader & hanged
Himselfe like a Bloodey Tiger.

W

Companyes of the Rebells meeting with the
English flyinge for their liues, falling downe
before them cryinge for mercy thrust theire
into their Childrens bellyes & threw them into
the water.

X

10

George Forde hanged on a tree in his owne ground
Cut his flesh a peaces, caruing it vp & downe
sayinge this is the flesh of one of the traitors against
our Holy Father the Pope.

Y

a Proclamation that nether English nor Irish should
either sell or keepe in their houses any Powder vpon
the losse of goods & life nether any Armes whatsoeuer,
exept with a licens & then but fine pound at
most at 4 Shill. p pound

11

12

were massacred by the rebels. This was not part of any policy, but rather the result of indiscipline and the wreaking of private vengeance. The Irish commanders punished their soldiers found guilty of murder, and many times Catholic priests intervened to save planters' lives. But for Northern Irish Protestants, the murders confirmed their worst fears of being surrounded and outnumbered by enemies, often in their midst. The myth that the wholesale extermination of Ulster Protestants was the purpose of the 1641 rebellion is still proclaimed on banners on Orange marches in Northern Ireland today. In 1646, Sir John Temple believed that three hundred thousand people had been slaughtered — about three times more than the total Protestant population at the time. Lurid wood-cuts and scarifying stories circulated widely as both sides in the English civil war sought to make capital out of the events of the Irish rebellion and as opportunists saw the chance of using the allegations to justify the confiscation of more property. Twenty-eight years later, the founder of the Quakers, George Fox, visited Ireland and believed that he could still smell the victims' blood in the atmosphere from over a hundred miles away: 'The earth and air smelt methought of the corruption of the nation, so that it yielded another smell to me than England did; which I imputed to be Popish massacres that had been committed, and the blood that had been spilt — from which a foulness ascended.' Lecky, the Anglo-Irish historian whose dispassionate examination of the rising is still a model study, concluded that 'the Irish massacre of 1641 seems to me one of the great fictions of history, though a great number of murders were committed. The consensus of modern English historians, however, about it is so great that it is hardly possible to shake the belief in the English mind.'

In March 1642, the Catholic hierarchy, led by the Primate of Ireland, Archbishop O'Reilly of Armagh, took the lead in giving the rebellion a moral and parliamentary framework. At a provincial synod held at Kells, O'Reilly declared that the war was just, waged against Puritans 'who have always, but especially in recent years, plotted the destruction of the Catholics, the destruction of the Irish, and the abolition of the King's prerogatives'. All who did not support the war effort were excommunicated. In June at Kilkenny a group of clerics and Irish commanders met and formed the 'Confederate Catholics of Ireland', and organized a General Assembly which met in October. They were too loyal to the Crown to assume the title of 'parliament', which could only be called by the King. And despite clerical pressure, the Assembly over the next six years refused to discriminate against Protestants, instead preferring to concern itself with the perennial question of land and its ownership. In this the seeds of internal division were rife: Old English rebels were worried about their security of title and tenure while the native Irish were simply worried that they had no lands at all. The Confederation, in consequence, was only united in a nominal loyalty to the King and in military opposition to English attempts to regain Ireland.

In 1642 Hugh O'Neill's nephew, Owen Roe O'Neill, who had fled with his uncle in 1607 and three years later had entered Spanish military service, returned to lead the insurgents, and the revolt spread to the whole of Ireland. Until Oliver Cromwell landed in Dublin in 1649, O'Neill was the most successful military commander in the country.

In Britain, as the civil war progressed, Charles I was attracted on several occasions by the possibility of using O'Neill's Confederate army against the parliamentary army under Cromwell. However, this plan was upset when the Irish parliament on 22 June 1642 expelled Catholic MPs on the grounds that they were in rebellion, and the Confederation in return demanded that the King repeal Poynings' Law and grant religious toleration. Charles went a long way towards meeting the Confederate demands, but the clergy excommunicated those who favoured alliance with the Royalists on terms less than had been proposed. In February 1647 the Kilkenny Assembly rejected the King's proposals, and the royal Deputy, the Earl of Ormond, decided to surrender Dublin (practically the only area under government control) to the parliamentary forces, preferring, as he said, 'English rebels to Irish rebels'. In 1649 after the English rebels had executed the King and ended the civil war with the establishment of the Commonwealth, the pacification of Ireland was given priority by the new government.

Ireland represented a threat to the security of the Commonwealth because of the Kilkenny Assembly's Royalist predilections. Royalist forces still operated in Ireland, and under the command of Ormond threatened government enclaves there. In the battle of Benburb in 1646, O'Neill's army killed over three thousand soldiers of a Scottish Parliamentary Army, winning a major victory. In August 1649 Oliver Cromwell, with twelve thousand men of the New Model Army, landed in Dublin to join the eight-thousand-strong Commonwealth force already in the city. A month later, on 11 September, he stormed the Royalist stronghold of Drogheda, entering Irish history with a vengeance still not forgotten.

Cromwell's objectives in Ireland were to establish the Commonwealth's authority and government over the whole country; to enforce the Adventurers' Act of 1642 (by which 'adventurers' prepared to support Irish campaigns financially would be entitled to the lands of Irish rebels); and to avenge the Ulster massacre of 1641 which he was convinced had been a large-scale and deliberate slaughter carried out by Irish papists. This last purpose seems to have dominated his thoughts

Oliver Cromwell (1599–1658)

at Drogheda, where he treated the townspeople and the 2600 men of the Royalist garrison ruthlessly. On his orders, the garrison was shown no mercy and the Catholic English Royalist commander, Sir Arthur Ashton, was put to death. On 16 September Cromwell reported to John Bradshaw, President of the Council of State,

> *I believe we put to the sword the whole number of defendants. I do not think thirty of the whole number escaped with their lives. Those that did are in safe custody for Barbados . . . I am persuaded that this is a righteous judgement of God upon those barbarous wretches who have imbrued their hands in so much innocent blood; and that it will tend to prevent the effusion of blood for the future — which are the satisfactory grounds to such actions, which otherwise cannot but work remorse and regret.*

By his own testimony, supported by many others, the slaughter was indiscriminate. In January 1650, Cromwell made a convoluted attempt to blame the Irish for his excesses, stating in a broadsheet he had printed in Cork, 'You, unprovoked, put the English to the most unheard of and most barbarous massacre (without respect of sex or age) that ever the sun beheld.' From Drogheda, Cromwell went on to Wexford, where two weeks later he conducted another slaughter as ferocious as the first. New Ross surrendered to him without a fight, and by July 1650 Commonwealth armies were in command of all Ireland except Connaught.

There was a profound difference between Cromwell's slaughters at Drogheda and Wexford, which were acts of policy, and the massacres of settlers in Ulster in 1641 which were the results of indiscipline. In the Irish historical memory, where myths are often as important as facts, Cromwell's activities in contrast to the events of 1641 need no embellishment.

After returning to England in 1650, Cromwell next tackled Ireland legislatively. On 2 March 1653 the Westminster 'Rump Parliament' voted to unify Ireland with Britain, abolished the Irish parliament and stipulated that there should be thirty Irish representatives in a new Westminster parliament of 460 members. In a further series of acts it was decreed that Irish landowners were to be transplanted to the inhospitable terrain of Connaught and Co. Clare and their lands forfeited to adventurers and demobilized soldiers of Cromwell's armies. More than eleven million acres of land were confiscated in the interests of about one thousand adventurers and thirty-five thousand soldiers. Native Irishmen found east of the river Shannon after 1 May 1654 faced the death penalty or transplantation to slavery in the Barbados and West Indies. 'To Hell or Connaught' became a proverbial phrase among later generations of Irishmen. In 1685, when King James II came to the throne, only 22 per cent of the land of Ireland was in the hands of Catholics. Any lingering differences between the native Irish and the various groups of Englishmen outside the Pale who had come to Ireland during the previous centuries were now largely forgotten.

As in previous plantations, it proved impossible to enforce the Cromwellian land settlement. It is thought that fewer than a quarter of the soldiers granted Irish lands actually settled in Ireland; most preferred to sell their shares instead. The new owners who did settle found, as previous planters in Ulster had found, that they needed a supply of cheap labour in order to farm their new fields, and so in practice many native Irishmen drifted back across the Shannon. The new planters were to become the ruling class in Ireland over the next 250 years, gradually changing — like the Normans before them — into Irishmen themselves. Only in the north, where many new planters augmented the survivors of previous plantations, did differences remain. But where previous differences had been derived from political and economic oppression, in the north the new division of strong anti-Catholic Protestantism was added. Convinced of the innate wickedness and vengefulness of native Irish Catholics, planters in the north from the time of Cromwell onwards determined to defend their lands and their own way of life to the bitter end.

After the monarchy was restored in Britain in 1660, the Irish parliament was resuscitated and the Commonwealth union between Ireland and Britain ended. But there was no ending of Cromwell's land settlement. Some of his supporters had their lands confiscated and regranted to loyal Royalists like Ormond, but Charles II refused to reinstate most of the original owners. The new King never forgot that he ruled only by the grace of those who had been leaders under Cromwell, and he rewarded them with promotions and security. In 1672, Cromwellian settlers owned four and a half million of the twelve million profitable acres Ireland had. Catholics owned three and a half million, and older (mostly Ulster) Protestants the rest.

Along with the restored monarchy came the restoration of the established Church. Charles II, however, diplomatically did not enforce the laws against Catholics, and when he was succeeded by his professedly Catholic brother, James II, in 1685, many in Ireland thought that at last relations with Britain would be settled amicably. It is one of the 'Ifs' of history, but if James had been less wilful and more skilful, England's Irish problem might have been resolved. As it was, James' insistence upon his prerogative at the expense of parliament generated another English civil war with an even greater Irish involvement. After the Scots had been defeated in June 1689 by William of Orange at the battle of Killiecrankie, Ireland remained James' only hope.

William, Prince of Orange and ruler of the Netherlands, was the grandson of Charles I of England as well as James II's son-in-law. A Protestant, he was invited in 1688 by James II's parliamentary and ecclesiastical opponents to accept the British Crown on the strength of his Stuart blood and wife, Mary. He invaded England and became joint sovereign with Mary, rapidly forcing James to flee to France where Louis XIV agreed to help the deposed king. In March 1689 James landed at Kinsale with French money, arms and officers and was greeted as the lawful monarch by almost the whole nation, led by the Lord Deputy Richard Talbot, ennobled by James four years earlier with the lapsed title Earl of Tyrconnell. Tyrconnell was able to give James an army which included not only Catholic Irishmen, but also Protestant loyalists united against a Protestant British government. For the first time since Hugh O'Neill's rebellion a century before, Irishmen of all sorts were acting together as a nation, although this time they were not in rebellion and, in fact, were supporting an English king in his attempt to regain his throne.

The war started in Ireland with James' siege of Londonderry, an event which in Northern Ireland has since been celebrated every year. Amongst the settlers in the north, James' arrival in the country and the gathering of Tyrconnell's army in his support revived memories of the massacres of 1641. However, these settlers were also loyal to the Crown, and recognized James as their rightful king. When the people of Londonderry learnt that a Royalist and largely Catholic garrison was on its way to occupy the town, they decided that the troops should be allowed in. The Protestant Church of Ireland Bishop of Londonderry and other Protestant town leaders, including Lieutenant Colonel Robert Lundy, Londonderry's military commander, supported this decision, but they had not considered the apprentice boys. These youths and young men, apprenticed to trades, were often Presbyterian, and thus on the counts of age and inclination more likely to discard established authority. Thirteen apprentices took matters into their own hands, and just before the garrison arrived, they slammed the gates of Londonderry shut on 7 December 1688. By the boldness of their action, they swung opinion in their favour. Colonel Lundy had to escape from the town in disguise, and his name has been spoken with derision in northern Ireland ever since. From April the following year, the town was under siege for three and a half months, during which time the inhabitants were completely cut off. Finally, on 28 July 1689, as starvation faced the besieged townspeople, a Williamite fleet led by the ship *Mountjoy* breached the boom placed across the river Foyle by James' troops, and relieved the town. 'No Surrender' had been the apprentice boys' cry, and 'No Surrender' has remained the watchword of Protestant unionists in Northern Ireland ever since.

Two months before Londonderry was relieved, James summoned what has become known as the 'Patriot Parliament' in Dublin. It was the last Irish parliament until 1921 to have Roman Catholic members. Indeed, only six Protestants were among the 230 members of the Irish House of Commons. Many of the members were subsequently to die in exile, and it was the last parliament to include the voice of Gaelic Ireland. Even so, it was an overwhelmingly Anglo-Irish establishment assembly, and it attempted to legislate in the interests of those landlords dispossessed by Cromwell, rather than to seek redress for the poorer classes banished to Connaught. By the end of the century, Irish Catholics owned only 14 per cent of the useful land in Ireland — a third less than when James II came to the throne.

James finally lost his throne on the banks of the river Boyne on 1 July 1690 (which became 12 July when the calendar was changed in the eighteenth century). When Pope Innocent XI heard the news of William's victory, he ordered a *Te Deum* to be sung in St Peter's in thanks. For the Pope, James and his ally Louis XIV were a greater menace than the Protestant William, because of Louis' suport of the French Church's independence from Papal authority, raising the spectre of another breach with Rome. The battle itself was not particularly hard fought, and James distinguished himself by retreating first, railing against his Irish army. It is said that Lady Tyrconnell, hearing the king condemn her kinsmen for running away, pointed out to him, 'But your Majesty won the race.' James gave up the struggle and hurried to France where he died in 1701, never again setting foot in the British Isles.

Patrick Sarsfield (c. 1650–93), first Earl of Lucan

For over a year after the battle of the Boyne, an Irish army continued to resist William. It was under the command of some French generals, sent by Louis XIV, and Patrick Sarsfield, an Irish soldier who had been trained in France and served in James II's Life Guards. In September 1691 Sarsfield finally surrendered, and the war ended with the Treaty of Limerick. The Treaty was an honourable one, guaranteeing the rights and property of the defeated Irish in return for loyalty to the new British King and Queen. Along with eleven thousand officers and men, Sarsfield was allowed to sail into exile to join five thousand Irish soldiers already in France in the Irish Brigade of the French army. His troops made their choice of loyalties on 5 October outside Limerick. The royal standards of William and Louis XIV were set up in a field and as Sarsfield and Ginckel, William's commander, watched together, the Irish army led by the Foot Guards almost all gathered round the French banner. Of the fourteen thousand men under Sarsfield, only one thousand joined Ginckel; and two thousand swore allegiance to King William and Queen Mary.

The Battle of the Boyne
was fought on 1 July 1690
three miles west of Drogheda.
This engraving is by the Dutchman
Theodor Maas who came to Ireland with
William of Orange and witnessed the battle.
William's victory is commemorated annually
as Orange Day (12 July in the new calendar)
in Northern Ireland.

110

III

Patrick Sarsfield caught the imagination of Ireland, and has remained a hero in Irish history. In a way quite different from the Londonderry apprentice boys, his message to posterity was also 'No Surrender'. Shortly after the Treaty of Limerick, a large French fleet sailed up the Shannon with reinforcements and arms for the Irish army. But Sarsfield, having made terms, felt in honour bound to instruct the French not to land. James created him Earl of Lucan in 1691, and in France Louis XIV made him a Marshal of the army. Two years later he was mortally wounded fighting William again at the battle of Landen in Flanders. 'Oh, that this were for Ireland!', he is credited with saying as he watched his blood pour away. His Irish Brigade was soon christened the 'Wild Geese' by his countrymen, and for generations to come Irishmen were to flock to the Brigade's colours as opportunities were denied them at home. Other Irish Brigades were formed in other European armies, and the Wild Geese and their descendants achieved renown from Moscow to Madrid. Fourteen Irishmen became Field Marshals in the Austrian army. Count Peter de Lacy, born in Limerick and one of the original Wild Geese, became a General in the Russian army and died in 1751 as Governor of Livonia. Don Alexander O'Reilly, born in Ireland in 1725, became a Spanish Field Marshal and Governor of Spanish Louisiana, before dying in Paris in 1794. In the nineteenth century, President MacMahon of France could trace his descent directly to an eighteenth-century Irish exile. The Hon. Emily Lawless, in her collection of poems *With the Wild Geese* (1902), portrayed the turmoil of these exiles perfectly:

> *War-battered dogs are we*
> *Fighters in every clime;*
> *Fillers of trench and grave,*
> *Mockers bemocked by time.*
> *War-dogs hungry and grey,*
> *Gnawing a naked bone,*
> *Fighters in every clime —*
> *Every cause but our own.*

7

PEOPLE AND PRIVILEGE: THE PENAL LAWS

And even I can remember
A day when the historians left blanks in their writings,
I mean for things they didn't know.

Ezra Pound, Cantos, XIII

When the text of the Treaty of Limerick arrived in London for ratification, part of the second clause had mysteriously been omitted. The clause guaranteed that officers and men in James' Irish army who swore allegiance to William and Mary should keep their properties, privileges, professions and estates, as should 'all such as are under their protection' — the missing phrase. William reinserted this in his own hand when he signed the Treaty on 4 February 1692. But it was a portent of what was to befall all those in Ireland who could possibly be accounted potential enemies of the State. The new Irish governors and their supporters were soon to show themselves as anxious as Cromwell had been to secure the Protestant faith and grab Catholic property.

The first step in the renewed campaign to coerce and suppress potential Irish enemies was the refusal of the Irish parliament (now completely Protestant) to ratify the Treaty of Limerick until 1697. By then Lord Sidney, as Lord Lieutenant the representative of the Crown in Ireland, had acted against the spirit and letter of the Treaty and dispossessed some four thousand landowners, confiscating 1.7 million acres. Only William III's personal influence moderated Sidney's activities, and sixty-five landowners and about 400,000 acres were restored.

In 1695 the Irish parliament began the legislation against Roman Catholics in Ireland known as the Penal Laws. Similar in many particulars to earlier anti-

Catholic laws, they were not completed until 1727, and they were to last for over a century. William III again did his best to abide by the Treaty of Limerick and resist this legislation, but England's 'Glorious Revolution' which had brought him to the throne had also limited the prerogatives of the Crown. British kings and queens could no longer claim the privileges of divine right, nor could they rule without the consent of regularly held parliaments. William and Mary's sovereignty was shared with parliament, and as time went by parliament came to have the final word. The Irish parliament rapidly became an adjunct of Westminster, and Poynings' Law became the instrument which confirmed Westminster's supremacy.

At first, the Cromwellians and Williamites who provided the bulk of representatives in the Irish Houses of Parliament were satisfied with their relationship with Westminster. They were colonists and, just like their colleagues in America, all they wanted of Britain was military and legal support for their schemes of exploitation. Later on, towards the end of the eighteenth century, again just like their American colleagues, they were to come to resent their subservient relationship with Britain as their commercial and economic success was perceived in Westminster as threatening British merchants' and landowners' interests. In Ireland, the colonists' success derived directly from their military subjugation of the native Irish, and from the economic licence granted by the Penal Laws.

The keep of Donegal Castle dates from 1505 and was built by Red Hugh O'Donnell. In 1610 the planter, Sir Basil Brooke, added to it one of Ireland's finest fortified houses.

By the end of the seventeenth century, Ireland had effectively been conquered. Almost every generation during the previous two hundred years had experienced military, economic and political attacks which at first had been contained in the area around the Pale, but then had expanded with the plantations to affect most of the country. Hugh O'Neill's rebellion had been the last attempt by the native Irish to withstand these encroachments, and his defeat had ended any real hope of a Gaelic/Old English resurgence. The 1641 rising was fundamentally different from any previous Irish resistance to British rule in that the members of the Confederation of Kilkenny accepted the rights of the Crown to govern Ireland, and were complaining only about the nature of the government. If their claims to ancestral lands and their religion had been recognized by Britain, they would probably have peacefully accepted the government's authority. After the Battle of the Boyne, which saw Ireland united in defeat in the cause of the Stuart monarchy, the vast majority of Irishmen who still had a sense of being Gaelic left their country for good, preferring exile in France to humiliation at home. The native Irish noble families and many Old English ones too formed a large part of the Wild Geese, and an estimated 120,000 left Ireland between 1690 and 1730. The loss of these leaders removed the last barrier between the Irish people and their foreign rulers. The eighteenth century in Ireland completed the process of subjugation as the Penal Laws witnessed the end of the ancient Gaelic order and the reduction to peasant-hood of the Irish nation.

The Penal Laws were passed by the parliament in Dublin, not Westminster. The first law, passed in 1695, ordered that no Catholic could have 'gun, pistol or sword, or any other weapon of offence or defence under penalty of fine, imprisonment, pillory or public whipping'. Like many of its successors, this law was modelled upon Louis XIV's anti-Protestant legislation in France. But unlike the French laws, which were directed against a minority and which were simply acts of persecution, the Irish Penal Laws were directed against the majority and used religion as a cloak for economic expropriation. Over the next thirty years, Irish parliaments passed acts which banished Catholic bishops; prohibited Catholics inheriting land from Protestants; from taking leases of more than thirty-one years; from buying land or enjoying mortgages. The estates of a Catholic landowner had to be divided equally among all his sons unless one of them converted to the Protestant, Anglican Church of Ireland, in which case he would inherit all the land. Priests were forced to register and take an oath of allegiance to the Crown. The Irish Privy Council even attempted to secure legislation to castrate unregistered priests, sending for permission to London:

The common Irish will never become Protestant or well affected to the Crown while they are supplied with Priests, Friars etc., who are the fomenters and disturbers ... The Commons proposed the marking of every priest who shall be convicted of being an unregistered priest ... remaining in this Kingdom after 1st May 1720 with a large 'P' to be made with a red hot iron on the cheek. The council generally disliked that punishment, and have altered it into that of castration which they are persuaded will be the most effectual remedy ...

These proposals were too much for the British government to accept, but they indicate the fevered anti-Catholicism that reigned amongst Ireland's Protestant rulers. Other Acts that were passed forbade Catholic churches to have belfries, towers or steeples. Pilgrimages to religious sites in Ireland were banned on the grounds that they constituted riotous assemblies, the penalty for which was flogging. Catholics were forbidden to enter a profession or to receive formal education. They were prohibited from living in the larger towns, and a whole code was passed which banned Catholics from the army, the electorate, commerce and the law. Rewards were offered for turning in Catholic bishops and unregistered priests. Catholics were not allowed to own a horse worth more than £5. The Hon. Standish O'Grady, a leading light of the nineteenth-century Irish revivial movement, told the story of the Catholic gentleman from Co. Meath who drove a splendid team of four matched horses. One day he was stopped by a Protestant who proffered £20 for them, whereupon the Catholic shot his horses dead rather than part with them for the legally stipulated amount. Protestant settlers of every class took ruthless advantage of these laws, petitioning parliament for the most particular satisfaction against Catholics. A typical example was reported in the *Commons Journals*:

A petition of one Edward Spragg and others in behalf of themselves and other Protestant porters in and about the City of Dublin, complains that one Darby Ryan, a captain under the late King James, and a Papist, buys up whole cargoes of coals and employs porters of his own persuasion to carry the same to customers, by which the petitioners are hindered from their small trade and gains.

The laws seized upon religious discrimination as the means of suppressing the Irish nation, and in so doing clearly stated the Irish Anglican, the 'Ascendancy', class's identification of Catholicism with nationalism in Ireland. The Ascendancy had been severely frightened by James II's willingness to secure Irish Catholic support in his fight to save his throne by promises of land reform and redistribution at their expense. The Penal Laws were, for them, a necessary, defensive series of Acts to keep Britain's Irish colony.

Still, the laws were soon seen as dastardly. Edmund Burke, in a much-quoted phrase some sixty years after these laws were passed, described them as 'a machine of wise and elaborate contrivance, as well fitted for the oppression, impoverishment and degradation of a people, and the debasement in them of human nature itself, as ever proceeded from the perverted ingenuity of man'. The Protestant Irish rebel and contemporary of Burke, Wolfe Tone, vented some of the hatred of the laws when he described them as 'that execrable and infamous code, framed with the art and malice of demons, to plunder and degrade and brutalize the Catholics'. 'There is no instance', said Dr Johnson, 'even in the Ten Persecutions, of such severity as that which the Protestants of Ireland exercised against the Catholics.' The explanation for the laws lay in greed, and fear that a Stuart restoration would mean Protestant suppression. However, as time went on, the laws were less strictly enforced and life for Irish Catholics in practice was not as severe as the laws dictated. Nevertheless, by the reign of George I, the Lord Chancellor was able to declare, 'The law does not suppose any such person to exist as an Irish Roman Catholic.' As the French observer Gustave de Beaumont noted about the Anglo-Irish Anglican Ascendancy, 'They said that they were Ireland and they ended by believing it.'

The law discriminated against some Irish Protestants as well. The majority of Protestants, especially in the north, were Dissenters and not members of the Established Church of Ireland. As such, their religious rites and ceremonies did not enjoy legal recognition so that, for example, a Presbyterian clergyman was not regarded as ordained in law. This meant that Dissenters could not be married legally unless an ordained clergyman (almost always therefore Church of Ireland) performed the ceremony. Like everyone else in Ireland, they also had to pay the tithe to the Church of Ireland clergy. The 1704 Act against Popery included a clause requiring office-holders under the Crown and Members of Parliament to be members of the Church of Ireland, thus disbarring Dissenters (as well as Catholics) from office and politics. Still, while galling, these disabilities were far less severe than those suffered by Catholics, and, unlike Catholics, Dissenters were able to inherit land and property and take part in most of the activities of the State. During the eighteenth century, the numerous and well-organized Presbyterians in the north became wealthy and influential as they developed their agricultural holdings and textile industries, and increasingly came to resent their second-class status. Many Scots-Irish Presbyterians preferred to follow the example of the Wild Geese and left Ireland for the American colonies.

The first wave of Irish emigration, which was to reach flood proportions in the nineteenth century, came from these northern settlers. Throughout the eighteenth century, an average of four thousand Ulster Dissenters emigrated every year to America or back to Britain. By the mid 1770s there were perhaps 200,000 Scots-Irish there. Catholic emigration was less because until 1780 they faced discrimination on religious grounds in the colonies too. 'The Presbyterians in the North,' wrote Lord Lieutenant Harcourt in 1775, 'are in their hearts Americans.' Eleven Presidents of the United States were descended from Ulster Protestant emigrants. Five signatories of the American Declaration of Independence, the man who printed it, and one of the four members of Washington's first Cabinet had all been born in Ulster or of Ulster-born parents. Sam Houston, Davy Crockett, Stonewall Jackson, Ulysses S. Grant and Woodrow Wilson were all of Scots-Irish descent.

As the eighteenth century progressed, the Irish Dissenters who remained in the country came to identify more and more with their Catholic countrymen in resisting governmental authority. In the eighteenth and nineteenth centuries, as a result of this common political and religious discrimination, many of the leaders of Irish nationalism were northern Irish Presbyterians. It was only in the later nineteenth century as the fires of religious antagonism were fanned for political purposes that northern Protestants returned to their separate identity in Ireland.

William III was always more moderate than his parliaments in his attitude towards the Irish. As we have seen, he tried hard to implement the terms of the Treaty of Limerick fairly, and against the opposition of the Church of Ireland he also fought for the rights of Irish Dissenters. He was partially successful in his endeavours, and the harsh discriminatory legislation of the Penal Laws did not take place until after his death, during the reign of his sister-in-law, Anne (1702–14). But while the laws made the Anglican minority apparently triumphant over Catholics and Dissenters in Ireland, Anglicans themselves faced discrimination from Britain. William had to agree to measures proposed at Westminster which were aimed at promoting English and discouraging Irish trade. In 1696 an Act was passed prohibiting goods from the colonies being exported directly to Ireland. In 1699, another Act placed heavy duties on Irish woollen goods and allowed them to be exported only to England, thus constricting the Irish woollen industry. Linen weaving was allowed because it did not compete with any English counterpart.

William Molyneux, an Irish Anglican philosopher and friend of John Locke, as MP for Trinity College, Dublin, published his famous 'The case of Ireland's being bound by Acts of Parliament in England stated'. Anticipating later Ascendancy politicians, Molyneux argued that England and Ireland were separate kingdoms bound by a common Crown, and that Ireland had a right to legislative and commercial independence. 'I have no other notion of slavery,' he wrote, 'but being bound by a law to which I do not consent.' His pamphlet was condemned by the Westminster House of Commons as 'of dangerous consequence to the Crown and Parliament of England', and was burned in public by the common hangman. However, although Molyneux's pamphlet was reprinted many times during the next hundred years, and quoted by Americans at the time of their revolution, its sentiments were before their time. Most Irish Anglicans in 1700 were in a state of political and social contentment. At the same time they realized that their supremacy was fragile, and fear of physical and economic destruction at the hands of Catholic Irishmen motivated their policy of determined suppression through the Penal Laws.

The Ascendancy had reason for their fears. The Stuart pretenders to the British crown represented a very real threat to their security, and a rallying point for Catholics. As a result of the Scottish campaign of Charles Edward Stuart, 'Bonnie Prince Charlie', between 1745 and 1746, the Irish government suspended some of the Penal Laws in an effort to ensure that the prince did not receive Irish support. In addition, new waves of Irish Catholic exiles kept the Irish Brigade in France alive. They also ensured that Britain's European enemies were always aware of Irish

During the war of the Austrian Succession, at the Battle of Fontenoy in the Low Countries on 11 May 1745, the French Army's Irish Brigade led by Lord Clare routed the Coldstream Guards and won the field for France. It was the Brigade's finest moment.

ENGLAND'S DEFEAT BY IRISH EXILES AT FONTENOY

discontent. The battle of Fontenoy on 11 May 1745 during the War of the Austrian Succession was the Irish Brigade's greatest moment. Led by Lord Clare, the Brigade routed the Coldstream Guards, and turned defeat for France into victory. The danger that these fighting men might return to Ireland was ever-present in the minds of the Ascendancy, and in 1756 an Act was passed which made death the penalty for any native-born Irishmen who returned to Ireland after fighting for France. Despite this, recruits for the Irish Brigade flocked to France throughout the eighteenth century. One regiment, commanded by Count Dillon, fought with the French and Washington during the American Revolution. Utterly loyal to the French kings, most of the Irish Brigade opposed the French Revolution. Count Daniel O'Connell, uncle of his namesake the 'Liberator', hated the Revolution so much that he offered the Brigade's services to George III. O'Connell was the last commander of the Brigade, which was dissolved by Louis XVIII after Napoleon's defeat at Waterloo.

Other Irish Catholic exiles in the later eighteenth century also kept Ireland's grievances alive in the world outside. Ambrose O'Higgins, who was born in Co. Meath in 1720, entered Spanish military service and became Viceroy of Peru where he died in 1801. His natural son, Bernado O'Higgins, became the liberator and national hero of Chile and its first President. John Barry of Tacumshane, Co. Wexford, founded and organized the American Navy. In command of the brig *Lexington* in 1776 he captured the navy's first warship, HMS *Edward*. Richard Hennessy of Killavullen, Co. Cork, who fought at Fontenoy, settled in Cognac and established the famous Hennessy distillery. The wealth and success of men like these contrasted strongly with the lethargy and despair of their kinsmen in Ireland. But they also served to remind the British and Irish governments that while poor and servile, Irishmen were not generically incapable of effective and enterprising organization. Dean Swift drew attention to this contrast when he commented upon the performance of Irishmen in foreign armies, 'which ought to make the English ashamed of the reproaches they cast on the ignorance, the dullness and the want of courage of the Irish natives; those defects, wherever they happen, arising only from the poverty and slavery they suffer from their inhuman neighbours'.

The Ascendancy society, in contrast to Ascendancy politics, was refined and sophisticated, befitting well the Age of Enlightenment. In many ways these privileged colonists patterned themselves on the English gentry and nobility, but they soon developed distinctions of their own. In 1827 Sir Jonah Barrington, a sharp observer of Ascendancy Ireland, perceived three sorts of Irish gentry: 'half-mounted gentlemen', 'gentlemen every inch of them', and 'gentlemen to the backbone'. The 'half-mounted' category were those who were on familiar terms with their servants, but who were also admitted to higher society. They habitually carried lead-weighted whips, according to Sir Jonah, with which to beat incautious peasants. The more fully fledged gentlemen tended to leave the trading professions to the urban middle classes, and concentrated instead on farming large estates, using peasants almost as slaves. Arthur Young, the English agricultural reformer, visited Ireland in 1776 and noted:

> *A landlord in Ireland can scarcely invent an order which a servant, labourer, or cottier dares to refuse to execute. Disrespect or anything tending towards sauciness he may punish with his cane or his horsewhip with the most perfect security ... Landlords of consequence have assured me that many of their cottiers would think themselves honoured by having their wives or daughters sent for to the bed of their masters, a mark of slavery that proves the oppression under which such people live.*

Social advancement was confined to members of Anglican society, and Catholics could harbour no social or economic hopes at all unless they were prepared to convert. Even Dissenters found that unless they were prepared to accept Anglican rites and beliefs, their prosperity was unlikely to improve much beyond that which they already enjoyed.

Becoming an Anglican clergyman or entering the legal profession were the two most usual paths to social improvement. Oscar Wilde's family found the Church to their advantage, with his maternal grandfather becoming Archdeacon of Leighlin. William Conolly, whose father was a native Catholic innkeeper at Ballyshannon, Co. Donegal, became an Anglican and entered the law. He made a fortune dealing with forfeited estates after the Treaty of Limerick and became Speaker of the Irish House of Commons in 1715. Before he died he was the richest man in Ireland, and he built the finest mansion, Castletown House, as his home in Co. Kildare.

Castletown House was constructed in the Palladian style with a central block and wings, set in a landscaped garden. Other great landlords and wealthy men copied Conolly's architectural choice time and again during the eighteenth century, establishing the beautiful Irish Georgian style. The Duke of Leinster, who had an income of £20,000 a year from his Irish estates, used it to build a Palladian mansion at Carton, Co. Kildare, and a town house in the centre of Dublin — Leinster House — so big that it now contains both houses of the Irish parliament, Dail and Seanad Eireann, and in its grounds are the National Library of Ireland, the National Museum and the National Gallery. Powerscourt House, Co. Wicklow, ruined by fire in 1974, was another eighteenth-century Irish Georgian mansion built for an

Ascendancy landlord. Less wealthy landlords, traders and merchants lived in smaller 'villas', and in large terraced houses which today are still the pride of Dublin and many other Irish towns. All of these fine buildings, with the wealth of painting, furniture-making and plastering that went with them, were testimony to the riches which Ireland afforded the Ascendancy classes. In these houses were provided the conditions of life which, as with the houses of the aristocracy and gentry in England, gave the eighteenth century a special lustre of elegance. One of the greatest pieces of European music, Handel's 'Messiah', had its first performance in front of an Ascendancy audience in Dublin, as *Faulkner's Dublin Journal* of 17 April 1742 reported:

> *On Tuesday last, Mr Handel's Sacred Grant Oratorio, the 'Messiah', was performed at the New Musick-Hall in Fishamble-street; the best judges allowed it to be the most finished piece of music. Words are wanting to express the exquisite delight it afforded to the admiring crowded audience. The sublime, the grand and the tender, adapted to the most elevated, majestic and moving words, conspired to transform and charm the ravished heart and ear.*

The Ascendancy middle class also prospered. Arthur Guinness, the brewer whose name and symbol, the harp, are today synonymous with Ireland, made a fortune by introducing 'Guinness's black Protestant porter' in place of ale. It became the sole product of his brewery in Dublin in 1799. Guinness himself became an esteemed member of Dublin Corporation, and the founder of a wealthy and notable Irish dynasty. Under licence, his 'porter' is today — and has been for some time — one of Ireland's most famed products.

However, for the vast majority of people in the country after 1692, the conditions of life were unspeakable. Nearly a century and a half after the Treaty of Limerick, Gustave de Beaumont tried to describe the housing conditions that the peasantry had endured for generations:

> *Imagine four walls of dried mud (which the rain, as it falls, easily restores to its primitive condition) having for its roof a little straw or some sods, for its chimney a hole cut in the roof, or very frequently the door through which alone the smoke finds an issue. One single apartment contains father, mother, children and sometimes a grandfather or a grandmother. There is no furniture in the wretched hovel; a single bed of straw serves the entire family. In the midst of all lies a dirty pig, the only thriving inhabitant of the place, for he lives in filth.*

The Mussenden
Temple, Downhill
House, Co.
Londonderry: a folly
modelled on the
Temple of Vesta in
Rome and built by
Frederick Augustus
Hervey (1730–1803),
fourth Earl of Bristol
and Anglican Bishop
of Derry, a notorious
collector of women
and objets d'art.
Despite the Penal
Laws, the
Earl-Bishop allowed
Catholics to celebrate
Mass in the room
under the Temple and
in his will insisted that
the practice should
continue.

One man, more than any other, drew attention to the gross social disparities of Irish life. Jonathan Swift, Dean of St Patrick's Cathedral, Dublin, was an unexpected lampooner of his own class, and a surprising social propagandist. Born in 1667 in Dublin, he graduated from Trinity College and became secretary to the Williamite statesman, Sir William Temple. In 1694 he took the vows of an Anglican clergyman, and for the next nineteen years spent most of his time in London where he gained a reputation as a wit and conversationalist. In 1704, he published two books anonymously, *A Tale of a Tub* and *The Battle of the Books*. He involved himself in politics as a supporter of the pro-Stuart Tories, writing broadsheets and articles in their cause. When his Tory patron, Robert Harley, became Chancellor of the Exchequer in 1710 and the following year was created Earl of Oxford, Swift hoped for advancement and a bishopric. However, Queen Anne would not hear of this for the man who in *A Tale of a Tub* had roundly attacked religious cant, and instead in 1713 he was made Dean of St Patrick's. He regarded this as banishment, and with the eclipse of the Tories by the Whigs at Anne's death the following year, any hopes he cherished of further recognition disappeared. For the rest of his life he remained in Dublin, becoming more and more incensed by the wretched condition of the people.

Swift's most famous work, *Gulliver's Travels*, was published in his own name in 1726, and gained him instant celebrity. A thinly disguised political satire, *Gulliver's Travels* does not deal with Ireland especially, although its rage at misery and depravity must have been drawn largely from the Dean's Irish experiences, and analogies with Lilliput and Brobdingnag are to be found in early Irish folktales. What is remarkable about Swift's attitude, however, is that it had changed so much over the previous decade. He had returned to Ireland in 1713 vehemently anti-Catholic and with a solid disregard for the peasant population. He was, after all, a Tory. But he was also an intelligent, sensitive and able man who harboured resentment against his political opponents, the Whigs, who were to rule Britain uninterruptedly until 1762. This resentment was almost certainly the starting point of Swift's espousal of the Irish cause.

Swift's first overtly Irish tract was published anonymously in 1720 and advocated a boycott of English fabrics. The *Drapier's Letters* (1724) — also published anonymously — came next and played a large part in preventing the corrupt introduction of a new copper coinage in Ireland. Readers guessed that Swift was the author, and he won immense popularity with this pamphlet, following it with *A Short View of the Present State of Ireland* in 1727, in which he attempted factually to describe Irish life to Englishmen:

> *One third part of the rents of Ireland is spent in England which, with the profits of employments, pensions, appeals . . . and other incidents, will amount to a full half of the income of the whole kingdom, all clear profit to England . . .*
> *The rise of our rents is squeezed out of the very blood, and vitals, and clothes, and dwellings of the tenants, who live worse than English beggars . . .*
> *The miserable dress and diet . . . of the people; the general desolation in most parts of the kingdom; the old seats of the gentry and nobility all in ruins, and no new ones in their stead; the families of farmers, who pay great rents, living in filth and nastiness without . . . a house so convenient as an English hog-sty to receive them.*

In 1729 he published his masterpiece of savage irony, *A Modest Proposal for preventing the children of poor people from being a burden to their parents or the country*. In this pamphlet he suggested that poor and rich alike might benefit by the sale of poor children as food for the rich. On his gravestone in St Patrick's is carved Swift's Latin epitaph which he wrote himself:

Here rests Jonathan Swift,
Where bitter indignation can no longer rend the heart.
Depart, traveller, and imitate, if thou canst,
So strenuous a champion of Liberty.

The philosopher George Berkeley, Church of Ireland Bishop of Cloyne, writing in the 1730s, confirmed many of Swift's observations. He asked rhetorically,

Whether there be upon earth any Christian or civilized people as beggarly,
wretched and destitute as the common Irish? ... Whether a foreigner could
imagine that one half of the people were starving in a country which sent out
such plenty of provisions? ... Whether it be not a vain attempt to project the
flourishing of our Protestant gentry, exclusive of the bulk of the natives?

Berkeley had lived for three years in the American colony of Rhode Island, where he had owned negro slaves; and he compared their lives to those of Irish peasants. He found the Irish 'more destitute than savages, and more abject than negroes. The negroes in our Plantations have a saying "If a negro was not a negro, Irishman would be negro". And it may be affirmed with truth that the very savages of America are better clad and better lodged than the Irish cottagers.'

LEFT]
Jonathan Swift
(1667–1745)

RIGHT]
Edmund Burke
(1729–97)

Edmund Burke, unlike Swift and Berkeley, developed his genius in England and concerned himself with English problems. He was born in Dublin to a Protestant father and a Catholic mother, and educated in a Quaker school in Ballitore, Co. Kildare. At Trinity College, Dublin, he was one of the founders of the college's Historical Society, leaving to study for the London Bar. He failed his legal examinations and turned to journalism and pamphleteering for his living, before returning to Dublin in 1761 as secretary to the Chief Secretary for Ireland. Two years later he went back to London, becoming in 1765 secretary to the Whig Prime Minister, Lord Rockingham, and MP for Wendover. As the crisis with the American colonies developed Burke made a strong impression on British politics by consistently arguing for conciliation rather than coercion. Between 1780 and 1792 he wrote three pamphlets on Ireland, drawing parallels with the American experience, and arguing that insensitive handling of colonial aspirations by Britain was the cause of opposition to the British government in both places. He was elected MP for Bristol in 1774, but lost his seat six years later as a result of his advocacy of liberal economic policies towards Ireland. From 1780 to 1794 he represented Malton, a pocket borough of Lord Rockingham's. In 1790 he published his most famous work, *Reflections on the Revolution in France*, which was read throughout Europe and America, going into eleven editions. In it, Burke argued for the maintenance of the *ancien régime* and encouraged rulers to resist, thus directly opposing the later arguments of Wolfe Tone and the United Irishmen, and provoking Thomas Paine to write his *Rights of Man* in reply. As a political philosopher, Burke was one of the foremost in England, and his thought became, with Benjamin Disraeli's, the philosophy of modern British conservatism. He died at his home near Beaconsfield, Buckinghamshire, where he is buried.

Two other Irishmen, also from the Ascendancy, made a significant contribution to English literature in the age of Swift and Burke. Oliver Goldsmith and Richard Brinsley Sheridan were both graduates of Trinity College who, like Burke, made their careers in London. Goldsmith, after starting his professional life as a medical doctor with dubious qualifications, became one of the wittiest and most versatile writers of his generation. His play *She Stoops to Conquer* (1773) is a classic satire on eighteenth-century men and manners. Sheridan, like Goldsmith, won fame with his plays, particularly *The School for Scandal* (1777), one of the most frequently performed comedies in the history of the English theatre. He entered politics in 1780 as Whig MP for Stafford, serving for thirty-two years. He was an eloquent opponent of the Act of Union and, unlike Burke, an admirer of the principles of the French Revolution. Goldsmith, Sheridan and, to a slightly lesser extent, Burke, belong properly in the pantheon of English writers and thinkers: only the accident of their Dublin birth — and their wit — connect them with Ireland.

At the same time, the vibrant but hidden Gaelic Ireland of the seventeenth and eighteenth centuries expressed itself in poetry. The tone of lament common to almost all this literature reflects the condition of Gaelic society at the time; but its quality places many of the poets on a par with contemporary leading English poets of the metaphysical and romantic schools. These Gaelic poets — many of whose names have not survived — were also the heirs of the pre-Norman bards and scholars, and unlike the poetry of other European nations their works were important and relevant to ordinary people. To Gaelic Ireland, poets and poems always held a respected place in society, and as Tudor and Cromwellian suppression gained ground, so did a native literary flowering, almost as the only effective Gaelic reply.

The poets travelled all over the country, singing and reciting their own and ancient verses, tales and sagas wherever people gathered. Eogan O'Rahilly, Sean Clarach Mac Domhnaill and Owen Roe O'Sullivan are the three leading Irish poets of this period. They developed the 'aisling' form of poetry (all in the Irish language which translates imperfectly) where the poet has a vision of a beautiful maiden (the symbol for Ireland) weighed down with sorrow as she waits for her love to return from across the sea. The poet speaks to the maiden and asks why she grieves. Her answer reflects the state of Ireland: she is held in bondage by a cruel tyrant. The poet tries to restore her happiness by promising her release with a victorious Jacobite return. O'Rahilly's 'Brightness of Brightness', brilliantly translated by Frank O'Connor, is a masterpiece of the aisling art:

Brightness of brightness lonely met me where I wandered,
Crystal of crystal only by her eyes were splendid,
Sweetness of sweetness lightly in her speech she squandered,
Rose-red and lily-glow brightly in her cheeks contended.

Ringlet on ringlet flowed tress on tress of yellow flaming
Hair, and swept the dew that glowed on the grass in showers behind her,
Vesture her breasts bore, mirror-bright, oh, mirror-shaming
That her fairy northern land yielded her from birth to blind them.

There she told me, told me as one that might in loving languish,
Told me of his coming, he for whom the crown was wreathed,
Told me of their ruin who banished him to utter anguish,
More too she told me I dare not in my song have breathed.

Frenzy of frenzy 'twas that her beauty did not numb me,
That I neared the royal serf, the vassal queen that held me vassal,
Then I called on Mary's son to shield me, she started from me,
And she fled, the lady, a lightning flash to Luachra Castle.

Fleetly too I fled in wild flight with body trembling
Over reefs of rock and sand, bog and shining plain and strand, sure
That my feet would find a path to that place of sad assembling,
House of houses reared of old in cold dark druid grandeur.

There a throng of wild creatures mocked me with elfin laughter,
And a group of mild maidens, tall with twining silken tresses,
Bound in bitter bonds they laid me there, and a moment after
See my lady laughing share a pot-bellied clown's caresses.

Truth of truth I told her in grief that it shamed her
To see her with a sleek foreign mercenary lover
When the highest peak of Scotland's race already thrice had named her,
And waited in longing for his exile to be over.

When she heard me speak, she wept, but she wept for pride,
And tears flowed down in streams from cheeks so bright and comely,
She sent a watchman with me to lead me to the mountainside —
Brightness of brightness who met me walking lonely.

The Jacobite defeat at the Battle of the Boyne, Sarsfield's last stand at Limerick, and the Wild Geese provided much of the material for these poets. In Bardic Schools in the seventeenth century, and in their smaller successors, the Courts of Poetry, in the first half of the eighteenth century, native Irish poets met privately and determined the style and subject-matter of poems to be submitted at the next School or Court. As a result, a special coherence characterizes these Irish poets and their works, centring on personal and national misfortunes, satirizing the new planters and rulers of Ireland, and extolling the virtues of independence and native pride despite all calamities.

Only two other native Irish writers of this period managed to make a lasting mark. Brian Merriman, the son of a travelling stonemason, was one of the last Gaelic poets. He was educated in hedge schools and earned a living as a small farmer. His reputation rests on one poem, 'The Midnight Court' (c. 1780), a rollicking account of peasant life mixed with the emotion of nationalism:

And it saddened the heart of the fairy king
And his lords and influential men
When they studied the cause of each disaster
That happened your people, man and master;
Old stock uprooted on every hand,
Without claim to their rent or laws or land;
The country waste and nothing behind
Where the flowers were plucked but the weeds and wild;
The best of your breed in foreign places
And upstart rogues with impudent faces
Planning with all their guile and spleen
To pick the bones of the Irish clean.

The poem enjoyed enormous popularity among the peasantry, and numerous manuscript copies circulated.

Much more successful, and a major literary figure, was Thomas Moore, who in his lifetime was as popular a poet as his friend Lord Byron. The son of a Dublin grocer and a highly patriotic mother, Moore studied at Trinity College, where he was friendly with Robert Emmet. He then went to London to become a barrister. In England he published a number of poems, culminating in his *Irish Melodies* (1807–34), which won him acceptance as the national poet of Ireland. He glorified its countryside and history in poems like 'The Meeting of the Waters':

Sweet vale of Avoca! how calm could I rest
In thy bosom of shade, with the friends I love best,
Where the storms that we feel in this cold world should cease,
And our hearts, like thy waters, be mingled in peace.

'The Minstrel Boy' is perhaps his most widely known song:

The Minstrel fell! — but the foeman's chain
Could not bring his proud soul under;
The harp he loved ne'er spoke again,
For he tore its cords asunder;
And said, 'No chains shall sully thee,
Thou soul of love and bravery!
Thy songs were made for the brave and free,
They shall never sound in slavery!'

Moore's songs remain to this day favourite expressions of Irish feeling.

For the majority of the Irish people during the eighteenth century, the physical conditions of life were harsh. Some chose to go into exile, others could only resort to protest and violence. Generations of impoverishment and deprivation provoked several secret peasant societies which now sprang up around the country. The Munster 'Whiteboys' in 1760 were the earliest agrarian protesters against high rents, evictions, tithes and the enclosure of lands contrary to ancient rights. For quite similar reasons, Presbyterians in Ulster followed the Whiteboys with their own secret organizations, the 'Oakboys' in 1763 and the 'Steelboys' in 1771. In all cases, these societies used violence, but because they lacked coordination and educated leadership, they never gained the dignity of national movements. What was important, however, was that oppressed Protestants and Catholics came together in these organizations against landlords and the government, forging from common distress an alliance which was to attempt national revolt in 1798. 'The gentlemen of Ireland,' wrote Arthur Young, 'never thought of a radical cure, from overlooking the real cause of the disease, which in fact lay in themselves, and not in the wretches they doomed to the gallows.'

The American Revolution (1776–82) sparked a resurgence of Irish national feeling. Many of the complaints of the American colonists were echoed by the Ascendancy in Ireland — neatly summed up by Jonathan Swift:

> *Were not the people of Ireland born as free as those of England? Is not their Parliament as fair and as representative of the people as that of England? Are they subjects of the same King? Does not the same sun shine on them? And have they not the same God for their protector? Am I a free man in England, and do I become a slave in six hours by crossing the Channel?*

The removal of British regiments from Ireland to America in the 1770s presented not only the Ascendancy, but the other sections of the Irish community, with an opportunity to press for reform. Merchants and industrialists were anxious for the removal of the trading restrictions they had suffered since the reign of William and Mary. The Ascendancy wanted more power and freedom to run Ireland without Westminster interference, and Catholics and Dissenters wanted relief from religious persecution. George III's government yielded to pressure for Irish reform, and in 1779 removed many of the duties which hampered Irish trade. In that same year the Irish parliament was persuaded that British military weakness in Ireland made relaxation of the Penal Laws advisable, and Catholics were allowed to buy land freely for the first time in nearly a century. The Catholic seminary at

Maynooth was allowed to open; in 1780 the legislation preventing Dissenters taking part in politics was repealed; and in 1782 the Ascendancy Irish parliament obtained Westminster's agreement to remove Poynings' Law and renounce its claim to the right to legislate for Ireland directly.

The legislative independence of the Irish parliament had been the principal demand of the Irish Volunteers, an Ascendancy-led militia formed in 1779 nominally to defend Ireland against a French invasion, but also to press the British government for reform. They were led by three Irish parliamentarians, Henry Grattan, Henry Flood and the Earl of Charlemont, who had developed a 'Patriot Party' demanding greater rights for the Ascendancy. Within a year, over one hundred thousand Irish Protestants — 'the armed property of the nation' as Grattan called them — were drilling under the eye of Charlemont, while Grattan and Flood lobbied in Dublin and London. In 1782, with the repeal of Poynings' Law, Grattan hailed the 'King, Lords and Commons' of Ireland in national terms:

> *I found Ireland on her knees. I watched over her with an eternal solicitude; I have traced her progress from injuries to arms and from arms to liberty. Spirit of Swift! Spirit of Molyneux! Your genius has prevailed! Ireland is now a nation. In that new character I hail her!*

Grattan came to realize that the Irish nation consisted of far more than the Protestant Ascendancy, and he urged both religious toleration and political representation for Catholics. 'The Irish Protestant,' he declared, 'could never be free till the Irish Catholic had ceased to be a slave.' In 1796 he proposed a Bill in the Irish House of Commons which would allow Catholics to become MPs; but it was defeated by 143 votes to 19, and the following year in bad health and dejection Grattan resigned his seat. He returned to politics to oppose the Union of Britain and Ireland, and spent the rest of his life compaigning for Catholic emancipation. His career was a testament to the fact that Irish history cannot be seen as purely Catholic versus Protestant: he is another example of a nationalist coming from the advantaged side. Nevertheless, while a noble Ascendancy representative, Grattan and his supporters were also the landlords whose coercion and exploitation of Ireland had reduced the bulk of the nation to peasanthood. Unlike Grattan, most of the Ascendancy were simply interested in strengthening their position as the dominant minority in the country, as Henry Flood said in 1783:

> *Ninety years ago four-fifths of Ireland were for King James. They were defeated. I rejoice in that defeat. The laws that followed were not laws of*

persecution; they were a political necessity. What will be the consequence if you give Catholics equal powers with Protestants? We will give all toleration to religion. We will not give them political power.

This refusal to share political power led Theobald Wolfe Tone, the son of a Protestant Dublin tradesman, to campaign and eventually rebel against his co-religionists in Ireland.

Born in Dublin in 1763, Wolfe Tone graduated from Trinity College and was called to the Irish Bar. Fired with enthusiasm by the American and French Revolutions, and influenced by radical Belfast Presbyterians themselves possessed of the revolutionary liberalism of the age, he formed the Society of the United Irishmen in Belfast in 1791, and published a pamphlet, *An Argument on Behalf of the Catholics of Ireland*, setting out the Society's aims:

> *To subvert the tyranny of our execrable government, to break the connection with England, the never failing source of all our political evils and to assert the independence of my country ... and to substitute the common name of Irishmen in place of the denominations of Protestant, Catholic and Dissenter.*

Theobald Wolfe Tone (1763–98)

In 1792 he successfully organized a Catholic Convention of elected delegates which played a large part in securing the Catholic Relief Act of 1793 from the Irish parliament. The Act gave propertied Catholics the right to vote and enter the professions, though not to stand in elections. This was so much less than the democratic rights of 'Liberty, Equality, Fraternity' proclaimed by the revolutionaries in France, that Tone determined on revolt. 'The French Revolution,' he wrote in his *Autobiography*, 'became in little time the test of every man's political creed, and the nation was fairly divided into two great parties, the Aristocrats and the Democrats.' Tone's followers included men like Henry Joy McCracken, a Belfast Protestant textile manufacturer, and Lord Edward Fitzgerald, cashiered from the British army for proposing the abolition of hereditary titles at a Paris banquet in 1792.

After the execution of King Louis XVI of France on 21 January 1793, the French Revolutionary Convention proceeded on 1 February to declare war on the Netherlands and their ally Great Britain. Once again, England's difficulty was seen as Ireland's opportunity, and Tone travelled to France for help in organizing a rebellion. In the winter of 1796 a French fleet of forty-three ships carrying fifteen thousand soldiers sailed for Bantry Bay, where they were to meet United Irishmen and overthrow the government. Stormy weather broke up the invasion fleet and prevented those ships that managed to reach Bantry Bay from landing their troops, and they returned to France. But as Leonard McNally, an Irish barrister, playwright and founder-member of the United Irishmen, who was also a British spy, in one of his secret reports warned his paymasters, they were still in danger:

> The whole body of the peasantry would join the French in case of an invasion … The sufferings of the common people from high rents and low wages, from oppressions of their landlords … and tithes are not the only causes of disaffection to Government and hatred of England; for though these have long kept the Irish peasant in a state of slavery and indigence, yet another cause, more dangerous, pervaded them all … This cause is an attachment to French principles in politics and religion, and an ardent desire for a republican Government.

The United Irishmen were social as well as political revolutionaries, and Tone indicated the lengths they might be prepared to go to if their demand for political

Protestants and loyalists were massacred in Wexford during the 1798 rising as mass violence turned the ideals of the United Irishmen into a sectarian bloodbath.

independence from Britain was not granted by the establishment: 'If the men of property will not help us they must fall; we will free ourselves by the aid of that large and respectable class of the community — the men of no property.' He was making it clear that while he preferred to work with the Irish *status quo* in a free Ireland, he was prepared if the Ascendancy did not support him to challenge their authority and position too.

Two years after Tone's abortive invasion attempt, the United Irishmen planned another rising. Warned by their spies, who had succeeded in penetrating the United Irishmen from top to bottom, the government cracked down in the middle of May 1798. All over Ireland United Irishmen were arrested, including most of the leaders except for Wolfe Tone who had returned to France after the Bantry Bay fiasco. Lord Edward Fitzgerald was betrayed four days before 23 May, the day set for the rising, and he died two weeks later from wounds he received while being arrested. Others were pitch-capped and flogged as the authorities sought out arms stored for the rising. Thomas Judkin Fitzgerald, high sheriff of Tipperary, had great success in Carrick-on-Suir with the cat o' nine tails:

> *My flogging Mr Wells had so satisfactory an effect that sixty of the Carrick yeomanry were obliged to confess publicly on their parade that they were United and that eight of them were sworn sergeants . . . I think I showed great mercy in not flogging the whole parcel of them . . . You know it was the cat alone that brought out the truth and 9,500 pikes and 1,500 stand of arms.*

As a direct consequence of the savagery of men like this in attempting to prevent the rebellion, it happened. Despite the loss of their leaders, thousands of United Irishmen took up scythes and pitchforks on the appointed day and ambushed British soldiers, especially in Wexford, Wicklow and Mayo. But as a result of the arrests of the idealistic leaders, these local risings were disorganized and easily degenerated into Catholic peasants attacking Protestant landlords and tradesmen. Most of the rebels were soon put to flight or captured by the 65,000 Irishmen in the yeomanry and militia forces of the government. Only in Wexford did rebels achieve any measure of success. Father John Murphy of Boolavogue, Co. Wexford, who unexpectedly found himself leading the insurgents, noted in his diary on 26 May, 'Began the Republic of Ireland in Boolavogue' after a successful ambush.

But the 'Republic' was short-lived and marred by horrible massacres of Protestants in the towns of Wexford and Enniscorthy. Captured gentry were spitted upon pikes, and near New Ross 184 Protestant men, women and children were trapped in a barn and slaughtered. There was an equally grim retribution for the Wexford

GREAT COURT YARD, DUBLIN CASTLE.

London, Publish'd according to Act of Parliament July 1793 by Ja.ⁿ Malton and George Cowen, Grafton Street, Dublin.

CHARLEMONT-HOUSE, DUBLIN.

London, Pub.ᵈ by Ja.ⁿ Malton & G. Cowen, Dublin, June 1793.

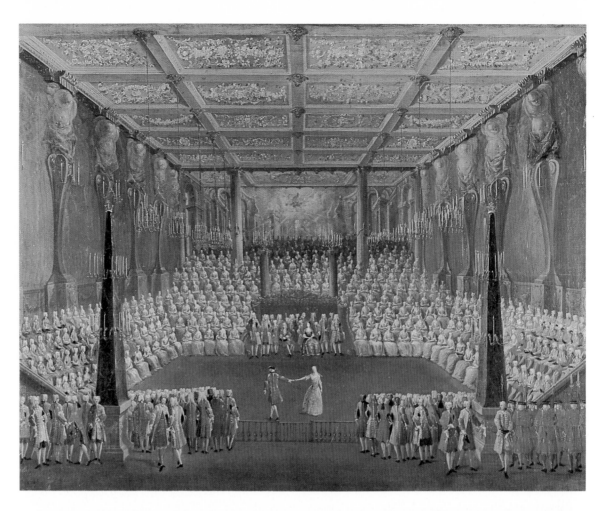

rebels after their defeat at Vinegar Hill on 13 June. Murphy and the other leaders were hanged. Henry Joy McCracken in Ulster had led an improvised attack on Antrim town on 7 June where the rebels sang the 'Marseillaise', but was captured a few days later and also hanged in Belfast. For those who had taken part and were not executed, the fiendish pitch-cap and floggings were meted out, and John Beresford, a Dublin riding-master, turned his school into a torture chamber to intimidate those still contemplating revolt in the capital.

In France, Wolfe Tone anxiously organized what help he could. On 22 August, a force of one thousand men under the French General Humbert landed at Killala, Co. Mayo, but were forced to surrender after some skirmishes. James Napper Tandy, who had started as a rent collector and land agent but had become a founder of the United Irishmen, had also been in France in May and June 1798. In September he landed with a small force on Rutland Island off the Donegal coast, but sailed away upon hearing of Humbert's surrender. Immortalized in ballads and songs, Napper Tandy, as Sir Jonah Barrington recalled, 'acquired celebrity without being able to account for it and possessed an influence without rank or capacity'. On 12 October, Tone himself was captured with three thousand French soldiers after his fleet of nine ships was defeated by a British squadron in a naval battle in Lough Swilly. Tone was brought to Dublin, tried by court martial, and sentenced to be hanged. When his plea to be shot like a soldier was unsuccessful, he committed suicide with a penknife instead.

The rebellion was seen by the Ascendancy as a Catholic one, but it was not. While sectarian killings had taken place, especially in Co. Wexford, the Lord Lieutenant, Lord Cornwallis, who had surrendered to George Washington at Yorktown in 1781, was quick to denounce 'the folly' he saw in 'substituting Catholic instead of Jacobin as the foundation of the present rebellion'. Sir Hercules Langrishe, a conservative independent Irish MP and a friend of Edmund Burke, agreed with Cornwallis. In effect, he blamed Tone's threat of unleashing 'the men of no property', and stated that 1798 was 'French politics and French success, it was the jargon of equality which had been diffused through a deluded multitude by designing men' together with 'the spirit of plunder and popular domination' which had led to the attempt 'to break the bonds of society and set up the capriciousness of the popular will against the stability of settled government'.

The Catholic Church also made clear its opposition, which was based on the French revolutionaries' hostility to the Pope. On 31 May, within days of the rebellion breaking out, the President of the Catholic seminary at Maynooth and twenty-eight prelates signed a public address calling on Irish Catholics not to take part, and to rally instead to the defence of 'our constitution, the social order and the Christian religion'. The overwhelming majority of priests and Catholics followed this advice, and in the whole of Ireland only sixty priests were ever accused of being involved. But the non-sectarian nature of the rising was demonstrated when fifteen Presbyterian ministers and nine licentiates or probationers were also implicated, and of these one Presbyterian minister and one licentiate were executed.

It was during this rebellion that green was established as the national colour, and many of the most memorable songs of Irish nationalism date from this period. 'The Wearing of the Green', banned by the government right into the twentieth century, linked the colour directly with rebelliousness:

> *I met with Napper Tandy, and he took me by the hand,*
> *Saying how is old Ireland? and how does she stand?*
> *She's the most distressful country that ever yet was seen;*
> *They are hanging men and women for the wearing of the green!*
>
> *I care not for the Thistle, and I care not for the Rose;*
> *When bleak winds round us whistle, neither dawn nor crimson shows,*
> *But like hope to him that's friendless, when no joy around is seen,*
> *O'er our graves with love that's endless blooms our own immortal green.*

Wolfe Tone and Lord Edward Fitzgerald were the first heroes of modern Ireland. Patrick Sarsfield belonged to an older, more aristocratic world, whose chivalry was not suited to the democratic and republican forces unleashed by the American and French Revolutions. Tone's son was declared an adopted child of the French Republic, and fought under Napoleon at Leipzig. Tone's United Irishmen became the forerunners of later Irish national movements. The rebellion of 1798 was a watershed and its ideas of an Irish republic, attractive to all Irishmen, to the present-day has inspired Irish nationalists. Wolfe Tone's grave at Bodenstown, Co. Kildare, is the site of annual pilgrimages by the leading nationalist groups, and in the early twentieth century the Wolfe Tone Memorial Committee was a cover for those dedicated to the use of force, in Tone's words, 'to break the connection between Ireland and Great Britain'.

8

UNION AND DISASTER

When two people are under the influence of the
most violent, most insane, most delusive, and most transient
of passions, they are required to swear that they will remain
in that excited, abnormal, and exhausting condition
continuously until death do them part.
GEORGE BERNARD SHAW, GETTING MARRIED

The connection between Britain and Ireland was in fact between the ruling class of both countries. For most of the eighteenth century, before the Industrial Revolution attracted Irish labourers to English towns, ordinary people in both countries had little contact with one another. Travellers like Arthur Young and writers like Swift were describing to their English readers a country whose conditions were quite foreign. They were shocked both by the behaviour of the Ascendancy and by the condition of the peasants.

With the Cromwellian and Williamite settlers, the Irish language had ceased to be the property of any but the peasantry. A few old Gaelic noble families like the O'Byrnes of Wicklow, who managed to survive with some land, also maintained Gaelic cultural and social practices well into the eighteenth century. The hedge schools flourished, with the descendants of the ancient Gaelic poet-class teaching Irish children in secret the history and stories of Gaelic Ireland, keeping their language as well as Latin and Greek alive among them. Owen Roe O'Sullivan, who had been educated in a Kerry hedge school, gained recognition as a poet after he translated a passage into Greek for his master's son. Catholicism gained a new hold on the people as priests were often their only comforters. Thousands of Irish priests were educated in seminaries and colleges in Europe, and many of them returned home to persecution and misery in the practice of their faith. John Mitchel, a

Protestant Irish nationalist who was himself transported as a convict in 1848, marvelled at the perseverance of these priests:

> *Imagine a priest ordained at Seville or Salamanca, a gentleman of high old name, a man of eloquence and genius, who has sustained disputations in the college halls on questions of literature or theology, and carried off prizes and crowns — see him on the quais of Brest, bargaining with some skipper to work his passage. He throws himself on board, does his full part of the hardest work, neither feeling the cold spray nor the fiercest tempest. And he knows, too, that at the end of it all for him may be a row of sugar canes to hoe under the blazing sun of Barbados ... See him, at last, springing ashore, and hurrying on to seek his bishop in some cave, or under some hedge — but going with caution by reason of the priest-catcher and the blood-hounds.*

Despite the inevitable disorganization and relaxed practices of the Church in Ireland after generations of persecution, the dedication of Irish priests was repaid in full by grateful flocks of devoted worshippers. Alexis de Tocqueville, travelling in Ireland in the 1830s, was told by a Connaught priest, 'The people give the fruit of their labours liberally to me, and I give them my time, my care, and my entire soul ... Between us there is a ceaseless exchange of feelings of affection.'

While this hidden Ireland struggled for survival, the face of the country was changing rapidly. Cities and stagecoaches, roads and industry spread through Ireland during the eighteenth century. Improved sailing techniques made her ports even more accessible to European traders. Forbidden to export live cattle, Irish merchants quickly turned to salted beef instead. By 1800, Cork was known as the slaughterhouse of Ireland and boasted a population of eighty thousand. The linen industry, concentrated in the counties of Antrim, Armagh, Down and Londonderry, accounted for over 70 per cent of Irish exports. It was the most important Irish industrial development of the age, and enjoyed a monopoly of the British market. With encouragement from the government (since there was virtually no English linen to compete), production expanded from 2.5 million yards in 1720 to over 37 million in 1790. Anglo-Irish trade alone expanded tenfold between 1700 and 1800, from £800,188 to £8,345,317 a year. Population growth kept pace with increased economic activity. From an estimated 1.1 million in 1672, it was 3 million by 1735; 4 million by 1785, and 8.2 million — the highest it has ever been — by 1841.

With this number of people, and with the enormous wealth generated by agriculture, industry and trade, Ireland became an even more valuable British possession. But after the 1798 Rising, the government at Westminster became convinced that Ascendancy rule in Dublin would only continue to foster unrest and make Ireland a potential danger to British security, especially in the face of the war with Napoleon's revolutionary France. Full-fledged union between Britain and Ireland was seen by William Pitt the Younger, perhaps George III's most able Prime Minster, as the solution to Irish grievances and British qualms. 'Ireland is like a ship on fire,' said Pitt, 'it must be extinguished or cut adrift.'

Pitt was well aware of Catholic alienation from the Ascendancy, and part of his calculation was that Catholic emancipation would have to be part of the union arrangements. However, before union or emancipation could be effected, Pitt had to secure the consent of the Irish parliament. Within weeks of the defeat of the 1798 rebels and Tone's execution, he set to work. Then, in January 1799, the Irish parliament rejected his proposals by 111 votes to 106. Ascendancy opposition to the union stemmed from their reluctance to surrender the profitable levers of power and position their own parliament and administration afforded them, even though, ultimately, the Ascendancy was always dependent upon British power.

Opposition to Pitt also came from another source. Despite the success of Tone's United Irishmen in attracting Ulster Presbyterian support, many Ulster Dissenters had come to regard their religion almost as a trade union, and they competed fiercely with Ulster Catholics for jobs. The 'Peep O'Day Boys' protected the interests of Protestants and the 'Defenders' those of Ulster Catholics from the 1770s onward. A violent clash between the two groups — the 'Battle of the Diamond' — took place in the streets of Armagh on 21 September 1795. The Defenders were routed and the Protestant victors decided to consolidate their

The Royal Coat of Arms from an Orange Association charter of membership

position by forming a society of their own, the Loyal Orange Association. The Association's original oath showed that more was involved than economic competition: 'I ... do solemnly swear that I will, to the utmost of my power, support and defend the King and his heirs as long as he or they support the Protestant Ascendancy.' The sectarian divisions among the Ulster Protestants were here again evident, and also their fundamentally conditional loyalty to the British government. They would be loyal and obedient only as long as the government maintained what they perceived as their interests. And Pitt's proposed union of the two countries was not, Orangemen considered, in their interest.

The crudely sectarian nature of the Wexford rebels of 1798 reawakened Protestant fears throughout Ireland of a Catholic backlash like that of 1641, and the Orange Association's membership swelled throughout the country. They saw no reason whatever to abolish restrictions on Catholics, and they regarded the union proposals as a Trojan Horse which would subvert their advantage. However, Orange and Ascendancy opposition to union was defeated with arguments, promises and money. The government spent £1,250,000 in bribes and over fifty Irish parliamentarians were given peerages or promoted in the peerage to win their votes for the union.

The union was corruptly secured. In 1800 the Irish House of Commons passed the Union Bill by 158 to 115 — Grattan reckoned that only seven who voted for the measure were unbribed — and the House of Lords agreed the measure by 75 votes to 26. Lord Cornwallis, as Lord Lieutenant, was entrusted with the job of 'managing' the parliament. He was disgusted with himself for his activities, writing to a friend, 'My occupation is of the most unpleasant nature, bargaining and jobbing with the most corrupt people under Heaven. I despise and hate myself for ever engaging in such dirty work, and am supported only by the reflection that without a Union the British Empire must be dissolved.' Lord Castlereagh, Chief Secretary of Ireland, was later scathingly attacked by Byron in his poem 'Don Juan' for his part in this work as a 'smooth-faced miscreant dabbling his sleek young hands in Erin's gore'. Yet despite the criticism that has been aimed at Pitt and his henchmen for their bribery and corruption of the Irish parliament, it must be remembered that political power was then regarded as a possession with a market value, like property. For the Ascendancy, their political power was worth a price that Pitt was prepared to pay. Thirty-two years later, the Great Reform Bill was passed by the Westminster parliament, also giving compensation to landlords who had previously owned parliamentary seats. But the argument for union was a strong one, and it was recognized. Lord Clare, who had ferociously suppressed Tone's United Irishmen, put the union case well:

The whole power and property has been conferred by successive monarchs of England upon an English colony composed of three sorts of English adventurers who poured into this country at the termination of three successive rebellions. Confiscation is their common title and from their first settlement they have been hemmed in on every side by the old inhabitants of this island, brooding over their discontents in sullen indignation. What was the security of the English settlers for their physical existence? And what is the security of their descendants at this day? The powerful and commanding position of Great Britain. If, by any fatality, it fails, you are at the mercy of the old inhabitants of this island, and I should have hoped that the samples of mercy exhibited by them in the progress of the late rebellion, would have taught the gentlemen who call themselves the Irish nation to reflect with sober attention on the dangers which surround them.

The Act of Union received the Royal Assent from George III on 1 August 1800, and came into effect on 1 January 1801, thus ending Ireland's five hundred-year-old parliament. Grattan and other opponents of the union spoke as if the Act had ended Ireland's national identity, but in truth it merely translated England's Irish representation to Westminster and affected the majority of people not at all. Cornwallis accurately reported, 'The mass of the people of Ireland do not care one farthing about Union.' Twenty-eight Irish peers, four bishops and one hundred Irish MPs were given seats in the new parliament of the United Kingdom of Great Britain and Ireland in London. The established Churches of the two countries were united as the Church of England and Ireland, and Ireland's financial contribution to the new United Kingdom was fixed at two-seventeenths of the total.

In the short term, the consequences of the union may have been negligible, but in the long term they were enormous. The union did nothing to alleviate the plight of the peasantry. As Irish emigration to Britain's industrial cities grew during the nineteenth century, the Irish became more and more involved in British politics, leaving a permanent mark on them, as the 1880s were to show. With the centre of Irish affairs removed to London, more Irish landlords remained absent from their estates, leaving their management in the hands of agents whose job was to secure the maximum rents and revenues. The Act also had the political effect in the nineteenth century of concentrating Irish nationalism on the demand for home rule rather than on the older demand for complete independence.

The first violent resistance to the new order came in 1803. It was a ludicrous attempt by a self-appointed general, Robert Emmet, to establish a 'Provisional

Government' with the support of none but a mob of fifty or sixty Dublin slum-dwellers. He was soon captured, and after a trial in which he was eloquently defended by the spy, Leonard MacNally, Emmet was executed. His insurrectionary imaginings had been the last gasp of the men of 1798. The youngest of seventeen children of the leading physician in Ireland, Emmet studied at Trinity College, but removed his name from the College roll in protest at being disciplined for his membership of the United Irishmen. He was in France at the time of the 1798 rising, and before his own effort in 1803 he tried to interest Napoleon in an invasion of Ireland. According to a subsequent government report, he used a £3000 inheritance from his father to purchase pikes and to rent depots in Dublin. He decided to launch his insurrection on 23 July 1803 to coincide with a French invasion of England planned by Napoleon.

Putting on a greatcoat to hide his uniform, carefully described at his subsequent trial as an officer's uniform of a green coat, gold epaulettes, white trousers and a cocked hat, Emmet led his mob in an attack on Dublin Castle, on their way dragging the Lord Chief Justice of Ireland and his nephew from their coach and murdering them. Some days later he was captured.

At his trial and in death, Emmet won enormous respect. 'I wished to procure for my country the guarantee which Washington procured for America,' he explained to the court, and when interrupted by the judge he calmly replied, 'My Lord, you are impatient for the sacrifice.' His last words from the dock have become the slogan of Irish nationalism: 'Let no man write my epitaph ... When my country takes her place among the nations of the earth, then and not till then, let my epitaph be written.' Refusing a clergyman, he was publicly hanged, drawn, quartered and beheaded with a huge crowd in attendance, outside St Catherine's Church in Dublin. In spite of the futility of his rising, he had won the hearts of the people.

> Bold Robert Emmet, the darling of Erin,
> Bold Robert Emmet will die with a smile.
> Farewell companions both loyal and daring,
> I'll lay down my life for the Emerald Isle.

Abraham Lincoln as a boy read Emmet's last speech by the firelight in his Kentucky cabin, and the text adorned the walls in many Irish-American homes, as it did in Irish cottages. James Connolly, the Irish labour leader, a century later loved to boast of Emmet's slum support, convinced that in 1803 the Irish proletariat first came of age. Its maturity, if this it was, brought with it a preference for constitutional activity that lasted for the next sixty years.

Robert Emmet
(1778–1803)

The Catholic Church had given its support to Pitt and the Act of Union because of his promise of emancipation and the ending of Ascendancy political power. As the Bishop of Waterford, Dr Hussey, said, he would rather live under the Mamelukes of Egypt than under 'the iron rod of the Mamelukes of Ireland'. Pitt, honourably, resigned as Prime Minister when faced by the King's refusal to accept Catholic emancipation. 'I would rather give up my throne,' said George III, 'and beg my bread from door to door throughout Europe than consent to such a measure.' His coronation oath to defend the Protestant faith was something the King refused to compromise. After Pitt's failure to secure emancipation, the Church threw itself behind the campaign for reform launched by a Dublin barrister, Daniel O'Connell.

O'Connell was born into an old Gaelic family in 1775. O'Connell's father had managed to hold on to much of the family's ancestral lands in the mountains of Kerry by leaving his property in the legal possession of a Protestant friend and thus circumventing the Penal Laws. Many Gaelic ways also survived in Kerry, and O'Connell was fostered by his uncle, Maurice 'Old Hunting Cap' O'Connell, at his home at Derrynane, where as a boy Daniel learnt Irish and became versed in the legends and songs of the people. Like many better-off Catholics, O'Connell was sent to France to finish his education. In Paris he was horrified by the terror and violence of the French Revolution, and there became convinced of the preference of constitutional over revolutionary action. Subsequent generations of Irish nationalists, remembering the failure of O'Connell's peaceful attempt to achieve home rule for Ireland and the horror of the famine which seemed to cap his career, blamed him for his approach and his respect for law. They forgot the abject poverty of the mass of the Irish people at the time, and the dismal failure of violent action in 1798. O'Connell was surely right to try another tack. And he recognized some harsh truths about his people, writing in 1793:

> *Ireland is not yet sufficiently enlightened to bear the sun of liberty. Freedom would soon dwindle into licentiousness. They would rob; they would murder. The altar of liberty totters when cemented only with blood, when supported with carcasses.*

The 1798 Rising only served to confirm O'Connell in his view that violence did not pay, 'that no political change whatsoever', as he put it, 'is worth the shedding of a single drop of human blood'. One of the first to take advantage of the 1793 Catholic Relief Act which allowed Irish Catholics to enter the legal profession, O'Connell was called to the Irish Bar on the same day that Lord Edward Fitzgerald was arrested — 19 May 1798. By 1808 he had not only made his mark in court, but had also become the leading spokesman of the Catholic Committee which had been established to press for emancipation, developing a powerful political movement by harnessing the Church to a quasi-national purpose. He became the acknowledged leader of Catholic agitation for reform, and even when he killed a member of Dublin Corporation in a duel in 1815, his position remained unchallenged.

In 1823, dissatisfied with the moderation of the Catholic Committee, O'Connell founded his own Catholic Association; and within months branches had been formed in almost every parish in Ireland. The object of the Association was to secure emancipation by all constitutional means. O'Connell soon had a mass following and considerable financial support through the 'Catholic rent' he instituted. This was the penny a month membership fee which his Association collected, with the support of the Catholic clergy, from the faithful after church services, and it averaged £2000 a week. In 1828, although prohibited as a Catholic from taking his seat, O'Connell won the Clare constituency in the general election. The following year, fearing another Irish rebellion, the Prime Minister, the Duke of Wellington, conceded emancipation. The Roman Catholic Emancipation Act received Royal Assent in April 1829 from a reluctant George IV. The King's objections to the measure were only overcome by Wellington's threat of resignation, and the Duke even had to fight a duel with a fellow Conservative peer, Lord Winchilsea, who opposed him (Wellington fired wide; Winchilsea fired in the air). The Act allowed Roman Catholics for the first time since 1691 to stand for and sit in parliament, and to hold all public offices except those of Regent, Lord Chancellor of England and Ireland and Lord Lieutenant of Ireland.

O'Connell was hailed as the uncrowned king of Ireland, 'The Liberator', and his success inspired him to further agitation, this time for the repeal of the Act of Union. But while in his campaign for emancipation he had found allies in British Catholics who had faced as much discrimination as their Irish co-religionists in the previous forty years, and in the Whig politicians who supported reform in principle, when it came to repeal of the union O'Connell was on his own. British politicians, with the memory of Napoleon still fresh and the strategic importance of Ireland for trade and defence in mind, would not support O'Connell's new campaign. In addition, there was frequent sectarian rioting in northern Ireland after 1828, in opposition to Irish nationalism. Even some of those who might have been expected to cheer on the Liberator were hostile to his whole purpose, seeing O'Connell as a 'West Briton', as someone prepared to make Ireland English in all but name in return for the spoils of office. Thomas Francis Meagher, a later revolutionary nationalist, dismissively scorned the Liberator's triumph of Catholic emancipation, which, he said, had only 'enabled a few Catholic gentlemen to sit in Parliament and there concur in the degradation of their country'.

O'Connell's method of seeking reform and change, by constitutional methods backed up by mass support, acted as a model for the Irish Home Rule Party of Parnell and Redmond in the last decades of the nineteenth and first years of the twentieth century. Emigration and the famine, however, combined to halve Ireland's population between 1841 and 1901, destroying the peasantry upon whom O'Connell had depended. Nevertheless, under Redmond, constitutional methods almost succeeded and only the First World War prevented Ireland achieving home rule peacefully. The Irish Republican Brotherhood, the 'Fenians' who launched the

1916 Rising, provided a contrasting model. The Fenians believed that O'Connell's failure to obtain repeal was the result of his refusal to resort to violence or illegal activity. Certain that constitutional agitation would only fail or lead to compromise through the manipulations of 'perfidious Albion', these revolutionary nationalists determined on violence from the start. However, before they could practise their theories, O'Connell's hold on the loyalty and affection of the Irish people had to be broken. In fact, this was never done, with the consequence that two strains of Irish nationalism developed: popular constitutional nationalism and secret physical force nationalism, both increasingly hostile to each other.

O'Connell's Catholic Association had been overtly sectarian in its aims and in its organization. In 1840 he formed his Repeal Association with exactly the same organization, including a church-collected subscription. In both cases, the Orange Order had been stirred, and O'Connell gave them plenty of reason for their opposition: he was making Irish Catholicism appear synonomous with Irish nationalism, so that many Protestants in Ireland again felt threatened. When O'Connell launched a campaign against the tithe paid by the Catholic peasantry for the support of the Church of Ireland, and when in 1838 the government agreed to a 25 per cent reduction in the tithe, Protestant fears were confirmed. They were not allayed by O'Connell's constitutionalism, and the Liberator's massive repeal meetings only served to strengthen Protestant opposition to Irish home rule. The Orangemen, whose numbers were now increasing, feared for their religious freedom and their land, and for their jobs in the linen, shipbuilding and engineering industries which depended upon Britain.

O'Connell's Repeal Association was also seen as a threat by the government, and in 1843 at the age of sixty-eight O'Connell was arrested and his meetings banned. He was in prison for three months before the House of Lords set aside his sentence, and when he emerged he recognized the hopelessness of his campaign. The peasantry who provided O'Connell with his mass support were becoming increasingly concerned with the failures of their potato crops in the early 1840s, a sinister prelude to the Great Famine. In failing health, O'Connell devoted his last years to attempts to secure land reform. He left Ireland in January 1847 to make a scarcely audible appeal in the House of Commons on behalf of his starving countrymen:

> *Ireland is in your hands, in your power. If you do not save her she cannot save herself. I solemnly call on you to recollect that I predict with the sincerest conviction that a quarter of her population will perish unless you come to her relief.*

He was absolutely right. Sensing his own imminent death, from Westminster he set out for Rome on a pilgrimage, but he only got as far as Genoa. His heart was sent on to Rome, and it now lies in an urn in the Church of St Agatha. His body was brought back to Dublin, and after the biggest funeral ever witnessed in Ireland, was buried in Glasnevin cemetery on 5 August 1847.

In later years, John Mitchel, a revolutionary who at the end of his life became a constitutionalist, named O'Connell 'next to the British Government the greatest enemy Ireland ever had'. He blamed O'Connell's influence for the failure of the Young Irelanders' insurrectionary attempt in 1848, and in his *Jail Journal* the following year wrote:

> *Poor old Dan! Wonderful, mighty, jovial, and mean old man! With silver tongue and smile of witchery and heart of unfathomable fraud! What a royal yet vulgar soul, with keen eye and potent sweep of a generous eagle of Cairn Tuathal — and the base servility of a hound, and the cold cruelty of a spider! . . . Think of the 'gorgeous and gossamer' theory of moral and peaceful agitation, the most astounding organon of public swindling since first man bethought him of obtaining money under false pretence. And after one has thought of all this and more, what then can a man say? What but pray that Irish earth may lie light on O'Connell's breast, and that the good God who knew how to create so wondrous a creature may have mercy upon his soul?*

Harsh words for a man who obtained for the mass of Irishmen greater liberty and greater coherence than they had enjoyed in over one hundred years. His very success was regarded by later radical nationalists as having been instrumental in weaning the mass of Irishmen away from revolution as the means of obtaining Irish freedom. But O'Connell was never able to exorcize the republican and physical force ideas of Wolfe Tone and thus, ultimately, he failed to establish constitutionalism as the mainstay of Irish politics. The Young Irelanders and the Fenians who followed them saw to it that there was a constant recurrence of republican revolt.

The Young Irelanders were the group of young intellectuals who attached themselves to O'Connell in the early 1840s. For them, the Liberator's campaign to repeal the Act of Union was the expression of their heartfelt, idealistic and romantic hopes for 'regenerating the spirit of Ireland'. At first, their support for O'Connell found expression in *The Nation*, first published in October 1842. It regularly sold over 10,000 copies and was the first magazine to circulate throughout the country. It was founded by three young men, Thomas Davis, Charles Gavan Duffy and John Blake Dillon. Davis, a graduate of Trinity College, was a Protestant barrister and

poet. Duffy was a northern Catholic journalist, and Dillon was a Catholic from a prosperous Co. Mayo commercial family who, like Davis, had graduated from Trinity College. They shared an earnest and lofty ideal of nationalism in keeping with the young romantic intellectuals in the Europe of their day. They envisaged a thriving nation which, by encouraging the entrepreneurial consciousness of all the people would develop a national identity with which all groups would have a sense of 'belonging'. Theirs was a generous vision, well-expressed in Davis' poems:

> *What matter that at different shrines*
> *We pray unto one God?*
> *What matter that at different times*
> *Our fathers won this sod?*
> *In fortune and in name we're bound*
> *By stronger links than steel;*
> *And neither can be safe nor sound*
> *But in the other's weal.*

Through the columns of *The Nation* Davis' songs and poems achieved wide popularity. One of them, 'A Nation Once Again', shouted defiance and became Ireland's unofficial national anthem. The power of its appeal to the present day was most recently demonstrated when in 1967 Northern Irish civil rights demonstrators spontaneously sang it at the end of their first mass meeting.

> *When boyhood's fire was in my blood,*
> *I read of ancient freemen,*
> *For Greece and Rome who bravely stood,*
> *Three hundred men and three men.*
> *And then I prayed I yet might see*
> *Our fetters rent in twain,*
> *And Ireland, long a province, be*
> *A nation once again.*

Davis also contributed the statement of Irish national purpose that was to become, along with Wolfe Tone's admonitions, the guiding light of revolutionary nationalists, and some constitutionalists too:

In one of the earliest photographs taken in Ireland, William Smith O'Brien (1803–64) is seen under arrest, flanked by his warders.

*We repeat, again and again, no hatred of the English. For much that England
did in literature, politics and war, we are, as men, grateful. Her oppression we
would not even avenge. We would, were she eternally dethroned from us,
rejoice in her prosperity; but we cannot, and will not try to forget her long,
cursing, merciless tyranny to Ireland; and we do not desire to share her gains,
her responsibility or her glory.*

Years later the founder of Sinn Fein, Arthur Griffith, was to describe Davis as 'the
prophet I followed throughout my life, the man whose words and teachings I tried
to translate into practice in politics'.

Another barrister and graduate of Trinity College, John Mitchel succeeded
Davis as editor of *The Nation* in 1845. Mitchel was born in Dungiven, Co.
Londonderry, the son of a Unitarian minister. Unlike Davis, who had supported
O'Connell's efforts to secure repeal of the union constitutionally, Mitchel espoused
more radical methods. By mid-1846 Mitchel openly opposed O'Connell, who had
made a political alliance with the Liberals in the Westminster parliament in return
for governmental positions for some of his supporters. For Mitchel and the Young
Irelanders, O'Connell had compromised the principle of Repeal. The destitution
wrought by the famine (1846 was one of the worst years) propelled them towards
revolution. In 1847 Mitchel published in *The Nation* a series of letters from James
Fintan Lalor, the son of an O'Connellite MP and gentleman farmer from Queen's
County (Co. Leix), who advanced the radical argument that the nature of land
ownership in Ireland lay at the heart of the famine. While recognizing the validity of
private property rights, Lalor held that 'the entire soil of a country belongs as of
right to the entire people of that country'. Mitchel, prodded by Lalor, speedily
translated this argument into a campaign for security of tenure for tenants. While
not attracting much support at the time as people struggled for survival, Lalor's
ideas came to dominate later nineteenth-century land reform agitation.

Mitchel and Lalor, early in 1848, split from the majority of Young Irelanders
who preferred Duffy's and Dillon's arguments that a strong and independent Irish
Party at Westminster offered the best hope of achieving their national aspirations,
and founded a new paper, the *United Irishmen*. In it Mitchel urged a 'holy war to
sweep this island clear of the English name and nation'. He was arrested in May
1848 on a charge of treason-felony, found guilty and sentenced to fourteen years'
transportation, which he served first in Bermuda and then in Tasmania before
escaping to the United States in 1853. Lalor, always in poor health, was also
arrested in 1848. He was soon released on health grounds and died in 1849.
Without their leadership, an abortive rising was organized by another Young
Irelander, William Smith O'Brien.

Emancipation Pudding; or, <u>Who</u> are the Carvers

An ATTEMPT to CHOKE JOHN BULL with IRISH-<u>MADE</u> DISHES.

O'Brien had been born in 1803 in Co. Clare and educated at Harrow School and Cambridge University. A Protestant landowner, at the age of twenty-one he became the Conservative MP for Ennis; ten years later, in 1835, he changed constituencies and sat, still a Conservative, for Co. Limerick. His opinions were changed by O'Connell, and with the zeal of a convert he first became an ardent Repealer and then a Young Irelander. Fired by the Chartist campaign for political reform in Britain and by the popular risings taking place all over Europe in 1848, O'Brien decided on an armed rising himself. However, before he could properly develop plans, many of his supporters were arrested and O'Brien had to go on the run. Surrounded by famine destitution, O'Brien, while addressing a motley assembly of half-starved peasants in the closing days of July 1848, clashed with forty-six Irish Constabulary in what has become known as the 'battle of the Widow McCormack's cabbage patch' at Ballingarry, Co. Tipperary. O'Brien was arrested soon afterwards and sentenced to death. The sentence was commuted to penal servitude for life, and he joined John Mitchel in Tasmania. He was released in 1854, but played no further part in Irish politics. 'The people,' he explained, 'preferred to die of starvation at home, or to flee as voluntary exiles to other lands, rather than to fight for their lands and their liberties.'

Mitchel and O'Brien determined the future pattern of Irish republican nationalism. They maintained the principles of Wolfe Tone and the United Irishmen with their ideal of an independent Irish republic and with a nationhood based upon ancient cultural traditions. They ignored the growing mass Orange opposition to this ideal, calling for reconciliation without seeing that their goal made this impossible. In this, every one of the Young Irelanders' successors followed suit. Even when the Irish civil war was fought in 1922–3, over the Anglo-Irish Treaty which partitioned Ireland as a result of Orange and Unionist opposition to home rule, the actual cause of the fighting was not partition but the question of whether men, who between 1916 and 1921 had fought for a republic, could in all conscience take an oath of allegiance to the British king.

In 1848, however, the Irish people were concerned with the basic problem of survival. Between 1841 and 1851 the population fell from 8,175,124 to 6,552,386, over 20 per cent. Total deaths (including deaths from natural causes) in the same period came to over one and a half million; and an estimated million more emigrated — mostly to America. The direct cause was the persistent failure of the potato crop in the years 1845–6, and in the partial failure of the crop in almost every other year of the decade. By tradition, Sir Walter Raleigh is credited with the introduction of the potato to Ireland from America in 1586. A century later, it had become almost the sole vegetable food of the peasantry. It needed little labour to plant and harvest. It yielded a large amount on small acreage, and so was ideally suited to the small tenant farmer. By 1700 the potato had displaced grain as the staple food of the majority of the people, providing enough nutrition with the addition of milk to sustain life and a reasonable state of health.

The effect of crop failure was devastating. It was caused by *phytophthora infestans* — potato blight — whose spores were carried to Ireland from Britain and the European content by wind, rain and insects. A fungus growth affected the potato plants, producing black spots and a white mould on the leaves, soon rotting the potato to a pulp. Cholera and typhoid epidemics killed off hundreds of thousands of people in various stages of starvation, nearly all of them from the poorest section of the community, the landless labourers and small tenants. By the summer of 1847, three million people, nearly half the total population of Ireland, were being fed by private charities — often organized by the Quakers — or at public expense. Mass graves littered the countryside. Emigration soared from 61,000 a year in 1845 to 250,000 in 1851.

The famine was worst in the west of Ireland, where since Cromwell the bulk of the population had been concentrated. In Co. Mayo in 1841, for example, there were 475 people for every acre of arable land, and in the province of Connaught 64 per cent of the farms were less than five acres in size. In these congested districts, famine diseases spread like wildfire.

The famine in Ireland: 'Funeral at Skibbereen' from a sketch by Mr H. Smith, Cork

The government in London was aware of the danger of famine inherent in dependence upon one particular source of food. In a previous famine a century earlier, in 1740–1, an estimated 400,000 Irishmen had died. At the same time, in common with nineteenth-century European political practice, British political parties were wedded to a policy of *laissez-faire* and the unrestrained forces of the market-place were considered to be most efficient in securing relief. Nevertheless, at first the response of the Conservative government under Sir Robert Peel was prompt and efficient. By the autumn of 1845 growing distress in Ireland convinced Peel of the need to abolish the Corn Laws (which raised tariff barriers on grain imported into the United Kingdom and so in effect subsidized British farmers) so as to lower the price of corn and therefore bread. The strong farming and landowning interests in the Conservative Party opposed their leader on this issue. But Peel perservered, splitting his Party the following year when, with Opposition support, he forced an Act through parliament repealing the Corn Laws. (The young MP for Maidenhead, Benjamin Disraeli, was soon to leap to prominence and ultimately the leadership of the Conservative Party by spearheading a successful revolt against Peel's leadership on this issue.)

Peel took other measures to relieve Irish famine victims. The first priority of his policies was to provide food. He sent a team of experts to Ireland to decide what measures were required: they incorrectly diagnosed the nature of the potato blight, but this was not Peel's fault. In November 1845 he set up a Relief Commission to coordinate relief work, and he authorized the purchase of £100,000 worth of maize from the United States which the Commission subsequently distributed in Ireland. To provide employment (and therefore money for starving Irishmen to buy food), early in 1846 he secured the passage of Acts which authorized improvements for Irish harbours and roads. He encouraged voluntary relief committees (about 650 were formed by August 1846) and established special food depots which released food supplies on to the open market so as to ensure that local traders would not be able to raise prices and capitalize on misery.

Peel's measures worked. No one died from starvation alone in the season of 1845–6. But this also reflected the fact that in 1845 only half the potato crop was blighted. When in 1846 the whole crop failed for the first time, the new Liberal Prime Minister, Lord John Russell, was faced with famine in Ireland of a drastically greater magnitude. Unlike Peel, who had pragmatically concentrated upon ensuring that there was enough food available to feed those in desperate need, Russell was a doctrinaire exponent of *laissez-faire*. In 1847 he set out his approach:

Ration cards used during the Great Famine under the Soup-kitchen Act of 1847. Adults were entitled to a full ration each day while children under nine years of age were given a half ration.

It must be thoroughly understood that we cannot feed the people . . . We can at best keep down prices where there is no regular market and prevent established dealers from raising prices much beyond the fair price with ordinary profits.

Russell's policies emphasized employment rather than food for famine victims. He and his supporters believed that food provision was the job of private enterprise, not of government, and that the cost of Irish relief work should be paid for by Irishmen. Peel's Relief Commission was wound up, and all public works were placed under the control of the Board of Works instead. Long delays in the deployment of relief and in the organization of work schemes resulted as the 12,000 civil servants in the Board tried to find work for nearly 750,00 starving people on top of all their other responsibilities. Workhouses were established where, in return for hard work, starving peasants were paid starvation wages. Tens of thousands of people died during the winter of 1846, and by the end of the year the government was forced to accept that its policies were not working, and that however reluctantly it would have to involve itself in food distribution.

Many individual landlords did the best they could to help their tenants in every way, and private relief works — most notably those undertaken by the Society of Friends and the British Relief Association — joined landlords in setting up soup kitchens. In early 1847 the government followed suit, and by August that year 3,000,000 people a day were being fed in soup kitchens. But Russell and his colleagues never conceived of interfering with the structure of the Irish economy in the ways that would have been necessary to prevent the worst effects of the famine. There was no capital investment in agriculture, no reclamation of land, and no reform of tenancies. Instead, landlords (who were completely responsible for the rates of their tenants on holdings below £4 valuation, even if rent was not paid) were able to continue to evict tenants as a way of reducing their rate bill (in 1850 alone, 104,000 people were evicted), and merchants were able to export grain and cattle without hindrance. One of the most remarkable facts about the famine period is that Ireland throughout exported more food than it imported.

In practice the Poor Law Unions, which were supported by local rates, were entrusted with the principal responsibility of dealing with famine relief, and as a result whole districts through the Unions' expenditure were soon bankrupted by the famine. The extent of their work can be judged by the numbers employed in relief works: 114,600 in October 1846; 570,000 in January 1847 and 734,000 in March. Over £500,000 was spent by the government in grants to local authorities for public works' projects.

It must be said that no government of the time would have done more. But the sheer magnitude of the famine even to contemporaries contrasted horribly with the apparent indifference of the British government. The *Times* leader of 30 August 1847 reflects British attitudes to the Irish in their plight:

> *In no other country have men talked treason until they are hoarse, and then gone about begging for sympathy from their oppressors. In no other country have the people been so liberally and unthriftily helped by the nation they denounced and defied, and in none have they repeated more humble and piteous supplications to those whom they have previously repaid with monstrous ingratitude. As a matter of state economy, some relief will be given to Ireland, in case she needs it, but we warn her that such relief will not be carried to the extent, or dealt forth, after the measure of former years.*

Sir Charles Trevelyan (knighted for public service in 1848), permanent head of the Treasury, was the civil servant most involved in Irish famine relief. But he, too, was a guardian of *laissez-faire* principles, and in an ivory tower of intellect he never properly appreciated the extent of distress or the effect of government measures.

Earthen and turf cabins like this one built in the 1870s were common habitats for many Irishmen from earliest times until the nineteenth century.

The overpopulation of Ireland, he wrote in October 1846, 'being altogether beyond the power of man, the cure had been applied by the direct stroke of an all-wise Providence in a manner as unexpected and as unthought of as it is likely to be effectual'. Two years later, after perhaps a million people had died, he wrote, 'The matter is awfully serious, but we are in the hands of Providence, without a possibility of averting the catastrophe if it is to happen. We can only await the result.' Sir Charles Wood, Trevelyan's political superior as Chancellor of the Exchequer, in 1848 replied to an Irish landlord who had written to inform him of what was actually happening in Ireland, 'I am not at all appalled by your tenantry going. That seems to me a necessary part of the process . . . We must not complain of what we really want to obtain.' 'The great evil with which we have to contend,' Trevelyan declared in 1846, 'is not the physical evil of the famine, but the moral evil of the selfish, perverse and turbulent character of the people.' Imprisoned by their attitudes, these men could stand by, convinced that they should not interfere in the divine retribution of the famine.

Many of the victims also seemed to accept their misfortune as providential. There were few food riots, and apart from O'Brien's attempted insurrection on a cabbage patch, no political violence either. Irish peasants had few allies and no defence against the death and devastation of the 1840s. 'The forbearance of the Irish peasantry,' the 1851 Census Commission declared, 'and the calm submission with which they bore the deadliest ills that can fall on many can scarcely be paralleled in the annals of any nation.'

The most important long-term consequence of the famine was the tradition established by 1851 of emigration to the United States of America. Between 1845 and 1855, nearly two million people had emigrated to America and Australia, and another 750,000 to Britain. By 1900, over four million Irishmen had crossed the Atlantic, and as many lived outside Ireland as in it. It is estimated that in the century up to 1930, one out of every two people born in Ireland made their homes elsewhere. In the 1950s, an average of sixty thousand people left the country every year, and emigration is still an important element in Irish life.

There were other drastic consequences too. Potatoes declined rapidly in importance, and the remaining farmers and tenants in Ireland after the famine changed over from tillage to grazing sheep and cattle. This in turn ended the practice of farm subdivision, and eldest sons tended to inherit farms intact. Emigration or a threadbare existence were the choices of younger children, and every census from 1851 to 1961 showed a decline in Ireland's population as people either left, married late or not at all. In 1900, in rural Ireland, the average age at marriage for men was

thirty-nine and for women thirty-one. In 1960 there were only 4.4 marriages per thousand people in the Irish Republic compared to 7.5 in England and Wales.

For the Irish language, the famine was fatal. Already under attack by the 1831 Education Act which established English as the language of Ireland's first National School system, the Irish language, which was spoken by four million people in 1841, was spoken by only 1.7 million in 1851. By 1911 only 12 per cent of the population could still speak the language. 'The Famine,' wrote Douglas Hyde in 1891, 'knocked the heart out of the Irish language.' Speaking Irish had become firmly identified with poverty and peasanthood and in the later decades of the nineteenth century Irish-speaking parents joined wholeheartedly with teachers to force their children to speak only English. English was identified with success and

'Ireland and America: before and after', from Mary Cusack's Illustrated History of Ireland, *1868, shows how emigration offered the best hope of prosperity for millions of Irish families.*

Bata scoir

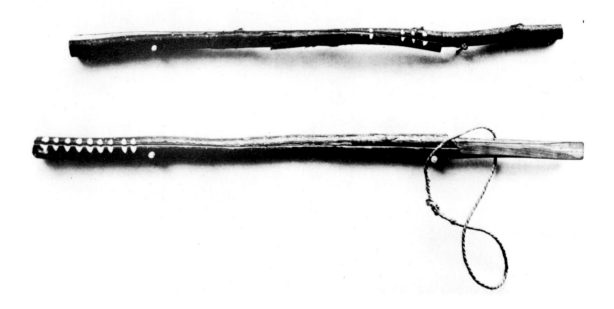

well-being. It was the language of commerce, and the language of emigrant relatives too. Hedge-school teachers, before the National Schools were introduced, had used tally sticks, the *bata scoir* which Irish-speaking children wore around their necks, and National School teachers adopted this practice for the same purpose. Every time the child spoke in Irish, a notch was carved on the stick, and at the end of the day the marks were counted and the child punished for each offence. In many ways, Patrick Pearse and his colleagues in 1916 represented the last generation which had a coherent sense of Irish language and culture. Even then, while admiring a legendary past through romantic spectacles, they could only pay lip-service to their national language. Despite their rejection of the thought, their country had been anglicized by a combination of education, social pressure and the famine.

There was one other significant effect of the famine: Irish emigrants in the United States came to form a body of political opinion consistently hostile to British interests. In both World Wars, American isolationism was strongly supported by Irish-Americans. Financial support for every Irish national movement from the Home Rule Party to the IRA today has flowed from America. American politicians and successive American Presidents have found it prudent, for domestic political reasons, to use their influence on Britain in Irish interests. Eamon de Valera, Ireland's political leader during the IRA's 1919–21 campaign, considered that his best course of action was to go to America in 1919 to drum up support for Irish independence, and to try to influence the 1920 American presidential candidates in the Irish cause. He raised over five million dollars in less than two years, and succeeded in making Presidents Woodrow Wilson and William Harding exert diplomatic pressure for an Irish settlement upon Lloyd George's government. It was from America too, that the Irish Republican Brotherhood, the most effective of all Ireland's national movements, was financed and sustained from the time of its foundation in 1858.

Despite the horror of the famine, and despite the memories of hate that it left, we must remember that similarly awful conditions plagued others too. Between June and October 1848, for example, over 72,000 people died of cholera in England and Wales. George Bernard Shaw was one of the first to make this point:

Surely the English people, in factory, mine, and sweater's workshop had reason to envy the Irish peasant, who at the worst starved on the open hillside instead of rotting in a fetid tenement rookery . . . When book after book from the press, and speech after speech from the platform, lay upon England the odium of misdeeds that no Irishman can contemplate without intense bitterness — that too many cannot think of without bloodthirsty rage — it is surely expedient to point out to that most distressful country that she has borne no more than her share of the growing pains of human society, and that the mass of the English people are not only guiltless of her wrongs, but have themselves borne a heavier yoke?

But in his play *Man and Superman* Shaw succinctly presented the Irish perception of what had happened:

MALONE   *My father died of starvation in Ireland in the Black '47. Maybe you've heard of it?*
VIOLET   *The Famine?*
MALONE   *(with smouldering passion) No, the Starvation. When a country is full of food and exporting it, there can be no Famine.*

9

'THE SONG
SHE WAS SINGING'

*They who assert that all is well have said a foolish thing,
they should have said all is for the best.*

VOLTAIRE, CANDIDE, CHAPTER I

The journey across the Atlantic for millions of Irish emigrants mirrored the horror of the famine and seared its memory on their minds. Emigrant ships were often disease-infested 'coffin ships' plying a speculative trade. In 1847, for example, the *Larch* carried 440 passengers and had 108 deaths on board before reaching Canada. Thousands more died in fever hospitals after landing. At Grosse Island near Detroit a plaque reads, 'In this secluded spot lie the mortal remains of 5294 persons who, flying from pestilence and famine in Ireland in the year 1847, found in America but a grave.' After the failure of the Young Irelanders, escaped transportees like John Mitchel and Thomas Francis Meagher also went to America, rapidly giving political expression to Irish-American hatred of Britain.

Mitchel vociferously supported the Confederate cause in the American civil war, refusing to accept that negroes or Jews had the same rights as Irishmen. He returned to Ireland in 1874 and was elected MP for Tipperary, only to be declared unseated as an undischarged felon. He was re-elected in 1875, but died shortly afterwards in Newry where he is buried. His compatriot, Meagher, after escaping from Tasmania in 1852, settled in New York and was admitted to the Bar there. When the Civil War started, he raised an Irish Brigade for the Union and was commissioned with the rank of Brigadier General. He planned to battle-train Irish soldiers who would return to Ireland at the end of the war and liberate their own country. But his Brigade was cut to ribbons at the battles of Antietam and Fredericksburg in 1862, thus thwarting his hopes. After the surrender of the Confederate States, Meagher was appointed temporary Governor of the Montana territory, and was accidentally drowned in a Missouri river flood in 1867.

Quite independently, others shared Meagher's hopes for an Irish-American supported rebellion. James Stephens, a Young Irelander who had avoided arrest, in 1848 fled to France where he learnt about the Carbonari, a Franco-Italian secret society dedicated to revolutionary activity. He returned to Ireland in 1856 determined to form an Irish society, modelled on the Carbonari, to work single-mindedly for Irish national freedom. For a year he journeyed mainly on foot through Ireland, covering three thousand miles, assessing public opinion and making contacts. Then, on St Patrick's Day, 17 March 1858, in Dublin, he formally established the Irish Revolutionary Brotherhood, later named the Irish Republican Brotherhood, the IRB. In rural areas, the new society quickly benefited from the traditions of the old agrarian secret societies, and hundreds of men took the membership oath:

> I . . . do solemnly swear in the presence of Almighty God that I will do my utmost at every risk while life lasts, to make Ireland an independent democratic republic; that I will yield implicit obedience in all things not contrary to the law of God to the commands of my superior officers, and that I shall preserve inviolable secrecy regarding all the transactions of this secret society that may be confided in me. So help me God. Amen.

In October 1858, Stephens sailed to New York to raise money for his organization, and there he contacted another Young Irelander, John O'Mahony, who had escaped with him to France ten years earlier before settling in America in 1852. Together they formed an Irish-American sister society to the IRB which O'Mahony, who was something of a Gaelic scholar, named the 'Fenian Brotherhood' after Finn MacCool's legendary band of warriors. The 'Fenians' rapidly became the popular name for the IRB which, for the next nine years, prepared for another rising. Stephens promised his American supporters that there would be a rising in 1865, and with typical optimism claimed that there were 85,000 Fenians in Ireland with 50,000 guns, and a further 15,000 Fenians in the British army waiting to rebel. A Fenian organizer in Britain, Michael Davitt, confirmed Stephens' assessment of Irish soldiers' support, and in Ireland another organizer, John Devoy, estimated that out of a British garrison of 25,000, 7000 were members of the IRB. As events were to prove, these estimates were wildly exaggerated.

Before Stephens' plans could come to fruition, he was arrested on 11 November 1865 and imprisoned in Richmond Gaol in Dublin. A fortnight later, with the help of some Fenian warders in the gaol, he escaped and made his way to Paris and then New York. Using the title 'Chief Organizer of the Irish Republic', with this escape Stephens caught the imagination of the people and became a national hero. But by his dictatorial ways, he had alienated much of the IRB and the Fenian Brotherhood, and he soon had to leave New York and return to Paris in fear for his life. For the next twenty years he lived as an impoverished journalist in France until in 1886 a public subscription in Ireland raised enough money for him to return and live in comparative comfort in Dublin.

Stephens had been betrayed by an informer who worked in the offices of the *Irish People*, a newspaper established by Stephens in 1863. The men involved in this newspaper in many ways came to dominate later years of Irish nationalism. John O'Leary, Thomas Clarke Luby, and Charles Joseph Kickham were the joint editors of the paper, and Jeremiah O'Donovan Rossa was the business manager. Along with Stephens and John Devoy they were arrested in 1865 and sentenced to terms of long imprisonment. O'Donovan Rossa, Luby and Devoy spent five years in English prisons before being released by amnesty in 1871 on condition they never returned to Ireland. They went to New York where Luby and Rossa became journalists and Devoy became one of the most influential leaders of the Clan-na-Gael, the successor organization to the Fenian Brotherhood. Devoy came to personify exiled Ireland. He played a crucial role in the IRB's attempt to secure German help during the 1916 rising, and despite a stormy relationship with Eamon de Valera in 1919–20, acted as the chief Irish-American organizer and fund-raiser for the IRA.

Kickham was released in poor health in 1869 and O'Leary in 1874, both becoming active supporters of the revival of Gaelic literature which dominated late-nineteenth-century Irish writing. Kickham's patriotic novel *Knocknagow* became the most popular book in Ireland. In 1915, after his death, O'Donovan Rossa's body was brought back to Dublin and given a massive funeral through the streets of the capital to Glasnevin cemetery on 1 August. Patrick Pearse gave the funeral oration, ending with the famous cry: 'The fools, the fools, the fools! — they have left us our Fenian dead, and while Ireland holds these graves, Ireland unfree shall never be at peace.'

For the Fenians who had not been arrested in 1865, the objective of a rising remained paramount. However, as in previous Irish risings, arrests and internal dissension ruined their plans. They first planned to rise in January, but then postponed the rising, and on Easter Sunday 1867, the day eventually appointed for

John Devoy (1842–1928)

In one of the last public executions in the United Kingdom, the Fenians Allen, Larkin and O'Brien died for the murder of Police Sergeant Brett in Manchester in 1867. The song 'God Save Ireland' commemorates their deaths.

THE PENNY
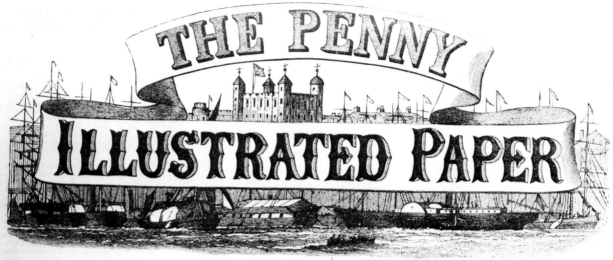

ILLUSTRATED PAPER

REGISTERED AT THE GENERAL POST OFFICE FOR TRANSMISSION ABROAD.

No. 322   LONDON, SATURDAY, NOVEMBER 30, 1867.   Vol. XIII.

EXECUTION OF THE FENIANS, ALLEN, GOULD, AND LARKIN, FOR THE MURDER OF SERGEANT BRETT, AT MANCHESTER, LAST SATURDAY.
SEE NEXT PAGE.

a national rebellion, only a few Fenians turned out. If 1848 was a tragi-comedy, 1867 was farce. The rebels' efforts were thwarted by a blizzard, and nearly all their leaders were captured. An Irish-American veteran of the civil war, Colonel T. J. Kelly, had succeeded Stephens as the Fenian chief. He came from America to lead the rising, and avoided arrest in England until 11 September when, betrayed by another informer, he was apprehended in Manchester with a colleague, 'Captain' Deasy. A week later, the two men were freed from a police van by a Fenian rescue party, and one of the police guards was shot dead. Kelly and Deasy were never recaptured, but three of their rescue party were — William Allen, Michael Larkin and Michael O'Brien. All three were charged with the policeman's death, found guilty, and hanged on the morning of 23 November.

Three weeks later, on 13 December 1867, another Fenian rescue attempt was made to release some prisoners from Clerkenwell Gaol in London by blowing a hole in the prison wall. The explosion misfired, twelve people were killed at once and another eighteen died as the result of their injuries over the following weeks. Another 120 were wounded. Public opinion was horrified and the Fenians became firmly established in British minds as odious murderers and terrorists. A Fenian named Michael Barrett was eventually executed for the Clerkenwell explosion in the last public hanging in England.

The explosion at Clerkenwell Gaol, 13 December 1867

LAW-COURTS AND WEEKLY RECORD.

No. 201.]   Registered for transmission abroad   LONDON, SATURDAY, DECEMBER 21, 1867.   Office—275, Strand, London   [PRICE ONE PENNY.

HOUSE OF DETENTION, CLERKENWELL—SCENE AFTER THE EXPLOSION

To the Irish, however, the Fenians were heroic warriors fighting against hopeless odds. Allen, Larkin and O'Brien soon became the 'Manchester Martyrs', and there are still annual commemorations of their execution in Ireland. Peadar Kearney, Brendan Behan's uncle and the man who in 1912 wrote 'The Soldier's Song' (Ireland's national anthem since 1926), wrote a ballad in 1917 which summed up the Fenian memory:

Down by the glenside, I saw an old woman,
Plucking young nettles, she ne'er saw me coming,
I listened awhile to the song she was singing,
Glory-oh, Glory-oh! to the bold Fenian men.

Some died by the glenside, some died 'midst the stranger,
And wise men have told us their cause was a failure;
But they loved dear old Ireland and never feared danger,
Glory-oh, Glory-oh! to the bold Fenian men.

I went on my way, God be praised that I met her,
Be my life long or short, I shall never forget her;
We may have good men, but we'll never have better,
Glory-oh, Glory-oh! to the bold Fenian men.

In America, a group of Fenians who were civil war veterans attempted to attack Britain by launching an 'invasion' of Canada in the summer of 1866. Under the command of a former Union army general and Indian fighter, John O'Neill, between six and eight hundred Fenians crossed the Niagara river in flat boats near Buffalo, New York, and occupied Fort Erie. Some days later another Fenian force crossed into Canada from Vermont. Both groups were easily routed, but not before they had operated under the name 'Irish Republican Army', the Fenian Army of the Irish republic which they regarded as existing in theory, if not in fact. For the Fenians, the existence of their republic was made necessary for the opposition they faced from the Roman Catholic Church.

The two forces of religious loyalty and nationalism have long pulled on Irishmen. For centuries they were not in conflict, and O'Connell had welded them together in a powerful combination. But with the formation of the IRB, the Church came to identify more and more with British government. The Act of Union and Catholic emancipation meant that during the nineteenth century the Church could count on the support of between seventy and ninety Irish Catholic MPs in the parliament of the greatest empire in the world. In addition, under the extremely

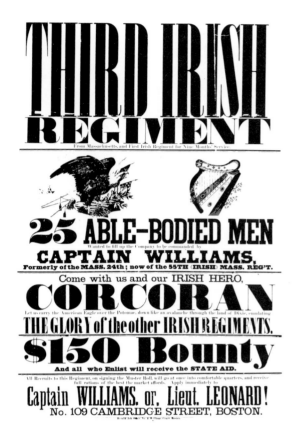

Union Army recruiting poster for the Irish Brigade

Members of the Irish Brigade in the Confederate Army during the American Civil War

conservative influence of Paul Cullen (who was reputed to have drafted the dogma on Papal infallibility at the first Vatican Council), Archbishop of Dublin from 1852 until his death in 1878, the Church became increasingly hostile to any movement that threatened the political or social *status quo*. Not until 1886 did the Church formally endorse home rule for Ireland, and even then only as 'representing the *legitimate* aspirations of the Irish people'. To the Church, legitimacy meant remaining within the framework of British law and practice. It rapidly distanced itself from rebellious nationalism after O'Connell's early successes, condemning the Fenians, the 1916 Rising and, in 1920, the IRA. In return for Catholic bishops' influence on behalf of constitutionalism in Ireland, successive British governments acknowledged the special position of the Church: a position so strong that in 1885 the Church secured the Irish Party's acceptance of a major voice for the clergy in the selection of parliamentary candidates. In 1870 Cullen secured governmental agreement that the wishes of the Catholic Church would be followed in State schools.

The Church's pro-government bias began in the eighteenth century as the Penal Laws were abolished. The Catholic seminary at Maynooth had since its foundation in 1795 received an annual government grant of £9000, and in exchange its staff and students took an oath to be loyal to and fully support the British monarch:

I . . . do take Almighty God and his only Son Jesus Christ my Redeemer to witness, that I will be faithful and bear true allegiance to our most gracious sovereign lord King George the third, and him will defend to the utmost of my power against all conspiracies and attempts whatever, that shall be made against his person, crown and dignity; and I will do my utmost endeavour to disclose and make known to his Majesty, and his heirs, all treasons and traitorous conspiracies, which may be formed against him or them; and I do faithfully promise to maintain, support and defend, to the utmost of my power the succession of the crown in his Majesty's family against any person or persons whatsoever.

It was not surprising, therefore, that the President of Maynooth College had led the condemnation of the 1798 rebellion, and that the Church, increasingly staffed with Maynooth-educated priests, should more and more oppose Irish nationalists and nationalism.

In 1845, despite furious opposition from Orangemen and the Church of Ireland, the grant to Maynooth College was increased to £45,000 a year. In the same year the government set up Ireland's second university, Queen's University, with teaching colleges in Cork, Galway and Belfast, open to Protestants and Catholics alike. At first the Queen's Colleges were accepted by the Church, but being denied the right to control the curriculum, the bishops denounced the 'godless colleges' and in 1854 founded their own independent Catholic University in Dublin. In 1871 the hierarchy banned Catholics from attending Trinity College, which had itself never imposed such a ban. In 1908 the Queen's Colleges in Cork and Galway were amalgamated with the Catholic University in the National University of Ireland. Queen's College, Belfast, remained separate and overwhelmingly Protestant, joining Trinity College, Dublin, and Magee College in Derry in a split, sectarian Irish higher education system: as late as 1956 Catholics were specifically forbidden by their Archbishop of Dublin to enter Trinity College, and the ban on attendance was not removed until 1970. The Church's influence on Irish life demanded respect and in the north generated renewed fear and opposition. But in the 1860s the Fenians were the first to feel the full weight of Catholic power.

The Church's growing opposition to extreme Irish nationalism throughout the nineteenth century may have been partly reflected by the fact that so many Protestants came to lead the more revolutionary sections of the Irish national movements. However, the mass of support for these movements came from the Catholic peasantry, and so at all times the concerns of the Catholic hierarchy were taken seriously. Constitutional nationalists came to enjoy the support of the Church in return for defending what the Church regarded as its vital interests, particularly in education. But in the case of the Fenians, there was little room for compromise. The IRB, as a secret oath-bound society, was anathema to the Church. This stemmed from a series of Papal Bulls, 'In Eminenti' (1738), 'Providas' (1751), 'Ecclesiam' (1821) and 'Quo Graviora' (1825), which condemned secret societies. In addition, the IRB was pledged to rebellion. Four conditions for justifiable rebellion were laid down by the Church, and it was usually pointed out that one or more had not been met when Fenian rebellions were discussed. First, the government must be habitually and intolerably oppressive. Secondly, rebellion must be a last resort after other means of opposition had been tried and failed. Thirdly, there must be a reasonable prospect of success and of not making matters worse. Fourthly, the resistance must enjoy approval by a popular majority. This is a formula designed to maintain the *status quo*, if only because there is little hope of testing public opinion beforehand on the merits of a rebellion.

In 1861, three years after their formation, the Fenians were condemned by the Archbishop of Dublin, Dr Paul Cullen, Ireland's leading churchman. He warned of the evils of secret societies and declared that those joining them were excommunicated *ipso facto*. But the pull of nationalism proved stronger than Church strictures, and Fenian recruiting continued. However, a lack of popular support for the 1867 Rising was ascribed by the Fenians to the hostility of the Church, and it was a constant source of worry to them. John O'Mahony had foreseen this in 1859:

> *We must calculate upon a certain amount of opposition from some of the priests. I do not, however, consider it judicious to come into collision with them openly. Those who denounce us go beyond their duties as clergymen. They are either bad Irishmen, who do not wish to see Ireland a nation, or stupid and ignorant zealots . . . Our association is neither anti-Catholic nor irreligious. We are an Irish army, not a secret society.*

This line of argument was advanced by the IRB throughout its life, and James Stephens in 1859 hurriedly changed the IRB's original oath, dropping reference to a secret society. In 1864, the *Irish People* refined the argument in a clear call for the separation of Church and State: 'We saw from the first that ecclesiastical authority in temporal affairs should be shivered to atoms before we could advance a single step towards the liberation of our suffering country.' This call, together with their dedication to physical force, was Fenianism's most important legacy. But it did not hold water with the Church. In February 1867 in Kerry, local Fenians, unaware that the planned rising had been postponed, attacked some officials and land agents around Kenmare. In response to this Bishop Moriarty of Kerry delivered the most furious and resounding clerical condemnation of the Fenians from the pulpit of Killarney Cathedral on 17 February:

> *Oh, God's heaviest curse, his withering, blighting, blasting curse on them . . . When we look down into the fathomless depth of this infamy of the leaders of the Fenian conspiracy, we must acknowledge that eternity is not long enough, nor hell hot enough, to punish such miscreants.*

Ecclesiastical hostility to the IRB reached a climax in 1870 when the Sacred Congregation of the Holy See, otherwise known as the Inquisition, with the authority of Pope Pius IX, banned the society and declared its members excommunicated by the very fact of membership. This was later extended to the IRA on 12 December 1920 with a decree of excommunication by Bishop Cohalan of Cork. On 10 October 1922 during the Irish civil war, the Catholic hierarchy in Ireland declared in a joint pastoral that the Irish Free State Government was the legitimate government and that the IRA, 'the Irregulars', were guilty of 'murder', 'robbery', 'criminal destruction' and 'molestation'.

Yet, while the hierarchy vehemently opposed the IRB and the IRA, many priests did not. When the Manchester Martyrs were executed, priests throughout Ireland said prayers at Mass for them. Requiems were held in their honour in many places. A procession was held for them in Killarney, despite the blasting opposition of Dr Moriarty.

This division within the Church was constant. It enabled members of the IRB to convince themselves that ecclesiastical opposition to the Brotherhood was based in ignorance. Charles Kickham in the 1860s and 1870s had masterminded the Fenian reply to the Church, and in 1873 he drew up a constitution for the organization which declared the president of the IRB to be the president of the Irish republic. The constitution also provided for a government with military and judicial powers. Ever after, for the IRB there was only one legitimate authority in Ireland — their own — and thus they gave themselves all the moral authority which, as good Catholics, they needed. So the chaplain of the 3rd Cork Brigade, IRA, Fr Dominic, OFM, Cap., was able to explain Bishop Cohalan's excommunication away:

Now kidnapping, ambushing and killing ordinarily would be grave sins or violations of Law. And if these acts were being performed by the [IRA] as private persons (whether physical or moral) would fall under the excommunication [sic]. But they are doing them by and with the authority of the State and Republic of Ireland. And the State has the right and duty to defend the lives and property of its citizens and to punish even with death those who are aiming at the destruction of the lives or property of its citizens or itself.

The Fenian deaths and atrocities of 1867 reawakened British interest in Ireland. A mixture of coercion and reform had marked Irish policies. *Habeas corpus*, for example, was suspended in 1804–5, 1807–10, 1824–5, 1833–4, 1848–9, and 1866–8, while in the same period measures of educational reform and religious toleration were enacted. The meekness with which the horror of the famine had been accepted by the Irish people was taken as a mark that the government's policy of gradual political and social reform tempered with firmness when necessary was working in Ireland. But in 1867 this assumption was proved wrong. 'Fenianism,' wrote the philosopher and MP John Stuart Mill, burst 'like a clap of thunder in a clear sky, unlooked for and unintelligible'. Mill turned his full attention to Ireland in 1868, publishing his essay *England and Ireland* in which he analysed England's Irish problem. He was the first man to realize that in many ways a better description would be Ireland's English problem. He saw that Fenianism was more than congenital criminality, and that a moral issue was involved: the ideal of freedom. 'The difficulty of governing Ireland,' he wrote, 'lies entirely in our own minds; it is an incapability of understanding.' Too many Englishmen, wrote Mill, liked to explain Irish rebelliousness as the result of 'a special taint or infirmity in the Irish character', but, he went on:

There is probably no other nation of the civilized world, which, if the task of governing Ireland had happened to devolve on it, would not have shown itself more capable of that work than England has hitherto done. The reasons are these: first, there is no other nation that is so conceited of its own institutions, and of all its modes of public action, as England is; and secondly, there is no other civilized nation which is so far apart from Ireland in the character of its history, or so unlike it in the whole constitution of its social economy; and none, therefore, which if it applies to Ireland the modes of thinking and maxims of government which have grown up within itself, is so certain to go wrong.

Mill's foresight went largely unnoticed at the time. 'Mill ought to be sent to penal servitude as a Fenian' was the reaction of Lord Bessborough, himself an Irish landlord. The *Saturday Review* called Mill 'the most recent and most thorough-going apostle of Communism'. Some, however, listened to Mill and were affected. One such was William Ewart Gladstone, who termed Mill 'the saint of rationalism'. In 1868 Gladstone fought a general election as leader of the Liberal Party with the slogan 'Justice for Ireland', and upon learning the results which made him Prime Minister for the first time, he said, 'My mission is to pacify Ireland.' For the rest of his life he tried.

Gladstone's first step was to disestablish the Church of Ireland in 1869. The 1861 census had revealed that in a population of 5.7 million there were only about 690,000 Anglicans with their churches and clergy supported by the tithe paid by the whole country. Gladstone's Act was the logical supplement to Catholic emancipation, and that it had been freely granted, without rebellions and mass demonstrations demanding it, was of major importance to the future of constitutional politics in Ireland. He followed this up in 1870 with a Land Act which, for the first time, involved government in landlord–tenant relations. Landlords were required to pay up to £250 compensation to unjustly evicted tenants. However, it was found easy to circumvent the Act, and agrarian discontent which had been simmering since the famine once more began to boil.

In 1850 the Tenant Right League had been founded by Charles Gavan Duffy, one of the Young Irelanders who had founded *The Nation* and who was tried for sedition five times, but whom no jury would convict, and William Sharman Crawford, a Co. Down landlord. The aim of the League was to protect tenants, 300,000 of whom were evicted between 1849 and 1852, from rapacious landlords. The League proposed the statutory extension of the custom of 'Ulster tenant right' to the whole country. This involved financial compensation for tenants for eviction and improvements they made to their properties, summed up in the 'three Fs'; fair rents, fixity of tenure while that rent was paid, and freedom of sale of one tenant's rights to another. However, the League and the Irish Independent Party, which Gavan Duffy also helped to found to press for reform and home rule, were successfully opposed by the Church as 'revolutionary'. Gavan Duffy emigrated in disgust to Australia where he also entered politics, becoming Prime Minister of Victoria in 1871, and being knighted for his services two years later. He retired in 1880 to the South of France and died in Nice. His son, George, was one of the five Irish signatories to the Anglo-Irish Treaty of 1921 which established the Irish Free State.

After Gavan Duffy's departure, attention was focussed on the Fenians until their 1867 fiasco. Gladstone's Acts produced a reaction in favour of peaceful politics as the best way of securing political and social reform which was increasingly seen in terms of the repeal of the Act of Union. In 1871, Isaac Butt, the son of a Protestant rector, who became O'Connell's successor as Ireland's leading barrister, founded the Irish Home Rule League. Butt had eloquently defended Smith O'Brien and other Young Irelanders in 1848, and in the 1860s he defended many Fenians too, including John O'Leary. He was personally persuaded of the case for Irish self-government, but he rejected outright repeal on the grounds that no British government would stand for it. Instead he proposed home rule, whereby Ireland would have control of all domestic matters, but Britain would retain control of all international affairs. With the introduction of the secret ballot in 1872, Butt's ideas were given a fair test, and changing the League into a Party he won 59 out of the 103 Irish seats in the House of Commons in the 1874 general election.

Butt himself, by common consent 'an old-fashioned gentleman', was ousted as leader of the Party shortly before his death in 1879. The more vigorous, younger and radical Charles Stewart Parnell, a Protestant landlord and High Sheriff of Wicklow, was elected leader in 1880. Under the influence of his strong-minded American mother (the daughter of Admiral Stewart who had fought against England in the War of 1812) who had an obsessive dislike of England, he entered politics as a home ruler, winning the Co. Dublin seat in 1875 at the age of twenty-nine. He quickly devastated British parliamentary traditions by developing the filibuster (first used by Irish MPs under Butt) to disrupt the proceedings of the House of Commons. 'Something really must be done about Mr Parnell' was the cry of parliamentarians and political journalists within a year of his entry to the House. Dr Walter McDonald, Professor of Theology at Maynooth, recalled once hearing Parnell speak:

> *He was very nervous; not however as if he were afraid of the audience or doubtful of his own powers, but as if he were one seething mass of energy, seeking to burst into violent eruption, but kept under firm control. He spoke a good deal with clenched right hand, and one could see the nails digging into the flesh, while up along his back the tightly-fitted frock coat showed the muscles playing as an instrument.*

Parnell's speeches electrified Ireland and created the most powerful political movement in Irish history. His parliamentary tactics enabled the votes of his party to sway Government policies, and in 1886 to bring down Lord Salisbury's Conservative administration and hold the balance of power between Gladstone's Liberals and their opponents. He placed the Irish question to the fore of British politics. He was little short of hated by English politicians, and many years later Winston Churchill compared him savagely with Butt:

> *Butt honoured and cherished the House of Commons. Its great traditions warmed his heart. He was proud to be a member of the most ancient and illustrious representative assembly in the world. He was fitted by his gifts to adorn it. Parnell cared nothing for the House of Commons, except to hate it as a British institution . . . Butt trusted in argument; Parnell trusted in force. Butt was a constitutionalist and a man of peace and order; Parnell was the very spirit of revolution, the instrument of hatred, the agent of relentless war.*

In 1879, warfare again looked likely in Ireland. Bad harvests in the years 1877–9 revived the spectres of famine and agrarian disturbance. Thousands of small tenant farmers could not pay their rents, and evictions began to increase. Michael Davitt, imprisoned for his Fenian activities in 1867 and released in 1877 following Parnell's campaign for an amnesty for Fenian prisoners, became convinced that non-violent agitation for land reform offered more hope than Fenian physical force. On 21 October 1879 Davitt founded the Irish National Land League

Michael Davitt
(1846–1906)

in Dublin with Parnell as its president. The League's initial purpose was to secure reduced rents, but it quickly became a popular mass movement which gave Irish peasants a new self-respect. Some months before, in Westport, Co. Mayo, the Irish leader made a statement of obduracy which was to characterize the League when he told local tenants: 'You must show the landlords that you intend to hold a firm grip on your homesteads and lands. You must not allow yourself to be dispossessed as you were dispossessed in 1847. You must not allow your small holdings to be turned into large ones.' When he assumed the presidency of the League, Parnell launched what was called the New Departure in Irish politics: the successful cooperation for specific objectives of the constitutional nationalists with the revolutionary ones. The New Departure was devised by Michael Davitt and John Devoy. Davitt threw the prestige and secret influence of the IRB amongst the peasantry behind Parnell's 'constitutional' campaign for land reform, while Devoy secured the support of Irish-Americans. With Fenian support, the League mushroomed, giving Parnell a mass, organized movement whose members would vote faithfully for his Party. During a visit to America in the winter of 1879–80, Parnell delighted revolutionary Irish nationalists at Cincinnati where he said he wanted to cut 'the last link which keeps Ireland bound to England'.

In 1876 an official analysis of the rents of Irish landlords revealed that the country was owned by 32,610 men, fewer than 4000 of whom owned nearly 80 per cent of the profitable land. Twenty large landlords alone owned nearly 10 per cent of the whole country. Michael Davitt calculated that, on the basis of these figures, 110 landlords owned four million acres (20 per cent of the country); that twelve owned one million acres, but that five million peasants did not own a blade of grass between them. Accordingly, the League demanded the redistribution of land to tenants, with compensation for landlords. To achieve this, Davitt launched a campaign that was soon called the 'Land War', whereby tenants refused to have anything to do with landlords — boycotted them, in fact — and withheld their rents. One of the first victims of the Land War was the Co. Mayo land agent for Lord Erne, Captain Boycott, whose name has since become synonymous with ostracism. Despite being sent protection and food by northern Orangemen, the Captain was unable to secure his master's rents, and he found it best to leave Ireland. Throughout the country, hayricks were burned, landlords' cattle maimed, and some owners even murdered by members of the League. In 1880, over 2800 agrarian outrages were reported to the authorities. Obliged to restore order, the Prime Minister, Mr Gladstone, warned: 'If there is still to be fought in Ireland a final conflict between law on one side and sheer lawlessness on the other, then I say

gentlemen, without hesitation, the resources of civilization are not yet exhausted.'

In 1881, Gladstone first secured a second Land Act which guaranteed the 'Three Fs' to all tenants and set up Land Courts to fix fair rents. The League, however, continued to press for land redistribution, and Parnell refused to endorse the Act. Agrarian violence continued and Gladstone blamed the Irish leader directly, accusing him of 'marching through rapine to the dismemberment of the Empire'. Many members and supporters of the Irish Party were involved in Land League outrages, although not Parnell personally. Nevertheless, on 12 October 1881, Parnell was arrested under a new Coercion Act and imprisoned without trial in Kilmainham Gaol in Dublin. 'The Chief', as he was affectionately called by his supporters, became a hero by being imprisoned. All the country's leading patriots, throughout history, had at some time in their careers been incarcerated by the government, and now Parnell joined them in this distinction. Seven months later, in an informal, unwritten agreement known as the 'Kilmainham Treaty', Parnell was freed after arranging with Gladstone the release of Land League leaders from prison and the waiving of tenants' rent arrears with an Arrears Act. In return, Gladstone secured Parnell's support for the 1881 Land Act and his promise to try to end agrarian outrages.

181

IRELAND

On 6 May 1882, four days after Parnell's release, public opinion in Britain and Ireland recoiled at the assassination of the Chief and Under Secretaries of Ireland, Lord Frederick Cavendish and Mr T. H. Burke. They were horribly murdered with surgical knives in Dublin's Phoenix Park as they were walking together on Lord Frederick's first evening in Ireland as Chief Secretary. A breakaway group from the IRB, the 'Invincibles', claimed responsibility for the atrocity. Parnell immediately wrote to Gladstone offering to retire from politics completely as token of his abhorrence of the murders. Gladstone refused his offer, and in January 1883 twenty-seven men were arrested for the crimes. One of them, James Carey, turned Queen's evidence: four men were executed and two more exiled to penal servitude. Carey, who had taken a leading part in the murders, was released and with government help made his way secretly to South Africa. He was followed by an Invincible, Patrick O'Donnell, and shortly after Casey boarded the *Melrose* at Capetown for Natal O'Donnell shot him dead. O'Donnell was arrested immediately and hanged for the shooting in December 1883 at London's Newgate prison.

In March 1887, five years after the Phoenix Park murders, *The Times*, in a vindictive series of articles entitled 'Parnellism and Crime', accused the Irish leader

PUNCH, OR THE LONDON CHARIVARI.—May 20, 1882.

THE IRISH FRANKENSTEIN.

"The baneful and blood-stained Monster * * * yet was it not my Master to the very extent that it was my Creature? * * * Had I not breathed into it my own spirit?" * * * (*Extract from the Works of C. S. P-rn-ll, M.P.*)

Punch *cartoon of the style popular from the 1840s, depicting the Irish as simian monsters. As this caption indicates, the English press attempted to link Parnell with the murders of Lord Frederick Cavendish and Mr T.H. Burke in Dublin's Phoenix Park.*

LEFT]
Charles Stewart
Parnell (1846–91)

RIGHT]
William Ewart
Gladstone (1809–98)

of being involved in Land War crimes, including murder, and of condoning the deaths of Cavendish and Burke. For three years Parnell fought these charges: in February 1889 the letters *The Times* had used as evidence were proven forgeries and the forger, Richard Piggott, confessed to them, fled to Madrid and there committed suicide. In February 1890 a special High Court investigative commission finally cleared Parnell completely.

In the meantime, a bombshell had burst in British politics. After the 1885 election which gave the Irish Party a balance of power in the House of Commons, Mr Gladstone, at the age of seventy-seven, again became Prime Minister and publicly espoused Irish home rule. He was accused of simply trying to stay in power by gaining Parnell's support but he had in fact become convinced of the need for an Irish settlement well before the election. On 8 April 1886, despite Conservative and Orange opposition, Gladstone introduced his first Home Rule Bill to parliament:

183

IRELAND

I cannot conceal the conviction that the voice of Ireland as a whole is constitutionally spoken. I cannot say it is otherwise when five-sixths of its lawfully-chosen representatives are of one mind on this matter . . . I cannot allow it to be said that a Protestant minority in Ulster, or elsewhere, is to rule the question at large for Ireland . . . I think that the Protestant minority should have its wishes considered to the utmost practical extent in any form which they may assume . . . Various schemes have been proposed including the exclusion of a proportion of Ulster from the operation of the Bill, or separate autonomy for that portion of Ulster. But there is no one of them which has appeared to us to be completely justified . . . The concession of local self-government is not the way to separation and independence, but the way to strengthen and consolidate unity. I ask that we should apply to Ireland the happy experience we have gained in England and Scotland.

SUPPLEMENT GIVEN AWAY WITH THE **WEEKLY FREEMAN** 16TH OCTOBER, 1886.   PRICE THREE HALF-PENCE

"DIVIDE AND CONQUER."
AN OLD ENGLISH CUSTOM

The Real "Separatist" —" They ask for *One* Ireland—I will give them *Four*, and then set them fighting—Ha! ha! Good old Tory game—not yet played out, I hope."

Lord Salisbury (1830–1903), leader of the Conservative Party and Prime Minister from 1886 to 1892, is linked in this cartoon from the Irish Nationalist Weekly Freeman *to Lord Randolph Churchill's attempt to encourage religious division in Ireland for political purposes.*

Parnell welcomed Gladstone's Bill as 'a final settlement', but ninety-three Liberals deserted their leader and joined the Conservatives against it. Their opposition was based not on a wish to keep the Irish down, but on the grounds that Irish home rule threatened the integrity of the United Kingdom and the Empire. On 8 June 1886, the government was defeated by 343 votes to 313. Six weeks later Gladstone resigned. In 1893 Gladstone's second Home Rule Bill was passed by the House of Commons but rejected by the House of Lords, and the 'Grand Old Man' of British politics, whose oleographed portrait had sprouted on Irish walls after 1886, retired at the age of eighty-five on 3 March 1894, having warned that 'ruder and more dangerous agencies' would grow up in Ireland again if home rule was not agreed. Parnell, however, was not alive to hear this prophecy.

In 1890 Parnell was at the height of his power and his fame. He was hated by Unionists and Orangemen, but he had been exonerated of any involvement in the Phoenix Park murders and was enjoying a wave of public sympathy throughout the United Kingdom. Like O'Connell before him, he was the uncrowned king of Ireland and his leadership of the Irish Party looked like achieving the passage of home rule in alliance with Gladstone's Liberals. Then, because of one of the most sensational divorce cases of the century, he was ruined.

In 1880 Parnell fell in love with Mrs Katherine O'Shea, the wife of the Irish Party MP for Clare, Captain William O'Shea. Between 1882 and 1884 she bore him three children. Parnell went to great lengths to keep his affair secret, even adopting extraordinary disguises, as William O'Brien, MP for Mallow and editor of the Land League journal *United Ireland*, recalled forty years after meeting Parnell one day in December 1886, in dense fog at Greenwich:

I suddenly came upon Parnell's figure emerging from the gloom in a guise so strange and with a face so ghastly that the effect could scarcely have been more startling if it was his ghost I met wandering in the eternal shades. He wore a gigantic fur cap, a shooting-jacket of rough tweed, a knitted woolen vest of bright scarlet and a pair of shooting or wading boots reaching to the thighs — a costume that could not well have looked more bizarre in a dreary London park if the object had been to attract attention.

It seems clear that despite Parnell's disguises and the Captain's later claims to the contrary, O'Shea was well aware of the relationship between his leader and his wife, and used it to secure political advantages for himself. In 1882 he acted as go-between for Parnell and Gladstone during the 'Kilmainham Treaty' negotiations, and in 1885, after being defeated for the Liverpool constituency in the general election, through Parnell he was quickly returned in a by-election in Galway. He resigned his seat soon afterwards, and in 1889 he filed for divorce on the grounds of his wife's adultery, naming Parnell in November 1890 as co-respondent. The effect on Parnell's career was shattering. The moral case for Irish home rule had been the basis of Parnell and Gladstone's campaign and was what had secured the vital support of British non-conformists for the Liberal Party. With one voice, the Catholic Church, the Conservative Party and non-conformists denounced Parnell as morally unfit to be in public life, let alone to lead the Irish Party.

Parnell fought back, refusing to step down. His Party at first rallied to him and re-elected him as leader, but then split on the issue, and at a famous meeting on 6 December 1890 in Committee Room 15 of the House of Commons forty-five of the seventy-two Irish MPs opposed Parnell's continued leadership. Three days earlier, the standing committee of the Irish hierarchy had condemned Parnell too. 'Parnellism,' proclaimed Bishop Nulty of Meath, 'springs from the root of sensualism and crime.' In failing health, the Irish leader launched himself on a speech-making tour of Ireland to regain his support, but in three successive by-elections his candidates were defeated. 'He looked like a hunted fugitive,' wrote one man who had seen Parnell speak in Cork in 1891, 'his hair dishevelled, his beard unkempt, his eyes wild and listless.' In May that year he married Katherine O'Shea in a civil ceremony and five months later on 6 October 1891, aged forty-five, he died in Brighton. His wife, years later, described his last minutes:

> *Late in the evening he suddenly opened his eyes and said: 'Kiss me, sweet Wifie, and I will try to sleep a little.' I lay down by his side, and kissed the burning lips he pressed to mine for the last time. The fire of them, fierce beyond any I had ever felt, startled me, and as I slipped my hand from under his head he gave a little sigh and became unconscious. The doctor came at once, but no remedies prevailed against this sudden failure of the heart's action, and my husband died without regaining consciousness, before his last kiss was cold on my lips.*

His body temperature was so high that no death-mask could be made, and his body had to be placed in a lead coffin at once, the weight of which quickly started a rumour that it was filled with rocks and that 'The Chief' was still alive.

Parnell's dogged determination to stay on as leader of the Irish Party won him both respect and enmity. The country, like the Party, divided over what became the question of loyalty to Parnell or to the Church, and as James Joyce depicted in his autobiographical *A Portrait of the Artist*, families feuded over him, even at Christmas dinner:

The bishops and priests of Ireland have spoken, said Dante,
and they must be obeyed.
Let them leave politics alone, said Mr Casey, or the people
may leave their church alone.
You hear? said Dante, turning to Mrs Dedalus.
Mr Casey! Simon! said Mrs Dedalus, let it end now.
Too bad! Too bad! said Uncle Charles.
What? cried Mr Dedalus. Were we to desert him at the bidding
of the English people?
He was no longer worthy to lead, said Dante. He was a public sinner . . . Dante
shoved her chair violently aside and left the table, upsetting her napkin-ring
which rolled slowly along the carpet and came to rest against the foot of an easy
chair. Mr Dedalus rose quickly and followed her towards the door. At the door
Dante turned round violently and shouted down the room, her cheeks flushed
and quivering with rage:

The northern end
of Grafton Street,
Dublin, in the 1890s:
Trinity College can be
seen at the end of the
street.

187

Devil out of hell! We won! We crushed him to death!
Fiend!
The door slammed behind her.
Mr Casey, freeing his arms from his holders, suddenly bowed his head
on his hands with a sob of pain.
Poor Parnell! he cried loudly. My dead King!

For Yeats and the members of the Irish literary revival, Parnell represented a proud, noble spirit brought down by love and the envy of lesser men. In *United Ireland*, Yeats published a prophetic poem in which he saw something of the significance of Parnell's death:

> *Mourn — and then outward, there is no returning,*
> *He guides ye from the tomb;*
> *His memory now is a tall pillar, burning*
> *Before us in the gloom.*

The Irish Party, rent, for over a decade lost its parliamentary effectiveness and came to the point of collapse. Tim Healy tried unsuccessfully to form a clerical party, while Parnell's supporters refused to compromise with those they came to scorn as 'traitors' and 'trimmers'. John Redmond, a Parnellite, who came to lead a reformed and effective Irish Party in 1900, graphically described the Party in 1894 as 'shattered, their funds bankrupt and their credit exhausted', while 'disunion, squalid and humiliating personal altercations and petty vanities' kept Irish MPs at each others' throats.

The prospect of Irish home rule seemed over after Gladstone, virtually single-handedly, tried to revive it with his second bill in 1893 and failed. However, as events were to show, two quite different movements were to keep it alive. Young writers like Yeats and Joyce carried the flag of Irish nationalism to a new generation which formed organizations like the Gaelic League and the Gaelic Athletic Association. Patrons and scholars like Lady Gregory and Douglas Hyde encouraged the Irish cultural revival and a reawakening of pride in Ireland's Gaelic past, providing a psychological refuge from the shabby behaviour of politicians. On the other side, the Orange Order had found new purpose and support with its outright opposition to home rule, and began organizing and training in such a way that the politics of home rule were always factious.

10

ORANGE AND GREEN

Success depends on three things:
who says it, what he says, how he says it;
and of these three things, what he says
is the least important.

JOHN, VISCOUNT MORLEY,
RECOLLECTIONS, II, 5, IV

About quarter of the people of Ireland were opposed to home rule and wanted to keep the union with Britain. Mostly concentrated in the north-east of the country, they were principally Protestant textile and ship-building workers and members of the Orange Order. Enjoying a higher standard of living than the rest of Ireland as a result of their hard work and successful industries, they feared persecution and the loss of their wealth and property in a united Ireland dominated by Catholicism. In 1886, hard on the heels of Gladstone's conversion to home rule, its Irish opponents came together under the auspices of the Orange Order which formed the Unionist Party as their political vehicle. Lord Randolph Churchill, Conservative Leader of the House of Commons and father of Winston Churchill, went to Belfast in 1886 to play, as he himself termed it, 'the Orange card' (by stirring up anti-home rule sectarian riots): 'I decided some time ago that if the Grand Old Man [Gladstone] went for home rule the Orange card would be the one to play. Please God it may turn out the ace of trumps and not the two.' And he publicly declared, 'Ulster will fight and Ulster will be right.' Within weeks, 73,000 Orangemen volunteered to resist home rule by force if necessary, but they did not have to. For the next twenty years the Unionists' allies, the Conservatives, enjoyed an almost unbroken monopoly of power at Westminster as the Liberals became irretrievably split on the question of home rule.

Liberal support for home rule, however, forced the Conservatives to come up with an Irish policy of their own. So they argued that there was no real demand for home rule in Ireland, but rather that unattended Irish complaints, particularly concerning land, had given rise to a spurious call for it. Accordingly, the Conservative governments of Lord Salisbury and his nephew Arthur Balfour in the years 1886–92 and 1895–1905 set about 'killing home rule with kindness' by a series of beneficial reforms.

In 1886 following the defeat of the Home Rule Bill, two of Parnell's close associates, William O'Brien and John Dillon, launched what was called the 'Plan of Campaign' against unfair rents, continuing evictions of tenants by landlords and the unfairness of Irish land ownership. Their hope was to revive the agitation and

disturbances which had characterized the earlier Land War and thus force conces-
sions which they believed the House of Commons would not otherwise make. For
five years they tried to maintain pressure on landlords. Just as in the Land League,
their supporters attacked and injured not only landlords, but also defenceless
animals. In Britain, where people were traditionally well-disposed to animals, the
maiming of them generated a growing racist dislike of the Irish. O'Brien and Dillon
had some success in securing lower rents, but in Arthur Balfour, Chief Secretary of
Ireland from 1887 to 1891, the Plan met staunch resistance. Balfour lent full
support to landlords carrying out evictions, often cooperating with them by arranging selective removals of Plan ringleaders, and on occasion by sanctioning wholesale estate clearances. He dealt with tenants who fortified their homes to resist

*Harland and Woolf
shipyards, Belfast,
c. 1909, during the
construction of the
Titanic, seen in the
background*

BATTERING RAM 1769 W.L.

An eviction scene on the Vandeleur estate near Kilrush, Co. Clare, in August 1888. Helmeted members of the Royal Irish Constabulary ('Royal' was added in 1867 after the Constabulary had helped to crush the Fenians) guard Vandeleur employees as they break down the cottage wall.

eviction by approving the use of battering rams in 1889 to force quick entry. By May 1891, the Plan had been beaten and there were only eighteen estates in Ireland where the tenants still held out. Dillon became a leader of the anti-Parnellite faction of the Irish Party after the O'Shea divorce case, but in 1900 accepted the Parnellite Redmond's leadership. In 1918 he became leader of the Party himself, but was defeated in the general election that year and retired from politics, dying nine years later in London. O'Brien also took the anti-Parnell side in 1891, but he left the House of Commons in 1895 to throw himself once more into land reform agitation, forming the United Irish League for this purpose in January 1898. Re-entering politics, he helped reunite the Irish Party and became convinced that Irish nationalists and unionists would have to cooperate if the country was to prosper economically. In 1918 he did not contest the election and ten years later, like Dillon, he died in London.

192

However, the efforts of O'Brien and Dillon to draw attention to land reform impressed Balfour despite his opposition to their methods. In 1891, as a result of Balfour's prodding, the Conservatives passed a major Land Act. The Act advanced £30 million for Irish tenants to borrow at preferential rates so that they could buy their farms. This had been done in the earlier Land Acts of 1870 and 1885 (the Ashbourne Act which had made £5 million available for this purpose), but not on so large a scale. In addition, Balfour set up the Congested Districts Board in 1891 to purchase land, redistribute it among tenants, and to make improvements to farm buildings and organization. By the time the Board was wound up in 1923, it had spent £11 million pounds, redistributed 2.5 million acres to 59,510 tenants, and had helped to develop some fisheries and home industries in the impoverished west of Ireland. In 1903 George Wyndham, Conservative Chief Secretary of Ireland, sponsored the greatest Land Reform Act of all. A further £100 million was advanced to tenants and in consequence over 250,000 of them acquired their holdings. Possibly the most far-reaching piece of social reform in Ireland since the union, the Wyndham Act was praised by John Dillon as having 'the effect of changing the whole character of the peasantry. Instead of being careless, idle and improvident, they have become like the French peasantry, industrious and economical, even penurious.' What is more, the Act irreparably weakened the economic and political base of the landlord class, and consolidated the post-famine development of an agrarian-based conservative Ireland, with catholic values centring on the family, land inheritance, and the Church. Many of Ireland's most creative spirits subsequently found that they had to leave their country to flourish and survive, and only in the 1970s did this begin to change.

It was left to the Liberals, who returned to power in 1906, to introduce the principle of compulsory purchase in 1909 in the final Land Act, which enabled a further 66,500 tenants to become landowners. By 1917, there were few agrarian outrages, 11.5 million acres — more than half the country — had changed hands, and almost two-thirds of all tenants had purchased their farms. With justifiable pride, British politicians looked upon these measures as solving the Irish problem. Together with Karl Marx, they made the mistake of thinking that economic problems were more important than political ones. Kindness worked, but not when confronted by the Irish perception of centuries of unkindness and injustice.

The memory of the past had been a strong element in the Young Ireland movement which had romantically tried to forge a new national identity transcending religion and ancestry. Their cultural idealism formed the basis of a Gaelic renaissance, of a reawakening of interest in every element of the Irish past. In 1841

the Archaeological Society of Ireland was formed as a direct result of renewed interest in the country's antiquities. In 1884 the Gaelic Athletic Association (GAA) was founded at a meeting at Hayes' Commercial Hotel in Thurles, Co. Tipperary, arranged by a teacher, Michael Cusak, who liked being called 'Citizen Cusak'. He drew up rules for Irish games, and clubs were set up in parishes throughout Ireland. Great emphasis was given to the game of hurling which, though today Ireland's national game, in 1884 had nearly succumbed to the English game of cricket.

From the start, the IRB was attracted to the GAA, seeing it not only as a practical step towards the separate Irish national consciousness the IRB wanted, but also as a recruiting ground for new members. In 1891, two thousand Fenian-minded members of the GAA marched with their hurley sticks draped in black in Parnell's funeral cortege. Just before and during the First World War, the GAA also provided an excellent cover for IRB men practising military drill, using hurleys as substitutes for rifles. So important was the GAA to the IRB that from the outset

194

British soldiers and police were banned from membership, and in 1914 IRB men gained control over the Association as a preliminary move towards the 1916 Rising.

The most important revival organization, however, was the Gaelic League. Founded in 1893 by two linguistic scholars, Douglas Hyde, a Protestant and later first president of Eire, and Eoin MacNeill, who was to found the Irish Volunteers twenty years later, the League set out to save the Irish language and to extend its use. Like the GAA, it established branches all over the country. It published Irish language textbooks and encouraged Irish games and dances. In 1901 Hyde's play *Casadh an tsugain (Twisting the Rope)* was the first play ever to be performed professionally in Irish. By 1904 there were 593 branches of the League with a total membership of over fifty thousand. Its agitation was successful in making Irish an essential subject for entry to the National University of Ireland, and Hyde became the first professor of modern Irish at University College, Dublin, in 1909. Membership of the League became almost a *sine qua non* of membership of the IRB, and it provided revolutionary nationalists with almost their only cover for reorganization after the failure of the 1916 Rising.

However, in its specific purposes the League itself was a failure. In 1891, before the Gaelic revival had taken hold, the census revealed that there were just over 680,000 Gaelic speakers in Ireland compared to 1.7 million in 1851. There was no census in Ireland in 1921, but the 1926 census showed what had happened to the Irish language. Despite over thirty years of League activity, there had been an eighteen per cent fall — 120,000 since 1891 — in the total number of Irish speakers. In addition, the League's insistence upon Irish as a qualification for most higher education and, after 1921, for civil service jobs in the Irish Free State, made the language more of a job ticket than a national exercise. Thus while in theory 27 per cent of the Irish Republic's population of 3,162,000 can speak Irish today, in fact only an estimated 55,000 actually do.

The Gaelic League nevertheless had a powerful effect on Irish literature. It kept alive the idealism which had left politics with the death of Parnell and helped restore a sense of dignity to Irish peasants by publishing collections of folktales and songs unlocked through the language. Douglas Hyde was largely responsible for this development, and it was he who rediscovered Cuchulain, quickly turned by Yeats and others into a symbol of nationhood. Lady Isabella Augusta Gregory, the wife of an Irish landlord, was one of those who became an ardent admirer of Gaelic legends and tales as a result of League publicity. Meeting Yeats in 1898, she became his patron and threw open her home at Coole Park, Co. Galway, to the young and brilliant generation of Irish writers inspired by the new awareness of Ireland's

Dion Boucicault (1822–90), Dublin-born author of about 150 plays including The Colleen Bawn *and* The Octoroon, *the first play to take seriously the predicament of American negroes. He died in New York.*

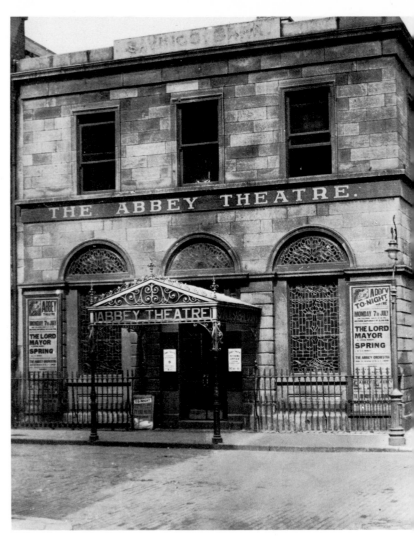

William Butler Yeats (1865–1939). This photograph was taken on 24 January 1908.

Dublin's Abbey Theatre was founded by W.B. Yeats and Lady Gregory in 1904 and was burnt down in 1951. The present theatre was opened in 1966 on the original site.

Gaelic past. In 1904 Lady Gregory and Yeats together took the lead in establishing Dublin's Abbey Theatre for the performance of Irish plays by Irish playwrights.

William Butler Yeats and James Augustine Joyce were the two greatest writers of the Irish literary revival. Yeats, born in Dublin, was brought up and educated in England. His family came from the Ascendancy class, and Yeats was instrumental not only in ensuring that Irish literature did not become a sentimental, nationalistic and parochial affair, but also in guiding and advising the younger writers of the revival. It was Yeats' insistence that there could be a distinctively Irish literature written in English that ensured the transmission of Gaelic myths, poems and folklore to a worldwide audience. In 1923 he was awarded the Nobel Prize for literature. Joyce, also born in Dublin, came from the Catholic middle class. Unlike most of the Irish revival writers, he was less interested in Ireland's past than in her present. He found Irish life, particularly the role of the Catholic Church, constricting and oppressive, on this basis describing Dublin as 'the centre of the paralysis of Irish life'. From 1904 until his death he lived in Switzerland, Italy and France, never visiting Dublin after 1914. However, Irish life was almost the sole subject of his writings, and he presented a vigorous and earthy picture of Dublin and its people to an international readership, its appetite whetted by the fact that his major novel, *Ulysses*, published in 1922, was banned in Britain and the United States.

George Bernard Shaw, together with Yeats and Joyce, was one of the greatest writers in English of the twentieth century. He was the son of an unsuccessful Dublin merchant. His mother was a singer and, when Shaw was eighteen, she left her husband and son and went to live in London with her music teacher. Four years later Shaw joined her, and spent nine years resolutely writing five novels, none of which was accepted by publishers. In 1884 he joined the socialist Fabian Society, becoming one of its best speakers, and the following year began reviewing art, music and books for various British newspapers and journals. He turned to writing plays next, but not until 1897 was he successful with *The Devil's Disciple*, which was acclaimed in New York. His works, however, have only a lively use of language and an unusual energy to indicate that their author was Irish. Only one major play, *John Bull's Other Island* (1904), concerns itself with Shaw's homeland. It was written at the request of W. B. Yeats for the Irish Literary Theatre, and in a preface to the play Shaw gave his Irish political testament:

> *What is an Irishman? When I say that I am an Irishman I mean that I was born in Ireland, and that my native language is the English of Swift... I am violently and arrogantly Protestant by family tradition; but let no English Government therefore count on my allegiance: I am English enough to be an inveterate Republican and Home Ruler... For let me halt a moment here to impress on you, O English reader, that no fact has been more deeply stamped into us than that we can do nothing with an English Government unless we frighten it.*

Apart from this, Shaw was never really involved in the Irish revival, making his life in England and taking his subjects from English life. Nevertheless, throughout his life he maintained his interest in Ireland, and in 1916 courageously defended the Easter Week rebels and Sir Roger Casement. In 1925 he won the Nobel Prize for literature. In 1946 he was made a Freeman of the city of Dublin, and in his will he endowed the National Gallery of Ireland where, as a boy, he had spent many hours finding the intellectual stimulus he craved. The enormous royalties from *My Fair Lady*, the film version of his play *Pygmalion*, have made the Gallery one of the richest in the British Isles.

LEFT TO RIGHT:
George Bernard
Shaw (1856–1950);
Oscar Fingal
O'Flahertie Wills
Wilde (1854–1900);
James Augustine
Joyce (1882–1941);
John Millington
Synge (1871–1909);
Sean O'Casey
(1880–1964)

A whole catalogue of literary giants sprang from Ireland at the end of the nineteenth and beginning of the twentieth century: George Augustus Moore, Oscar Fingal O'Flahertie Wills Wilde, George William Russell, better known as 'AE', John Millington Synge and Sean O'Casey. All except O'Casey were Protestant, and generated interest in Ireland and things Irish. In the process they often had to brave the anger of their countrymen. Synge's play, *In the Shadow of the Glen* (1903), in which the heroine runs off with a tramp, was denounced by Arthur Griffith because 'all of us know that Irish women are the most virtuous in the world'. *The Playboy of the Western World* was met with rioting when it was first performed at Dublin's Abbey Theatre in 1907 because of its 'unpatriotic' indications that Irish chastity was not all that it might seem. One line in particular from the play caused a storm: 'It's Peegeen I'm seeking only and what'd I care if you brought me a drift of chosen females standing in their shifts itself.' O'Casey's play *The Plough and the Stars* (1926) also led to riots after its first performance at the Abbey Theatre, because its portrayal of IRA men as less than heroic was taken as a slur by nationalist crowds. The fact that O'Casey had helped form the Labour movement's Irish Citizen Army in 1913, and had recruited for the IRB, was forgotten in the uproar.

Yeats consistently struggled against narrow nationalism. In 1894 he had joined the Irish National Brotherhood (as a result of which he met his life-long love, Maud Gonne McBride), a breakaway group from the IRB, entering the Irish police reports of the time as 'a literary enthusiast, more or less of a revolutionary'. So when in 1925, as one of the first Senators of the Irish Free State, he spoke against the new State's legislation making divorce illegal even for Protestants, his words carried more than usual weight:

I think it is tragic that within three years of this country gaining its independence we should be discussing a measure which a minority of this nation considers to be grossly oppressive. I am proud to consider myself a typical man of that minority. We against whom you have done this thing are no petty people. We are the people of Burke; we are the people of Grattan; we are the people of Swift, the people of Emmet, the people of Parnell. We have created the most of the modern literature of this country. We have created the best of its political intelligence.

Yeats' plea for liberalism was ignored, and the social oppression of the new State, like the political oppression of the old, maintained the pressure to emigrate on all those who would not conform. George Moore, James Joyce, George Bernard Shaw, Oscar Wilde and Sean O'Casey all found that they could only practise their art in voluntary exile. George Moore in particular blamed hypocritical piety and the overbearing influence of the Catholic Church in Ireland for his exile, and went so far as to convert to Anglicanism to express his feelings. To the present day it is noteworthy that many Irish writers, despite tax benefits and family ties, still prefer to live abroad.

Without doubt, a combination of Catholic and conservative religious and social attitudes was (and still is) responsible for this diaspora of Irish talent. In 1912, however, Irish Protestants, with fears that they would be forced into a Catholic State with the successful passage by the House of Commons of a Bill for Irish home rule that year, were galvanized into resistance.

In the general election of 1906 the Liberal Party, led by Sir Henry Campbell-Bannerman, won a landslide majority of 106 over all other parties combined. He had made no mention of home rule during the election campaign, and most Liberals were glad to be rid of the divisive policy. But in 1907 Augustine Birrell, MP for North Bristol, was appointed Chief Secretary for Ireland, and he became convinced of the need of home rule. No other Chief Secretary approached his task with Birrell's conscientious enthusiasm. He read Wolfe Tone's *Autobiography* and John Mitchel's *Jail Journal*. He admired the work of Synge and Yeats, and was a regular visitor to the Abbey Theatre. He became a friend of Redmond and other leaders of the Irish Party, winning their trust with his obvious love and concern for Ireland.

John Edward Redmond had reunited the Irish Party under his leadership in 1900 and had played a major part in the discussions which had led to the 1903 Land Act. Before entering politics in 1881, he had been a clerk in the House of Commons, and so he was one of the rare breed of politicians who had experience of the whole political process. He refused to regard the Liberals as betrayers of home rule after 1906, preferring instead to maintain the Irish Party's unofficial electoral alliance with them that had existed ever since 1886. He supported the tremendous social reforms undertaken by the Liberals, who from April 1908 were led by Henry Herbert Asquith. The costs involved in these reforms, which included the introduction of old-age pensions, labour exchanges, and other early elements of the British Welfare State, together with the growing expense of Britain's arms race with Germany, brought political conflict to a head. In 1909 the Chancellor of the Exchequer, David Lloyd George, introduced the 'People's Budget', which proposed the raising of the necessary revenue by increasing taxes, especially on higher incomes. The Conservative Party vehemently opposed the budget, and after it was passed by the Commons, used their majority in the hereditary House of Lords to defeat it. In December 1909 Asquith called a general election on the issue, winning with a greatly reduced majority which gave Redmond's seventy-five Irish Party MPs the balance of power for the first time since 1886. Asquith agreed to introduce a Home Rule Bill, and in return Redmond continued to support his government.

Arthur Griffith (1871–1922)

Redmond rejoiced in this political success. Apart from anything else, it put paid to the incipient threat from a splinter group called Sinn Fein to the domination of his Party in Irish politics. Sinn Fein (meaning 'we ourselves' in Irish) was founded by Arthur Griffith on 28 November 1905. Griffith was a convinced Irish nationalist who, after an early flirtation with the IRB, adopted constitutional methods. He developed his Sinn Fein Party in order to increase the pressure for home rule at a time when it seemed as if the Irish Party might never achieve it. He argued for a dual monarchy on the Austro-Hungarian model, with the reintroduction of Grattan's Irish parliament — 'the King, Lords and Commons of Ireland' — and proposed to work for this by influencing the Irish county councils to add their active support to the Irish Party's efforts. At the very first meeting of the new Party's executive, it was decided that no Sinn Fein candidate would oppose an Irish Party candidate in a parliamentary election, and this remained Party policy until 1917. For the first twelve years of its existence, the Party remained a miniscule affair, its members — often, like Griffith, connected to the IRB in some way — figuring more prominently in police reports than in elections. By 1911 it was almost moribund, with Redmond's success having made its purpose appear unnecessary.

In 1912 Asquith honoured his promise to introduce home rule, having in the previous year secured the reduction of the House of Lords' veto power to two years with the Parliament Act. Remembering that the peers alone had prevented the introduction of home rule in 1893, the Unionists became desperate. The Government of Ireland Bill was passed three times by the Commons in 1912, 1913 and 1914, and three times it was rejected by the Lords. Then, as specified in the Parliament Act, it automatically became law, receiving King George V's Royal Assent on 15 September 1914. The Act set up an all-Ireland parliament in Dublin, with control over all matters except defence and foreign policy. The dream of O'Connell, Parnell and Redmond seemed, at long last, to have come true. But six weeks before the Bill was signed, at 11 pm on 3 August, the United Kingdom had declared war on Germany and the implementation of the 1914 Government of Ireland Act was postponed.

The government chose to postpone the Act because of the inadvisability of major constitutional change at the start of war, coupled with the real prospect of civil war between unionists and nationalists in Ireland. Under the leadership of a Dublin-born barrister and MP for Trinity College, Sir Edward Henry Carson, unionists in northern Ireland in 1912 had proclaimed their decision to fight home

Sir Edward Carson (1854–1935), Dublin-born Unionist leader, signs the Solemn League and Covenant at the Belfast City Hall on 28 September 1912.

rule. Faced with the inevitable passing of the Home Rule Bill, Carson bent his powerful oratory to mobilize Orangemen against it. In 1895 he had devastated Oscar Wilde at the witness stand during the writer's libel action against the Marquis of Queensberry, thus bringing about Wilde's trial and imprisonment for homosexuality. On 31 January 1911, Carson won the hearts of Orangemen with his resounding promise, 'We will yet defeat the most nefarious conspiracy that has ever been hatched against a free people.' On 28 September 1912 the confirmation of Carson's sway over Unionists came when in one day 471,414 Ulstermen signed 'Ulster's Solemn League and Covenant':

> *Being convinced in our consciences that home rule would be disastrous to the material well-being of Ulster as well as to the whole of Ireland, subversive of our civil and religious freedom, destructive of our citizenship and perilous to the unity of the Empire, we whose names are underwritten, men of Ulster, loyal subjects of His Gracious Majesty King George V, humbly relying on the God whom our fathers in days of stress and trial confidently trusted, do hereby pledge ourselves in solemn covenant throughout this our time of threatened calamity to stand by one another in defending for ourselves and our children our cherished position of equal citizenship in the United Kingdom and in using all means which may be found necessary to defeat the present conspiracy to set up a Home Rule Parliament in Ireland. And in the event of such a Parliament being forced upon us we further solemnly and mutually pledge ourselves to refuse to recognize its authority.*

The conditional loyalty of unionists in Ulster to the British Government was once again clearly expressed. They would deny parliament's authority unless parliament did what they wanted. To give even more force to this position, Carson went as far as setting up a 'Provisional Government' for Ulster that would commence the day home rule was put into effect. In January 1913, with the help of Britain's most distinguished military commander, Lord Roberts, VC, the Ulster Volunteer Force was formed with General Sir George Richardson, a retired Indian army veteran, as commander-in-chief. Within months the UVF had over one hundred thousand men drilling and training regularly. A defence fund was set up and £1 million collected which was used to buy arms in Germany. Fourteen weeks before Britain went to war, on the night of 24 April 1914, the UVF illegally landed 35,000 German rifles and five million rounds of ammunition at the port of Larne, Co. Antrim, having taken over the town, cut telephone wires, and locked up the local police.

An eye-witness postcard sketch of the Larne gun-running

The actions of Carson and the UVF were clearly criminal, if not treasonable. They were as guilty of as much as the Young Irelanders and Fenians, who had been sent to prison and penal servitude in the 1840s and 1860s. Carson recognized this, telling a London audience before leaving for Belfast in 1912 that 'he intended when he went over there to break every law that was possible'. 'I do not care twopence whether it is treason or not,' he declared. 'I do not even shrink from the horrors of civil commotion. I am a rebel, a Sussex-Irish rebel, and all my Ulster friends are all rebels.' Carson and his Orange supporters feared for their economic and political well-being. Above all, they feared being swallowed up by an alien, Catholic culture.

Asquith's Liberal Government tried to ignore Carson's activities, unwilling to make him a martyr by arresting him, and unwilling to risk open conflict with the UVF. In addition, the Conservative Party, since 1911 under the leadership of Andrew Bonar Law, lent its support to Carson, so Asquith could not even count on broad political support at home in dealing with Carson's subversion. Bonar Law, who was the son of an Ulster Presbyterian minister, personally identified with

Carson, telling a rally of Conservatives at Blenheim Palace near Oxford on 29 July 1912, 'I can imagine no lengths of resistance to which Ulster will go which I shall not be ready to support, and in which they will not be supported by the overwhelming majority of the British people.' These were extraordinary words from the leader of the Party that prided itself upon its respect for law; but like Carson, Bonar Law genuinely believed that Irish home rule would lead to the breaking-up of the Empire. There were states in India and colonies in Africa and the Far East which had just as good a claim as Ireland — often even better — to self-government. For these men, home rule represented the thin end of the wedge of British demoralization and collapse at a time when the United Kingdom needed all its strength and resources for the war with Germany.

The young First Lord of the Admiralty, Winston Leonard Spencer Churchill, was the only member of Asquith's government with the courage to act. In February 1912 he went to Belfast, where he was threatened by a mob, burnt in effigy on the Shankhill Road and denied the use of the Ulster Hall where his father had played the Orange card in 1886. He returned to England determined to compel Carson to obey the law. At Bradford on 14 March 1914, Churchill spoke of a 'treasonable conspiracy' and made his intentions clear:

> If every concession that is made is spurned and exploited, if all the loose, wanton and reckless chatter we have been forced to listen to these many months is in the end to disclose a sinister and revolutionary purpose, then I can only say to you: 'Let us go forward together and put these grave matters to the proof.'

Three days earlier he had ordered the Royal Navy's Third Battle Squadron to hold its exercises in the Firth of Clyde, sixty miles from the Ulster coast. At his prompting, the Cabinet ordered Lieutenant General Sir Arthur Paget, commander-in-chief in Ireland, to take steps to defend its Ulster weapons depots and to send troop reinforcements to the province. Paget, who had a reputation for excitability, resisted these instructions on the grounds that they might fuel Ulster conflict and that the Great Northern Railwaymen, Orange to a man, would refuse to move his troops. At a final conference in London with the chief of the Imperial General Staff, Sir John French, on 19 March, Paget had to be told not to be 'a bloody fool' after he bellicosely admitted his unionist sympathies, but he obtained French's verbal agreement that officers domiciled in Ulster would be allowed to 'disappear'. All other officers would have to obey orders.

The following day in Dublin Paget called a conference of his officers and gave them a colourful account of his instructions, during which he referred to the government as 'those swine' and painted a picture of inevitable bloodshed in Ulster as a result of their decisions. That evening at the Curragh military camp, fifty miles from Dublin, Brigadier General Sir Hubert de la Poer Gough, his three colonels and fifty-five officers in the Third Cavalry Brigade notified Paget that they would resign rather than move against Ulster. Three days later, Gough and his three colonels were assured in London that 'the troops under our command will not be called upon to enforce the present Home Rule Bill in Ulster, and that we can so assure our officers', and they returned to Ireland in triumph. Major General (later Field Marshall) Sir Henry Wilson, a fanatical unionist and Director of Military Operations at the War Office, kept Carson and Bonar Law informed of the Cabinet's plans throughout. When Sir John French told him in confidence that the government proposed 'to spray troops all over Ulster as if it were a Pontypool coal strike', Wilson reported every word.

The 'Curragh Mutiny', as the episode was called, blunted the possibility of military action against Ulster. In Switzerland, the Russian revolutionary and communist, Lenin, followed the events closely, rejoicing in what he saw as the spectacle of the upper classes providing workers with a lesson in resistance to the law. In America President Woodrow Wilson, himself of Ulster Presbyterian ancestry, was horrified by Carson's resistance and felt that 'he ought to be hanged for treason'. All Asquith could say was, 'I have rarely felt more hopeless in any practical affair.'

While these events rocked the British political establishment, Redmond and the Irish Party blithely placed their trust in Asquith and the government, maintaining that Carson was merely 'bluffing' and would back down when presented with the fact of home rule. Having succeeded in obtaining the legislation for which his Party had been established, Redmond was prepared to relax and leave full responsibility for it with the government. He was more concerned with the implications of social unrest made evident by the activities of Dublin workers and the Dublin strike of 1913 than with the threats of Carson.

James Larkin, born in Liverpool of Irish parents, had launched the Irish Transport and General Workers' Union in Dublin in 1909 to organize unskilled labourers and campaign for better wages and living conditions. The slums of the Irish capital were among the worst in Europe. One-third of the population of the city lived in one-room tenements, without light, water or sanitation. Unemployment was always high, averaging 15 per cent, and for those lucky enough to have a job, average pay was £1 per week — 12½ per cent below the poverty line. Sickness, especially tuberculosis, was rife, and the death rate was the highest in any city in

James Larkin (1876–1947) at a Dublin rally after being expelled from the United States in 1924. This photograph inspired the statue of Larkin erected in 1979 in Dublin's O'Connell Street, and it catches the magnetic quality of the labour leader. Larkin is the central character in James Plunkett's immensely successful novel Strumpet City.

Belfast at the turn of the century: tenement inhabitants after a riot

Europe. From this background, 'Big Jim' Larkin soon gathered a mass following. 'I have got a divine mission,' he would declare, from the Union's headquarters at Liberty Hall, 'to make men and women discontented.' 'I am a rebel', he would shout, 'and the son of a rebel. I recognize no law but the people's law.' From 1910 onwards, Larkin's second-in-command was James Connolly, born in Edinburgh of Irish immigrant parents, and a convinced Irish nationalist and socialist. Together, Larkin and Connolly succeeded in forcing some employers. to improve wages. Alarmed, Dublin businessmen formed an Employers' Federation and in August 1913 they determined to try and destroy Larkin's Union by locking out its members. After six months, during which 25,000 workers were unemployed, the men capitulated and went back to work on the employers' terms. Larkin, defeated, went to America.

During the lock-out, Connolly had formed the 'Irish Citizen Army' to protect pickets in clashes with the police. After Larkin left, the army was reorganized on military lines by the playwright Sean O'Casey, with a flag depicting a plough and stars on a dark green background, the plough symbolizing the dignity of labour and the stars the hopes of man. Connolly and O'Casey wanted a socialist and nationalist counterpart to the Ulster Volunteer Force, but their efforts were unsuccessful. They did, however, manage to develop by 1916 a tightly knit 'army' of 220 men, which Connolly was able to use in conjunction with the IRB-controlled Irish Volunteers to launch a rising.

The Irish Volunteers had been formed on 24 November 1913 in the Rotunda Rink in Dublin by Eoin MacNeill as a direct response to Carson's UVF. From the very start MacNeill made plain that the object of the Irish Volunteers was 'to secure and maintain the rights and liberties common to the whole people of Ireland', and the motto of the Volunteers was 'Defence not Defiance'. MacNeill saw that if the UVF's defiance of home rule could be balanced by Volunteers defending it, then there was a greater likelihood of home rule coming into force as planned. What he did not realize was that from the start he was being manipulated by the IRB.

In December 1907, Thomas James Clarke returned to Ireland from the United States, sent by the old Fenian John Devoy to revive the IRB, which since the 1860s had gradually become more and more involved in Dublin Municipal politics. In 1883 Clarke, under the alias of 'Henry Hammond Wilson', had been sentenced to fifteen years' imprisonment in England for his part in an unsuccessful Fenian dynamite campaign. Upon his release he returned to Ireland and was made a Freeman of the city of Limerick before emigrating to America in 1899. Back in Ireland, in 1910 he published a vehemently nationalist paper, *Irish Freedom*, with a

Eoin MacNeill (1867–1945)

young business manager, Sean MacDermott. Together they master-minded the reorganization of the IRB, and by 1912 could boast fifteen hundred members. These two men were to be the mainspring of the 1916 Rising.

After the UVF was formed in 1913, Clarke and MacDermott saw that a counterpart to it would be an excellent cover for another Irish rising. When Eoin MacNeill, a respected member of the Irish Party, published on 1 November 1913 an article entitled 'The North Began' and proposed the creation of another force to ensure that home rule was put into effect, they seized the opportunity. One of their IRB colleagues, Bulmer Hobson, approached MacNeill, proposed the creation of an Irish Volunteer force, and asked MacNeill if he would head it. MacNeill agreed, and the Irish Volunteers were formed. But the IRB's control was short-lived. Within ten months over 100,000 men had enrolled, forcing Redmond and the Irish Party to take notice of what was happening. Frightened that the Irish Volunteers might challenge the government and thus upset the home rule arrangements, and frightened that they might also become a political force appealing to Irish nationalism over the head of the Irish Party, Redmond demanded control of the Volunteers. On the evening of 15 June 1914, the provisional committee of the Irish Volunteers voted by eighteen votes to nine to accept a majority of Redmondite nominees on their committee, and the IRB lost its direct control of the Volunteers.

Clarke and MacDermott were furious at this development, particularly because Hobson and five other members of the IRB had voted for the Redmondites. Hobson argued that since Redmond's enormous popularity would ensure his control of the mass of Volunteers whatever happened, the IRB's best course of action was to roll with the punch. Clarke and MacDermott would not accept this, as Hobson later recalled:

> I had expected disapproval of the action I had taken, but I was completely taken by surprise when I was met with a storm of hysterical abuse and accusations of having betrayed the movement . . . It was impossible to argue or state a case in such an overcharged atmosphere, and when I made a little attempt to do so, this seemed to increase their fury. When they demanded to know how much I had been paid by Redmond for selling the Volunteers, I realized I could not discuss policy on that level or work with people who thought like that. I was shocked to find that men so sincere and devoted had such paltry minds.

From now on the IRB became even more secretive, its leadership convinced that they had to take even more precautions to prevent informers penetrating their organization. Shortly after the outbreak of war, on 9 September 1914 they called a secret meeting of extreme nationalists in Dublin to plan a rebellion using guns which had been smuggled from Germany to the Irish Volunteers only days before the First World War started.

Robert Erskine Childers, an ex-Clerk of the House of Commons, was one of the most popular writers of his generation. His novel *The Riddle of the Sands*, published in 1903, was based on his own sailing experience in the North Sea and gave a dramatic, though fictional account of German plans to invade England. It was an instant best-seller and was cited for ten years after it first appeared as an indication of Britain's alleged military unpreparedness. Childers became convinced of the necessity of Irish home rule and with his friend, the distinguished diplomat and colonial administrator Sir Roger Casement, raised £1500 with which he purchased 1500 rifles and 45,000 rounds of ammunition in Germany and Belgium. On 26 July 1914, in a carefully planned operation, Childers sailed his yacht, the *Asgard*, with 900 rifles and 26,000 rounds of ammunition, into Howth harbour,

Co. Dublin, where he was met by eight hundred Dublin Volunteers. A week later the remaining rifles and bullets were landed at Kilcoole, Co. Wicklow.

In contrast to the Larne gun-running episode, the Howth affair galvanized the police into action. A mixed force of the Dublin Metropolitan Police and the King's Own Scottish Borderers tried to block the Volunteers as they marched with their new guns back to Dublin, but managed to confiscate only nineteen rifles. Jeered and booed, the soldiers and police returned to Dublin where, in Bachelor's Walk, the Borderers panicked and fired into the crowd around them. Two men and one woman were killed and thirty-two others wounded. The victims were given elaborate funerals, and memorial services were held for them in churches throughout the country. A commission of inquiry censured the authorities for the incident, and the Assistant Commissioner of Police was dismissed. The moral the police construed from this was that firm action on their part was likely to be penalized by the government, and this contributed to the ease with which Volunteers were able to march and train in public, even after war started.

With the outbreak of war, Carson and Redmond agreed to set aside their differences and pledged support to Britain in her fight 'for the freedom of small nations'. *En masse*, the Ulster Volunteers enrolled in the new 36th Division, the Ulster Division, while Redmond, in a speech to an Irish Volunteer parade at Woodenbridge, Co. Wicklow, on 20 September, told them:

> *Your duty is two-fold. I am glad to see such magnificent material for soldiers around me, and I say to you 'Go on drilling and make yourselves efficient for the work, and then account yourselves as men, not only in Ireland itself, but wherever the firing line extends, in defense of right, of freedom, and of religion.'*

160,000 of Redmond's followers joined up during the war. But to the IRB minority in the Volunteers, this speech proved that Redmond was a 'West Briton', prepared to sacrifice Irish youth in the cause of the age-old enemy. They had already decided to split with the Redmondites, and this speech gave them their excuse.

On 21 September, under IRB influence, twelve thousand Irish Volunteers under MacNeill split away from the hundred thousand who remained with Redmond. Four days later, a small group of Volunteers under the leadership of Tom Clarke and some Irish Citizen Army men under their commander, James Connolly, prepared with their guns to break up a Dublin recruiting meeting to be addressed by Mr Asquith, the Prime Minister, and John Redmond. They had to drop their plan when armed troops turned out to protect the meeting, but within the break-away Volunteers and the Citizen Army there could be little doubt as to the purpose of Clarke and his supporters. Even MacNeill was aware of the IRB's revolutionary purpose, although he believed that as chief-of-staff he and not Clarke could control the Volunteers. In this mistaken belief, MacNeill was encouraged by his closest henchmen who, unknown to him, were also members of the IRB.

The Press Secretary and Director of Organization of MacNeill's Volunteers was Patrick Henry Pearse, the son of an English stone carver who had come to Ireland and established a successful business in Dublin. At the age of sixteen Pearse joined the Gaelic League and thirteen years later he founded a bi-lingual private school, St Enda's, in Dublin. An admirer of MacNeill's, he was also a supporter of the Irish Party, but in 1913 he was converted by the IRB's arguments for physical force to achieve Irish freedom, and he joined the secret society. An excellent orator, he gained national fame in 1915 with his speech at the graveside of the Fenian Jeremiah O'Donovan Rossa, which ended with the reminder that 'while Ireland holds these graves, Ireland unfree shall never be at peace'. In May that year at its formation he had joined Tom Clarke's secret Military Committee which planned a rising and from which MacNeill was excluded. With Clarke and MacDermott, Pearse became one of the principal organizers of rebellion. Their first plan was for a rising in September 1915, but they had to cancel their arrangements after MacDermott was arrested and imprisoned for four months in May and when their attempts to get arms from Germany that year failed.

Sir Roger Casement in July 1914 had sailed to New York where he had made contact with John Devoy and the Clan-na-Gael. Devoy had already been in touch with the German Ambassador to the United States, and had asked for German military support for an Irish rebellion. On the outbreak of war, Casement travelled to Germany with Devoy's blessing, hoping to secure some kind of support for his revolutionary Irish friends, and to form an Irish Brigade from prisoners of war. In November 1914 he succeeded in bringing the German government to announce, in a document he himself drafted, that as far as Ireland was concerned 'Germany desires only a national prosperity and national freedom'. In forming an Irish Brigade from Irish prisoners of war to fight for Irish freedom, he was much less successful, recruiting only fifty-five men by 1916.

In great numbers, Irishmen volunteered for the British army. Over 200,000 of them had joined up by the end of the war, and 60,000 never returned. Sean O'Casey described the scene in Dublin as thousands marched to the troopships: 'The stoutest men from hill, valley and town came pressing into the British army. Long columns of Irishmen went swinging past Liberty Hall down to the quays, to the ships waiting to take them to a poppy-mobbed grave in Flanders.' As they marched they sang 'It's a long way to Tipperary' and gave the war its song. By joining up, Irishmen were voting with their feet and their lives in favour of the moderate, cooperative, constitutional approach to Anglo-Irish relations epitomized by Redmond, and against the complete separation of the two countries favoured by the IRB.

Undismayed, the IRB pressed ahead with its machinations. By the beginning of 1916 Clarke's Military Committee had grown to seven. James Connolly had been taken as a member because of his persistent threats to launch a rising with his miniscule Citizen Army. Clarke, MacDermott and Pearse were worried that if Connolly did go ahead on his own he would jeopardize their plans, and they were also stung by Connolly's ignorant but frequent taunts that the Volunteers might march well, but would they ever fight? A poet, Joseph Mary Plunkett, was also made a member of the committee after he travelled secretly to Germany in 1915 on IRB instructions to help Casement secure German soldiers and arms for a rising in Ireland. Eamonn Ceannt, a leading member of the Gaelic League, and a senior IRB man, was an original member of the committee. Thomas MacDonagh, another poet who had been Pearse's first member of staff at St Enda's school, in April 1916 was the last person to join the committee. Together, this IRB group — in effect a secret society within a secret society — organized the Easter 1916 Rising.

Unknown to Eoin MacNeill and the majority of his supporters, the IRB's Military Committee prepared the Volunteers and the Irish Citizen Army for an insurrection. In Dublin they drilled, practised shooting, went on route marches and even launched mock attacks on various strongpoints which the committee planned to seize on the appointed day. In the country, similar exercises were carried out, and 'battle plans' were drawn up for a nation-wide rising of Volunteers. The committee, through John Devoy in New York, remained in contact with Sir Roger Casement in Germany. Early in April 1916 they arranged with the German government for a ship, the *Aud*, disguised as a Norwegian trawler, to land twenty thousand rifles in Tralee Bay between Friday, 21 and Monday, 24 April, having set Easter Sunday, 23 April, as the day for their rebellion. They also asked the Germans for military personnel, and apparently expected much more help from Germany than the Germans were prepared to give. Casement, aware of the committee's misapprehensions, sailed from Germany to Ireland in a submarine, intending when he arrived to do his best to stop the rising.

The Lord Lieutenant, Lord Wimborne, the Chief Secretary, Augustine Birrell, and the Under-Secretary of State for Ireland, Sir Matthew Nathan, knew that some sort of trouble was brewing. Only Wimborne thought it might be serious. Police reports spoke of a 'German landing at an early date', but Birrell in November 1915 refused to take the Irish Volunteers seriously, saying 'I laugh at the whole thing', and Nathan insisted to the end that the Volunteer leaders did not intend insurrection. Wimborne, however, pressed for the arrest of Volunteer and Citizen Army leaders and a clamp-down on both organizations. Birrell and Nathan succeeded in allaying Wimborne's fears by arguing that repression might inspire the revolt Wimborne feared. A month before the rising, Birrell had written to Lord Midleton, the leader of the southern Unionists who, like Wimborne, was worried by Volunteer parades and posturings, 'to proclaim the Irish Volunteers as an illegal body would be in my opinion a reckless and foolish act and would promote disloyalty to a prodigious extent'. Clarke and his Military Committee had succeeded in keeping the plans for an Irish rising secret from the government for longer than any other Irish rebels in the previous 250 years.

Then, in the week leading up to Easter Sunday 1916, the plans went wrong. British intelligence early on in the war having cracked the German codes, the army authorities in Ireland learned news of the arrival of the *Aud* and of the intended rising which they passed on to Nathan. The authorities quickly put the police on alert and on Easter Saturday prepared to arrest the Volunteer leaders.

MacNeill, whose support as chief-of-staff of the Volunteers was essential to the rising, proved difficult to convert to rebellion. He all along maintained that the Volunteers' purpose was to defend the 1914 home rule settlement and that the only other circumstances in which the Volunteers should fight should be in defence of their arms. Accordingly, the IRB Military Committee had decided to pretend to him that the mobilization which they were planning was simply another routine drill. They also hoped that the majority of the Volunteers, whether approving or not, would thus find themselves taking part in an uprising. But in order to ensure that a rising actually took place (and not simply the ostensible manoeuvres), most of the officers in the Volunteers were sworn into the IRB and made privy to the plans.

On the Tuesday before Easter MacNeill was shown a document by Plunkett which announced that the Irish Volunteers' arms were to be confiscated and the leaders arrested. This 'Castle Document', which purported to be drawn up by the authorities in Dublin Castle, was probably forged by Plunkett and MacDermott (though quite possibly on the basis of a genuine draft document). MacNeill, however, believed the document and on Wednesday, 19 April ordered the Volunteers to prepare to defend their arms. The following day Bulmer Hobson found out that the planned rising was only forty-eight hours away, and told MacNeill.

Realizing he had been duped all along MacNeill wrote out orders cancelling the arrangements he had authorized for Easter Sunday nation-wide Volunteer manoeuvres. But then, instead of issuing these orders, he sought out the members of the IRB Military Committee and argued with them. Eventually, when they revealed the full extent of their preparations, and the help they expected from Germany, MacNeill reluctantly agreed to their plans. But when on Easter Saturday he heard that the *Aud* had been intercepted by ships of the Royal Navy, and that Sir Roger Casement had been captured near Tralee within hours of landing from his submarine, he decided that a rising was hopeless after all and finally issued his orders cancelling the Easter Sunday parades. He sent couriers all over the country telling Volunteer commanders to do nothing on Sunday, and he published his order in the *Sunday Independent* for all to see. The authorities saw it too and decided that they could relax, believing that there would be no trouble. Wimborne alone still insisted on arresting between sixty and a hundred of the Volunteer and Citizen Army leaders, and on Easter Monday finally obtained the authority to do so. It was too late.

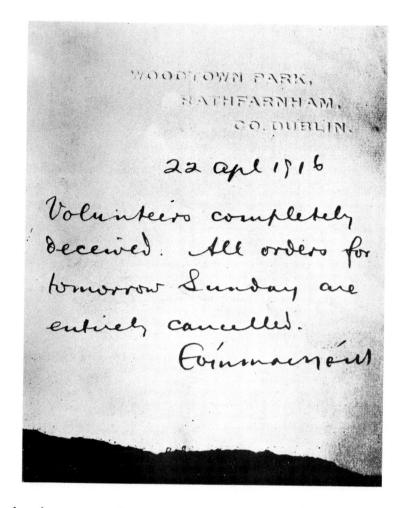

WOODTOWN PARK,
RATHFARNHAM,
CO. DUBLIN.

22 apl 1916

Volunteers completely
deceived. All orders for
tomorrow Sunday are
entirely cancelled.

Eóinmacnéill

Despite the almost complete collapse of their plans, the IRB Military Committee decided to press ahead, merely delaying the rising by twenty-four hours. Patrick Pearse, using his position as Director of Organization of the Volunteers, ordered the Volunteers to mobilize on Easter Monday instead. James Connolly did the same with the Citizen Army. It was a sunny bank holiday, and while the insurgents gathered their forces thousands of Dubliners were leaving the city to go to the Fairyhouse races. Because of the confusion about MacNeill's Sunday cancellation, altogether perhaps only seven hundred men and boys gathered at Liberty Hall during the morning, watched by holidaymakers. Then, at mid-day, they divided into several different groups to take over various city strongpoints.

IRISH CITIZEN ARMY.

SPECIAL MOBILISATION.

All ranks will parade at *Liberty Hall*

with full equipment, on *Sunday* at *3.30*

James Connolly

COMMANDANT.

Connolly and Pearse marched with one group into Sackville Street (renamed O'Connell Street in 1924), wheeled left half way up and rushed into the General Post Office, which became the rebel headquarters for the next five days. Once inside the GPO the rebels arrested a British officer who had been buying stamps, and turned everyone else out of the building. Then James Connolly addressed his men and told them that they were no longer members of the Citizen Army or the Volunteers, but of the 'Army of the Irish Republic'. For the first time since the Fenian invasion of Canada forty-nine years earlier, the IRA was back in the field.

Another group, under Eamon de Valera, commandant of the third battalion, Dublin Brigade, Irish Volunteers, occupied Boland's Bakery, which commanded the principal route into Dublin from the port of Kingstown (now Dun Laoghaire). De Valera, born in New York of an Irish mother and Spanish father, was to become the dominant personality in Irish politics after 1922 and the political leader of Irish nationalists after 1918. Men under his command in houses on Northumberland Road in Dublin put up the most determined resistance during the rising, killing and wounding 230 British soldiers, over half the total British casualties of the whole rising. Another group tried to capture Dublin Castle, but after killing the policeman on duty, they were repulsed by the guard. Dublin's Four Courts, the College of Surgeons, South Dublin Union, Mendicity Institution and Jacob's Biscuit factory, all imposing buildings covering access roads to the city centre, were occupied and held in the name of the Irish Republic, which was proclaimed in posters hurriedly put up by the rebels all over the capital. On two occasions during the afternoon, Pearse read the proclamation to curious crowds in Sackville Street, appealing to the tradition of Irish national resistance:

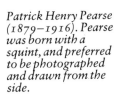

Patrick Henry Pearse (1879–1916). Pearse was born with a squint, and preferred to be photographed and drawn from the side.

Thomas James Clarke (1857–1916)

Irishmen and Irishwomen: In the name of God and of the dead generations from which she receives her old tradition of nationhood, Ireland, through us, summons her children to her flag and strikes for her freedom. Having organized and trained her manhood through her secret revolutionary organization, the Irish Republican Brotherhood, and through her open military organizations, the Irish Volunteers and the Irish Citizen Army, having patiently perfected her discipline, having resolutely waited for the right moment to reveal itself, she now seizes that moment, and, supported by her exiled children in America and by gallant allies in Europe, but relying in the first on her own strength, she strikes in full confidence of victory.

With Thomas J. Clarke heading the list, the seven members of the IRB Military Committee signed the proclamation. It was their rebellion, and it was to be both one of the most short-lived and the most successful in Irish history.

The first news of the rising caught the authorities completely unawares, as the Countess of Fingall in her memoirs *Seventy Years Young* later recalled:

Sir Matthew had spent that morning at the Viceregal Lodge with Lord Wimborne, and he assured us that with Casement's arrest and the cancelling of the next day's Volunteer parade by John MacNeill, all immediate danger had been averted. We could go to Fairyhouse races on Easter Monday as we had planned . . . I had planned to take Mrs Nathan to the Abbey Theatre that night, and during the morning I rang up the Under Secretary's Lodge but could not get any answer. Then I tried Sir Matthew's offices at the Castle.

'I want to speak to Sir Matthew Nathan.'

'You can't.' The voice was that of the old man who looked after the Under Secretary's telephone.

'Why not?'

'There is a rebellion on! Can't you hear the shooting? They have just shot a policeman at the gate.'

I rushed to the window. Outside, in the peaceful spring sunlight, Horace and one of his male guests were playing 'old man's golf'.

'Horace!' I shouted out of the window. 'There is a rebellion on in Dublin!' He turned and looked at me.

'What nonsense! Someone is pulling your leg.'

'But they say so at the Castle — Sir Matthew's office.'

'Well', he said. 'Ring up the Kildare Street Club.'

And went back to his golf.

I rang up the Club and spoke for Sir Horace Plunkett. Was there a rebellion on in Dublin?
"Never heard a word of it', said the porter.
A few minutes later the telephone rang.
'Tell Sir Horace that there is a rebellion. They have taken the General Post Office and shot a policeman.'

For forty-eight hours after Pearse read the proclamation, hardly any fighting took place. Looters ransacked the shops in and around Sackville Street. An unsuspecting party of Lancers were fired on as they rode by the Post Office. On Wednesday afternoon, troops from Britain and the Curragh military camp began to close in on the rebel strongpoints. Many of the soldiers who arrived from Britain during the week at first thought they were in Belgium and only realized their true location as Dubliners cheered and encouraged them. One member of the Sherwood Foresters (a regiment in the 59th Division which began landing at Kingstown on Tuesday night) later recalled that they could have had ten breakfasts a day if they had wanted; the Irish people could not have treated them better than if they had been their own. By Thursday they had penetrated the side streets around the Post Office and began shelling the building. On Friday evening the centre of the capital was a mass of flames, and on Saturday, 29 April at 3.45 pm Pearse, now as commander-in-chief of the IRA, surrendered.

Elsewhere in Ireland MacNeill's couriers and cancellation order effectively stopped other Volunteers taking part in the rising. Only in Galway and at Ashbourne in north Co. Dublin did some Volunteers clash with soldiers and police. Five Volunteer brothers, the Kents, at their farmhouse in Castlelyons, Co. Cork, fought a gun-battle with police on 2 May 1916, three days after the rising leaders surrendered in Dublin. In Co. Wexford, Dundalk and parts of Munster and Ulster, Volunteers mobilized, but no other fighting took place. The rebellion was confined almost completely to Dublin, where £2.5 million worth of damage was caused, and where Patrick Pearse's theory that a 'blood sacrifice' was necessary to keep the revolutionary demand for Irish freedom alive was justified in the end.

11

THE FIGHT FOR FREEDOM

*'I go to encounter for the millionth time
the reality of experience, and to forge in the smithy of my soul
the uncreated conscience of my race. Old father, old artificer,
stand me now and ever in good stead.'*

JAMES JOYCE, PORTRAIT OF THE ARTIST AS A YOUNG MAN

Confusion and dismay were the feelings of Irishmen as they surveyed the ruined centre of Dublin in the weeks following the rising. Everybody realized that the rebels had been more than foolhardy. In the eyes of the government they had betrayed a United Kingdom embroiled in total war with Germany: in the Proclamation of the Republic they had publicly acknowledged support from 'gallant allies in Europe'. For General Sir John Maxwell, commander-in-chief of British forces in Ireland, martial law provided a clear course of action. He had seen years of service in Egypt and India, and now he had been sent to Ireland to put down the rebellion. To him the rising was a supreme act of treachery, for which he was going to teach 'these infernal fellows a lesson they would not soon forget', saying to the Lord Lieutenant: 'I am going to ensure that there will be no treason whispered for a hundred years.' Within four days of the rebels' surrender, he had convened courts martial.

Probably fewer than nine hundred men and women had taken part in the rebellion. They had killed 132 British soldiers and policemen and wounded a further 397 during Easter Week. Total casualties were over three thousand. In Dublin after their surrender the rebels were marched up O'Connell Street to the Rotunda Gardens where, for two cold and rainy days, they were kept wet and uncovered as troops and passers-by jeered and taunted them. One officer stripped

From Commander of Dublin Forces
To   P. H. Pearce

29. April/16

1.40 P.M.

A woman has come in and tells me you wish to negotiate with me.
I am prepared to receive you in BRITAIN ST. at the North End of MOORE ST provided that you surrender unconditionally—
You will proceed up MOORE ST accompanied only by the woman who brings you this note under a white flag—

W. H. Lowe
B. Genl.

Brigadier-General Lowe's surrender instructions to Patrick Pearse, written by Lowe's son (later the film actor John Loder) who was his father's ADC

The main hall of the GPO immediately after the rebels surrendered

Two flags flew over the GPO during the Rising: the tricolour of green, white and orange and a green flag with 'Irish Republic' painted on it in gold and silver, displayed here by British officers at the base of Parnell's statue in Sackville Street.

Dublin's General Post Office, gutted after the Rising

Irish Rebellion – May 1916.
A group of Officers with the captured rebel flag.

Tom Clarke naked and slapped him in front of the men there before they were all marched to prison. Over 2500 more people, including Eoin MacNeill and Arthur Griffith, were arrested throughout the country and charged with complicity in the rising.

The courts martial quickly went into action, trying one woman and 120 men and sentencing 90 of them to death. Patrick Pearse was the first to be condemned. At his trial even the judges came to respect his courage, and Lady Fingall reported that the president of the court 'was terribly affected by the work he had to do'. Pearse's mother was not allowed to see him, but on a sheet of paper which today can be seen at the National Museum of Ireland, he wrote his last poem for her:

> *Dear Mary that didst see thy first-born son*
> *Go forth to die amid the scorn of men*
> *For whom he died,*
> *Receive my first-born son into thy arms*
> *And keep him by thee till I come to thee.*
> *Dear Mary, I have shared thy sorrow*
> *And soon shall share thy joy.*

Early on Wednesday 3 May, he was stood with his back to the thick granite wall of Kilmainham Gaol and shot. With him that same morning the unrepentant Fenian, Tom Clarke, and the young poet, Thomas MacDonagh, were also executed in the stonebreaker's yard of Kilmainham. Clarke, defiant to the end, had announced at his court martial that he would do the same thing again if spared. The next day four more executions took place. On Friday John MacBride, husband of Yeats' love Maud Gonne, was shot in Kilmainham. MacBride had not known about the rising plans and had been as surprised as the rest of Dublin on Easter Monday but, seeing his friends, had joined them. He had been second in command of a small Irish brigade that had fought against the Crown in South Africa during the Boer War. Since then, however, he had become Yeats' 'drunken, vainglorious lout'. The rising and his execution speedily elevated MacBride into a national hero and martyr.

Six of Redmond's Volunteers had been killed fighting alongside Maxwell's troops in Dublin. Others patrolled O'Connell Street after the rising was over, helping soldiers and police maintain order. Nevertheless the executions alarmed Redmond. He realized that public opinion in Ireland, horrified as it had been by the rising, could still be swayed towards the rebels as people like Lady Fingall began to report that they were 'watching a stream of blood coming from beneath a closed door'. George Bernard Shaw warned the government that they were 'canonizing their prisoners'. The Prime Minister, Mr Asquith, responded to these warnings and sent two telegrams to Maxwell saying that he hoped there would be no more executions except in special cases. Maxwell paid little attention, and four more men were shot on 8 May, another the next day.

By now the slow methodical pace of the executions was beginning to change men's minds just as Redmond had feared. His colleague and deputy as leader of the Parliamentary Party, John Dillon, demonstrated this change when on 11 May in the House of Commons he lost control of himself, shouting, 'I am proud of their courage and if you were not so dense and stupid, as some of you English people are, you could have had these men fighting for you . . . it is not murderers who are being executed; it is insurgents who have fought a clean fight, however misguided.'

The following day Sean MacDermott and James Connolly were executed. MacDermott, one of the principal organizers of the rising, captured the romantic spirit as well as the leaders' justification for it in his last letter to his family. 'You ought to envy me,' he wrote. 'The cause for which I die has been rebaptized during the past week by the blood of as good men as ever trod God's earth . . . It is not alone for myself I feel happy, but for the fact that Ireland has produced such men.' Connolly, whose ankle had been shattered by a bullet in the GPO, was executed strapped to a chair. He was the last to die: the seventy-five others who had been sentenced to death had their sentences commuted to terms of imprisonment.

In the circumstances, the execution of fifteen men was not particularly harsh as far as Maxwell and many in authority were concerned. On 21 February the struggle for Verdun had begun with tremendous loss of life. Preparations were being made for the crucial battle of the Somme which began on 1 July and which was to cost 600,000 Allied lives — 400,000 of them British. Pearse in his last poem had written of people's scorn for the rising, and it was universally condemned in Ireland. The poet and storyteller, James Stephens, who witnessed the events in Dublin at this time, noticed that women in particular were 'viciously hostile' to the captive rebels as they were marched through the streets to prisons, barracks and the docks for transport to British gaols and, ultimately for many of them, the Frongoch internment camp in Wales. Seven bishops denounced the rising and the *Irish Catholic* described Pearse as 'a crazy and insolent schoolmaster', ridiculing the rebels as 'rogues and fools'. Local and district councils passed resolutions calling for 'the severest punishment' and deploring 'the outbreak which brings the blush of shame to every honest Irishman'. But by 10 June, Tim Healy, who had let the attack on Parnell and who was soon to become first Governor General of the Irish Free State, was writing to his brother:

I never knew such a transformation of opinion as that caused by the executions . . . They have lost the hearts of the people beyond all hope of retrieving their mistakes. Clerics have discovered that 'the probable hope of success' needed to justify rebellion does not necessarily mean military success, and that Pearse achieved his object and 'builded better than he knew'. His executioners would now give a good deal to have him and his brother back in jail alive.

The Pearse brothers, together with the twelve others executed in Dublin, were buried in quicklime in Arbour Hill barracks. Sir Roger Casement was still in the Tower of London charged with high treason. From a purely legal standpoint he had no defence to the charge, and to make sure that appeals on his behalf did not succeed copies of his diaries revealing his homosexuality were circulated by the authorities. Early on the morning of 3 August 1916 he was hanged in Pentonville Gaol. His speech from the dock on the fourth day of his trial is a classic, passionate statement of the Irish nationalist cause:

If true religion rests on love, it is equally true that loyalty rests on love. The law I am charged under has no parentage in love, and claims the allegiance of today on the ignorance and blindness of the past. I am being tried, in truth, not by my peers of the live present, but by the fears of the dread past; not by the civilization of the twentieth century, but by the brutality of the fourteenth; not even by a statute framed in the language of the land that tries me, but framed in the language of an enemy land — so antiquated is the law that must be sought today to slay an Irishman, whose offence is that he puts Ireland first. Loyalty is a sentiment, not a law. It rests on love, not restraint. The government of Ireland by England rests on restraint, and not on law; and, since it demands no love, it can evoke no loyalty . . . For if English authority be omnipotent — a power, as Mr Gladstone phrased it, that reaches to the very ends of the earth — Irish hope exceeds the dimensions of that power, excels its authority, and renews with each generation the claims of the last. The cause that begets this indomitable persistency, the faculty of preserving through centuries of misery the remembrance of lost liberty — this surely is the noblest cause ever man strove for, ever lived for, ever died for.

Casement became the sixteenth Irish martyr of 1916.

No one else was executed for involvement in the rising, but 1867 men and women were interned and gaoled in Britain. Most of them were kept in Frongoch Camp which became, as a result, a sort of university of rebellion. A young energetic

A group of 1916 rebels photographed in Stafford Gaol shortly after the Rising, and before being sent to Frongoch. Michael Collins is fifth from the right.

Corkman, Michael Collins, who had left his home to work in London but who had returned to Dublin to take part in the rising, soon organized history classes as well as military instruction for the prisoners. He gathered around him a group of men from West Cork — often referred to as 'The Mafia' by the other prisoners — and with their help reorganized the IRB, compiling lists of people who had helped insurgents during the rising. He made notes of friendly policemen, of arms dumps and of those who were willing to continue the fight for the Irish Republic proclaimed by Patrick Pearse. By the time most of the prisoners were released on 23 December 1916, Michael Collins had developed the contacts and the sense of purpose that were to combine to upset the best laid plans and the last desperate acts of the British government and the Irish Parliamentary Party.

Collins and the six hundred others released in December had been given their freedom, as the Chief Secretary for Ireland admitted, because the risk of keeping them any longer, untried, was greater than the risk of letting them go. Over 90,000 southern Irishmen had already volunteered for the British army since the outbreak of war, and on the battlefields of Belgium they might start to wonder for precisely which small country's freedom they were fighting. There was also the ever-pressing need for more and more troops, as German machine-guns, shells and poison gas found their targets on the Western Front. Indeed, extraordinary as it now seems, a serious attempt was made to conscript for the British army those prisoners in Frongoch who lived in England, Scotland or Wales. But perhaps most importantly, the need to take American opinion into account was pressed home upon the government. The chance of prising the United States away from neutrality to hasten an Allied victory over Germany was too precious for Britain to jeopardize. Within a week of the executions, the British Ambassador in Washington had reported a shift in American opinion against Britain. This had played a part in securing the commutation of the death sentence passed on Eamon de Valera who, because of his American birth, could claim United States citizenship. De Valera, who had commanded the Boland's Mill outpost during the rising, after the execution of James Connolly was the senior surviving rebel leader.

Flustered by the rapid change in Irish opinion, Asquith and Redmond agreed to try to implement the 1914 Government of Ireland Act before the end of the war. David Lloyd George, wartime Minister of Munitions, was put in charge of the negotiations. Since the Act had been passed and postponed, Irish Unionists and their Conservative partners had joined the Liberals in the wartime coalition, in which Redmond and his colleagues in the Irish Party were not included. Sir Edward Carson had even become a senior member of the Cabinet as Attorney-General, although he resigned in 1915 in order to throw himself into the job of opposing home rule when the war ended. Thus Lloyd George had the difficult task of reconciling the aspirations of the vast majority of Irishmen for home rule with the domestic political requirements of Asquith's coalition partners. With brilliance and duplicity, he negotiated separately with the Unionists and the Irish Party, thus sowing the seeds for the future partition of Ireland.

Carson and his followers, having opposed the principle of home rule for so long, were persuaded to agree to it for all but the six north-eastern Ulster counties. However, while Redmond was given to understand that this arrangement was to be for a temporary period only, Carson was assured, 'We must make it clear that at the end of the provisional period Ulster does not, whether she wills it or not, merge in the rest of Ireland.' On 22 July 1916 Redmond was officially informed that the proposed settlement was to be permanent. He refused to accept this decision, and the settlement broke down. Nevertheless, in the process, three clear facts emerged. First, as Tim Healy so pertinently said, 'Redmond has left the Irish cause in a worse position than it was ever placed in by his concession of the six counties, as it can't be obliterated.' Secondly, the Unionists, having accepted the principle of home rule, would not compromise any further by accepting a united Ireland. Thirdly, if Irishmen wanted self-determination in their own country quite possibly they would have to find another way of getting it.

In December 1916 Lloyd George succeeded Asquith as Prime Minister. He arranged an Irish Convention which met at Trinity College, Dublin, in another attempt to reach a settlement. In order to generate goodwill among Irish nationalists, the remaining 1916 rebels were released in June 1917 to thronging welcomes in Dublin. Eamon de Valera, as their senior surviving leader, was adopted as the Sinn Fein Party candidate for a by-election in East Clare, which he won with more than twice the number of votes cast for his Irish Party opponent. A rejuvenated Sinn Fein was now coming forward to give voice to the ideals of the rising. The Party boycotted the Convention, which ended in April 1918 without any agreement being reached and with Sir Edward Carson and the Unionists making plain that whatever happened their six northern counties would remain part of the United Kingdom. The Irish Party, which for two generations had dominated the politics of Ireland, was broken. Redmond died in March 1918 knowing that his life's work had failed.

Eamon de Valera in the uniform of a 1916 Irish Volunteer Commandant, with supporters after winning the East Clare by-election, June 1917

John Edward Redmond (1856–1918)

An early meeting of
Dail Eireann in the
Mansion House,
Dublin. Eoin
MacNeill can be seen
presiding. Dail
members sat in the
chairs around the
podium; pressmen
and spectators filled
the balcony and desks
around them.

Sinn Fein propaganda
cartoon of 1918.

"I'M AFRAID I'LL HAVE TO DROP MY PARCEL!"

SINN FEIN

IRISH PARTY

£400 PER YEAR

GENERAL ELECTION

G.B

Sinn Fein rapidly grew under the direction of Michael Collins and the leadership of Eamon de Valera. They held an Ard Fheis — Party Conference — in October 1917 and hammered out Party policy, dropping its monarchist home rule bias in the process. It was decided that successful Sinn Fein parliamentary candidates would not take their seats at Westminster and would work towards 'securing the international recognition of Ireland as an independent Irish republic'. De Valera was elected President of Sinn Fein in place of Griffith, the Party's founder. Throughout 1918 the Party gained support as it spear-headed opposition to the government's proposal to extend military conscription to Ireland, and by the time the first post-war general election came in December 1918, Sinn Fein's policy and organization were so effective that of the 105 MPs returned for Ireland, 73 belonged to Sinn Fein. John Dillon, Redmond's successor as leader of the Irish Party, was defeated in East Mayo, which had regularly returned him in every election since 1885. Only six Home Rulers were elected, and twenty-six Unionists. These results and the decisive victory for Sinn Fein were declared by de Valera, re-elected for East Clare, to be an endorsement of the Irish Republic proclaimed on Easter Monday 1916. Among the successful Sinn Feiners were Michael Collins (South Co. Cork) and the Countess Markievicz (St Patrick's, Dublin), the daughter of a wealthy Anglo-Irish landlord, who had taken part in the rising, been imprisoned and then released in June 1917. Now she became the first woman to be elected to the House of Commons. Refusing to take her seat, she left the way clear for Lady Astor to become the first woman actually to sit in the House twelve months later.

The problem that faced politicians on all sides at this point was the absolute refusal of all parties in Britain even to contemplate the breaking-up of the United Kingdom implicit in Sinn Fein's demand for an Irish republic. In Dublin, Sinn Fein

Countess Constance Markievicz (1868–1927)

10, Downing Street,
Whitehall, S.W.

5th February, 1919.

SIR,

On Tuesday, February 11th, His Majesty will open Parliament in person. An address will be moved and seconded in answer to the Gracious Speech from the Throne.

I hope you may find it convenient to be in your place.

Yours faithfully,

D Lloyd George

Envelope and letter addressed to a successful Sinn Fein candidate in the December 1918 general election who was in prison when the Westminster parliament (which Sinn Fein boycotted) assembled

maintained itself as a constitutional political party, setting up Dail Eireann — the Parliament of Ireland — in the Mansion House, Dublin on 21 January 1919. Forty-two of the Sinn Fein members, including de Valera, were in gaol, exiled or avoiding arrest, on suspicion of involvement in what was termed a German Plot to launch another rebellion in Ireland in 1918, or in some cases for opposing with too much fervour the government's proposals before the end of the war to introduce conscription to Ireland. The twenty-seven members who did attend the Dail's first meeting quickly drafted a Declaration of Independence reaffirming the 1916 republic and established a government of their own for it. Michael Collins was appointed Dail Minister for Home Affairs, two months later becoming Dail Minister for Finance instead in a reshuffle carried out by de Valera upon his appointment as Dail President on 1 April 1919.

Ever since his release from Frongoch, Collins had been busy reshaping the whole national movement, including the Irish Volunteers which, after 1916, are more properly known as the Irish Republican Army. He was determined to avoid a repeat of 1916 which he regarded as having been 'bungled terribly costing many a good life. It seemed at first to be well-organized, but afterwards became subjected to panic decisions and a great lack of very essential organization and co-operation.' He speedily came to dominate the Irish Republican Brotherhood, first as Secretary and later as President. Using all the contacts he had developed, including connections supplied to him by Mrs Tom Clarke, he arranged for IRB groups to provide the nucleus of a secret reformation of the IRA and later of Sinn Fein clubs all over Ireland. In November 1917, a month after the Sinn Fein conference, he had organized an IRA convention at which de Valera was elected President of the army, and in March 1918 he masterminded the formation of a new General Headquarters Staff of the IRA. He became Director of Organization and Adjutant-General, and the real moving spirit of the IRA. Throughout the national movement his ability and efficiency became legendary. A big courageous man, bursting with vitality and quick wit, Collins loved wrestling with his friends, often stealing into their rooms as they slept and leaping on them. Using members of the IRB he devised the stunning escape of de Valera and two others from Lincoln Gaol on 3 February 1919, smuggling them a key for the prison's locks. And still using IRB men in the IRA, reminding them of their oath to fight for Irish freedom, Collins in 1919 began to force the pace of revolt.

Divisions were already appearing in the national movement. Sinn Fein and the members of the Dail had won the 1918 election with the promise that they would take the case for Irish independence to the Peace Conference which had followed

Thomas Ashe (1885–1917) died after being fed forcibly while on hunger strike. Michael Collins gave the oration at his funeral, saying, after a volley was fired, 'That volley which we have just heard is the only speech which it is proper to make over the grave of a dead Fenian.'

Germany's surrender in the First World War. But as the Allied leaders proved reluctant to take up Ireland's cause and to interfere in what Britain maintained was a domestic political matter, so men of action like Collins began to have their way. The Dail was very hesitant about acknowledging the IRA or assuming responsibility for IRA activity.

The IRA's GHQ Staff, who were nearly all members of the Dail as well, were also reluctant (with the exception of Collins) to authorize attacks on British soldiers and constabulary. As a result, IRA activity was at first carried out by local units on their own initiative in open defiance of their superiors in Dublin. By 1920, however, the IRA's actions were tacitly recognized by the Dail. De Valera called the IRA 'our last reserve', and not until March 1921 did he admit, 'From the Irish Volunteers we fashioned the Irish Republican Army to be the military arm of the Government. This army is, therefore, a regular State force, under the civil control of the elected representatives.' However, some IRA leaders recognized by 1919 that while there was propaganda value in keeping the Dail distanced from the IRA, there was a greater danger in having two sources of authority competing for the loyalty of Irish nationalists. Therefore, in August 1919, members of the Dail and of the IRA both took an oath of allegiance to 'defend the Irish Republic and the Government of the Irish Republic which is Dail Eireann against all enemies, foreign and domestic'.

In order to accommodate this new oath, the IRA, which had previously been oath-bound to recognize only the authority of its own governing body, the Executive, now drafted a new constitution. The lingering suspicion of the IRA Executive for the Dail was reflected in this constitution, with the insistence upon the IRA's right to approve the appointment of the Dail's Minister of Defence. The oath of loyalty to the Irish republic and the IRA's suspicion of the Dail were shortly to have a profound effect upon Ireland's history. But until March 1921, when de Valera and the Dail finally accepted responsibility for the IRA, it was answerable only to itself, and many members of Sinn Fein became increasingly frightened of its systematic violence unleashed by Collins. For Collins the issue was clear: if there was to be any hope of obtaining British acceptance of an Irish republic, then Irishmen would have to fight for it; Redmond had proven the futility of negotiation. As early as 1918 a Tipperary IRA leader, Sean Treacy, disturbed by the peaceful, constitutional approach of Sinn Fein, had declared, 'If this is the state of affairs, we'll have to kill someone, and make the bloody enemy organize us!' On the same day that the Dail first met, Sean Treacy and a group of IRA men on their own initiative shot dead two men of the Royal Irish Constabulary (RIC) at Soloheadbeg in Tipperary. The IRA had fired its first shot since the rising.

After his escape from Lincoln Gaol, Eamon de Valera was elected President of Dail Eireann and head of the Irish republic's government. He was now President of the three main nationalist bodies: the Dail, Sinn Fein and the IRA. In the new Cabinet, Collins was appointed Minister for Finance and was immediately put in charge of raising a Dail loan of £250,000, for 'propagating the Irish cause all over the world' and for establishing a Dail administration in Ireland. De Valera had decided that the key to Irish independence lay in America; that if American opinion and money could be swung behind the independence movement, and the American-Irish mobilized in support, then American pressure would prove decisive in forcing Britain to relinquish Ireland to the Irish. In June de Valera, leaving Arthur Griffith as acting President of the Dail and of Sinn Fein, was smuggled to the United States by Collins. For the next eighteen months he journeyed across the country campaigning for Ireland's freedom, raising $5 million, and bringing Irish-American opinion to bear upon the two presidential candidates at the Democratic and Republican Parties' Conventions in 1920 in an unsuccessful attempt to secure their recognition of Irish independence. Meanwhile the news from Ireland was grave.

Undeclared war between the IRA and British forces in Ireland began in earnest in September 1919. By then, Michael Collins had succeeded in penetrating the Dublin Castle headquarters of the 'G' Division of the Dublin Metropolitan Police, the plain-clothes detectives who were the British government's principal intelligence group in Ireland. In September he also formed his 'Squad' of handpicked gunmen, who were entrusted with the killing of police agents and detectives. IRA groups had already launched attacks upon RIC barracks all over Ireland in August, as a result of which the Castle authorities banned most Irish nationalist organizations including the Dail, Sinn Fein and the IRA. The Dail continued to meet in secret, but its suppression sealed the attitude of the British Liberal—Conservative coalition government: from now on force would be met by force.

On the Irish side, despite the reluctance of politicians in the Dail formally to recognize or accept the IRA as their creature, more and more attacks were carried out by IRA groups against British forces. In December 1919 Lord French, the Lord Lieutenant of Ireland, was ambushed by Collins' Squad and Dublin IRA men, although the IRA's chief-of-staff, Richard Mulcahy, made it clear to the ambush party that the Dail might have to repudiate the ambush as part of its effort to present a peaceful, responsible front. As 1920 progressed, flying columns were developed by IRA leaders in the countryside, the most famous being that led by Tom Barry in Cork. Outside Dublin, Cork carried most of the burden of the war. Two Lord Mayors of Cork, who were also the city's IRA leaders, died in the national cause.

Thomas MacCurtain was shot dead in his own bed on the night of 19 March and the coroner's jury investigating his murder found that it 'was organized and carried out by the Royal Constabulary'. His successor, Terence MacSwiney, was arrested in the City Hall five months later and immediately went on hunger-strike in protest. Seventy-four days later he died in Brixton Gaol. These deaths played a major part in attracting the attention of the world to events in Ireland and in particular to the activities of the RIC's new recruits.

Collins had directed the main thrust of the IRA campaign against RIC men and their barracks. By the end of June 1920 fifty-five policemen had been killed and seventy-four wounded, and by July 1921 over two thousand of the ten thousand regular RIC had resigned from the force. In the spring of 1920 hundreds of RIC barracks were evacuated, in order to protect the men. Then, one night in April, 315 of the evacuated buildings were burned down in the IRA's single largest operation of the war. The *Irish Times* four weeks later baldly stated, 'The King's government has virtually ceased to exist south of the Boyne and west of the Shannon.' To the Prime Minister, Lloyd George, it seemed an obvious step to strengthen the RIC in the face of these attacks, and so ex-servicemen and officers were recruited in England to reinforce the beleaguered RIC.

Collins' Squad. From left to right: Joe Leonard; Jim Slattery; Joseph Dalton; Gearoid O'Sullivan; William Stapleton; and Charles Dalton. All except O'Sullivan (who was Adjutant-General of the IRA from 1920 to 1922) were members of the Squad. This photograph was taken during the 1921 truce: they had all dressed up as gentlemen, complete with canes, for the occasion.

The burnt-out shell of Bruree RIC Barracks and Courthouse, one of hundreds of barracks destroyed by the I.R.A.

Black and Tans round up IRA suspects, 1920.

No. 20.

BRIGADE PROCLAMATION

By Colonel Commandant N. J. G. CAMERON, C.B., C.M.G., A.D.C.,
Commanding 16th Infantry Brigade, and Military Governor.

On various occasions when members of the Royal Irish Constabulary or Loyalist Civilians have been brutally murdered by rebels or when the houses of Loyalist Civilians have been destroyed by rebels, it has been necessary as a punishment to destroy the houses of rebels or of persons who are known to be in active sympathy with the rebels who commit these outrages.

It has come to notice that in some cases the rebels have as a reprisal destroyed the houses of Loyalists.

Be it known that in such a case, for ever Loyalist's house destroyed by rebels TWO houses of rebels or sympathisers with rebels will be destroyed.

If the rebels repeat their action this proportion of TWO for ONE will be increased.

Signed at Fermoy this 23rd day of May, 1921.

N. J. G. CAMERON, Colonel Commandant,
Commanding 16th Infantry Brigade, and Military Governor.

In March 1920 the first reinforcements arrived in Ireland, dressed in a mixture of black and khaki 'pending the arrival of RIC uniform'. On 28 April a group of them went on a rampage through Limerick, breaking shop windows and assaulting civilians, so earning the title of 'Black and Tans' after a local pack of hounds. In July the first Auxiliaries arrived, in their distinctive dark blue uniforms and Glengarry caps. Together, these two adjuncts of the RIC earned the fear and hatred of nearly everyone in Ireland. In September they sacked and burned part of the town of Balbriggan as a reprisal for the shooting of an RIC Head Constable, bayonetting to death two townspeople in their nightshirts. As the *Westminster Gazette* pointed out, 'Unless the Government take very stern and convincing steps to stop reckless reprisals on Irish towns, these reprisals will begin to horrify the world even more than the crimes which provoked them.' Even Field Marshal Sir Henry Wilson, the dedicated Orangeman who as Director of Military Operations in 1914 had plotted with those involved in the Curragh mutiny, felt compelled to protest to the Prime Minister about the Black and Tans. Eight days after Balbriggan he recorded in his diary:

> I had 1½ hours this evening with Lloyd George and Bonar Law. I told them what I thought of reprisals by the Black and Tans and how this must lead to chaos and ruin. Lloyd George danced about and was angry, but I never budged. I pointed out that these reprisals were carried out without anyone being responsible; men were murdered, houses burned, villages wrecked . . . I said that this was due to want of discipline and this must be stopped. If these men ought to be murdered then the Government ought to murder them.

House-search, Dublin, 1920

A notice of the official Army reprisal policy in response to IRA attacks on loyalists' houses and property

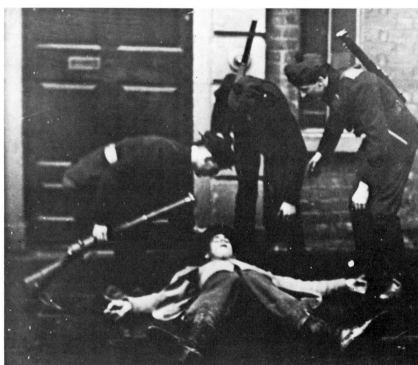

Lieutenant Price
shoots Sean Treacy on
14 October 1920 in
Talbot Street, Dublin.
At the same moment,
Price himself was shot
dead.

Instead, the government decided to institute a policy of retaliation against the IRA with official reprisals against property, and Sir Hamar Greenwood, Chief Secretary for Ireland, stated in the House of Commons, 'I have yet to find one authentic case of a member of those auxiliary forces being accused, of anything wrong.' The first official reprisal occurred on 29 December at Midleton, Co. Cork, where six houses were destroyed following an ambush nearby in which three RIC men were killed. But in the three months between the unofficial reprisal at Balbriggan and the official one at Midleton, the scale of the fighting in Ireland had dramatically increased.

On 14 October in broad daylight, Sean Treacy, the man who had started the shooting at Soloheadbeg, was killed in Talbot Street, Dublin, after a gunfight with soldiers and policemen. Ten days later Terence MacSwiney was dead. On 1 November, the eighteen-year-old IRA man Kevin Barry, a medical student at University College, Dublin, was hanged in Mountjoy Gaol. Barry's death, following so closely on the heels of MacSwiney's, made a profound impression on people everywhere. A ballad which swept the country was written:

At Mountjoy, one Monday morning, high upon a gallows tree,
Kevin Barry gave his young life for the cause of Liberty.

Lloyd George followed this with a speech at London's Guildhall on 9 November, revealing, 'We have taken the steps by which we have murder by the throat.' Then, on Sunday, 21 November, in the cause of liberty, the most momentous event of the war took place. In a carefully planned operation Collins' Squad shot dead fourteen British officers, most of whom were involved in intelligence work, some in their beds in front of their wives. 'Bloody Sunday' had only started. That afternoon at Croke Park, where the All-Ireland Gaelic Football Final was being played between Tipperary and Dublin, Auxiliaries and Black and Tans surrounded the grounds and then, obviously incensed by the shootings that morning, opened fire upon the spectators and the teams. Twelve people were killed including a child, a woman and a Tipperary player. In the evening three men being held on suspicion by the police were riddled with bullets by Auxiliaries in the guard room of Dublin Castle. Collins in a characteristic gesture attended their funeral while his colleagues went 'on the run' or, like Arthur Griffith, were arrested in the clamp-down that followed. A week after Bloody Sunday, Tom Barry's flying column successfully ambushed a convoy of eighteen Auxiliaries at Kilmichael, near Macroom in Cork, killing seventeen of them. Two weeks later, Auxiliaries and Black and Tans went on another rampage, burning the centre of Cork city to the ground. Damage was estimated at £3 million.

Ticket for the All-Ireland Gaelic Football final on 'Bloody Sunday'. During the match the grounds were surrounded by British Auxiliaries and Black and Tans who opened fire on the crowd, killing twelve people and wounding sixty.

The violence had now really frightened the politicians in Sinn Fein. Just as the IRA Executive had feared, peace moves began which showed Lloyd George that there were Sinn Feiners prepared to accept less than an Irish republic. On 30 November Roger Sweetman, the Dail member for North Co. Wexford, wrote to the Press suggesting a conference 'to put a stop to bloodshed in this country'. Three days later the Sinn Fein Galway County Council passed a resolution: 'As adherents of Dail Eireann request that body to appoint three delegates to negotiate a truce.' Two days after this, Father Michael O'Flanagan, acting President of Sinn Fein after Griffith's arrest, sent a telegram to Lloyd George: 'You state you are willing to make peace at once without waiting for Christmas. Ireland also is willing. What steps do you propose?' Michael Collins, who by now was acting as head of the Dail Government, was very worried by these peace moves and tried to stop them, warning, 'There is a very grave danger that the country may be stampeded on false promises and foolish, ill-timed actions'. Still, conversations between Sinn Feiners and emissaries from Lloyd George continued. In a note from Arthur Griffith smuggled out of Mountjoy Gaol, Collins learnt that Griffith had gone so far as to submit to Lloyd George a formula for a truce. Not surprisingly, Eamon de Valera decided that it was time he left America to return to Ireland, and on Christmas Eve 1920 he arrived in Dublin. Hearing of his return the British Cabinet decided that he should not be arrested unless some criminal charge could be laid against him: Lloyd George had seen the value of keeping a line open to those behind the IRA.

The day before de Valera's return, a new Government of Ireland Act came into force. The product of a year's debate and discussion at Westminster, this Act superseded the 1914 Act and legislated for the partition of Ireland along the lines set out by Lloyd George in 1916. It was an attempt to end the troubles. With this Act Sir Edward Carson and his northern Irish Unionists were guaranteed home rule of their own in their six counties, secured by a parliament in Belfast and not by a parliament in Dublin. As one leading Unionist had pointed out to the Cabinet Committee on Ireland, 'the people in the inner circles hold the view that the new province should consist of the six counties, the idea being that the inclusion of Donegal, Cavan and Monaghan would provide such an access of strength to the Roman Catholic Party, that the supremacy of the Unionists could be seriously threatened'. Provisions were made for the eventual unification of Ireland, but only when and if the Unionists wanted it. Having obtained self-determination for his supporters in the north, Carson retired from politics. Ironically, the Unionists were now the only ones to accept the principle of home rule. The Act also provided for a Parliament of Southern Ireland and a home rule government in Dublin for the remaining twenty-

Eamon de Valera
(1882–1975)

six counties. Yet, while partition was now a fact, the IRA and the Dail were still determined to fight on for their all-Ireland republic. They refused to accept the Act. However, under the terms of the Act a general election was held on 19 May 1921 in the twenty-six counties to elect the Parliament of Southern Ireland. The Dail decided to adopt these elections as its own and Sinn Fein, unopposed in 124 of the 128 new constituencies, swept the board. The four University seats of Trinity College, Dublin, returned southern Ireland's only Unionists. Five days later another general election was held in the six county area, where forty Unionists, six Nationalists (the party formed by the old Redmondites in the north) and six Sinn Feiners were elected.

The Sinn Feiners elected in both elections now formed the Second Dail, which still maintained itself as the parliament of an all-Ireland republic. It was to this Dail that de Valera resolved to demonstrate his authority, and to test the IRA's willingness to take his orders as head of the Dail government. The Dublin Customs House, the beautiful eighteenth-century masterpiece of James Gandon, was chosen by de Valera as his target. It was the centre of nine British government departments,

Dublin's Custom House was burned by the IRA on 25 May 1921.

including the Revenue and Local Government Board. Despite Collins' opposition to the scheme on the grounds that it was too risky and might involve the loss of more guns than the IRA could afford, de Valera's orders for the systematic burning of the building were carried out by the Dublin Brigade of the IRA on the afternoon of 25 May 1921. All night the fire blazed and the great copper dome collapsed. By morning, only a smoking shell was left.

The burning of the Customs House was carried out by about 120 IRA men. Most of them were arrested and their arms captured afterwards by the troops and police who quickly arrived in large numbers on the scene. These were losses the IRA could ill afford: Collins at one time reckoned that he could field a maximum of only three thousand men. He was constantly badgered for arms and ammunition by IRA commanders, and by June 1921, owing to lack of guns and bullets, the IRA had resorted to burning unionist houses and property. A new British policy of saturating areas of IRA activity with troops and police had placed the IRA on the defensive.

When King George V opened the new Northern Irish Parliament on 22 June and appealed 'to all Irishmen to pause, to stretch out the hand of forbearance and conciliation, to forgive and forget', the moment was opportune. Lloyd George responded, glad of an opportunity to convince his Conservative coalition partners and the country that he was doing all he could to reach a satisfactory Irish settlement. He wrote a letter to de Valera 'as the chosen leader of the great majority in Southern Ireland', inviting him to attend a peace conference with Sir James Craig, the newly elected Premier of Northern Ireland. De Valera, after conferring with his own supporters and Unionists from north and south Ireland, and with the increasingly hard-pressed IRA's approval, agreed. A truce was signed and at mid-day on Monday, 11 July 1921, fighting between the IRA and the British forces stopped.

For several months negotiations dragged on between Lloyd George and de Valera and they eventually agreed on a Conference without any preconditions as to the unity or independent republican status of Ireland. Nevertheless, Craig after a meeting with Lloyd George declared that 'it now merely remains for Mr de Valera and the British people to come to terms regarding that area outside of that which I am Prime Minister'. On 11 October, led by Arthur Griffith and Michael Collins, a delegation of five Plenipotentiaries appointed by de Valera and the Dail to negotiate an end to the war met Lloyd George, Winston Churchill and other members of the British Cabinet at 10 Downing Street. De Valera stayed behind in Dublin, not (as his enemies later said) because he wanted to avoid being tainted by the compromise he saw as inevitable, but because he perceived the inherent weakness of the republican movement: that dogmatic republicans might split away at the first indication that the Irish republic for which they had fought might not be obtained. Still, as William Cosgrave, later to become the first Prime Minister of the Irish Free State, argued in the Dail, it was a pity to have 'their best player among the reserves'. Just before 3 o'clock in the morning of 6 December the Irish delegation signed their acceptance of an Irish Free State, 'faithful to H.M. King George V, his heirs and successors by law', and a partitioned Ireland, in the 'Articles of agreement for a Treaty between Great Britain and Ireland' — commonly called the Treaty. For the next seventeen years Irish Free State ministers negotiated with the British government the details of each article. These agreements technically constitute the Treaty.

Right until the end the agreement of the Irish delegates was in the balance. Lloyd George had successfully insisted upon the partition of Ireland as established by the 1920 Government of Ireland Act, and that the proposed twenty-six county southern Irish government would owe allegiance to the British Crown. De Valera had instructed Griffith and Collins that they should not agree to such allegiance or to partition. However, Griffith early on in the negotiations had personally and privately agreed to Lloyd George's suggestion of a Boundary Commission which would adjust the border between north and south, on the grounds that a fair-minded Commission would doubtless reduce northern Ireland so much in size that it would become unworkable. As a monarchist, Griffith was more wedded to the hope of a united Ireland than to the establishment of an Irish republic. Only hours before the Treaty was signed, Lloyd George revealed Griffith's agreement on partition to the startled plenipotentiaries, and Griffith announced that he, personally, would sign the agreement even if none of the others did. Then, as Sir Austen Chamberlain, a member of Lloyd George's team, later recounted, the Prime Minister declared that the agreement of each member of the Irish delegation was necessary and held up two envelopes, saying:

> I have to communicate with Sir James Craig to-night. Here are the alternative letters I have prepared, one enclosing the Articles of Agreement reached by His Majesty's Government and yourselves, the other saying that the Sinn Fein representatives refuse the oath of allegiance and refuse to come within the Empire. If I send this letter it is war — and war in three days! Which letter am I to send?

Together with Griffith and his colleagues, Collins signed. Then, before going to bed, he sat down and wrote to a friend: 'Think, what have I got for Ireland? Something she has wanted these past seven hundred years. Will anyone be satisfied at the bargain? Will anyone? I tell you this: early this morning I signed my death warrant.'

Men and women in Downing Street praying for peace during the Treaty negotiations, November 1921

Michael Collins (1890–1922): a still from a ten-minute film he made secretly in October 1919 to help raise money for the Dail Loan. He is standing on the steps of St Enda's School with Robert Emmet's execution block in front of him.

In the country as a whole, people were delighted by the prospect of a permanent peace offered by the Treaty. However, the oath they had taken to their republic weighed heavily with those who had fought for it, and one by one all the groups in the national movement split, the majority opposing the Treaty in every organization except the Dail. The IRB, pledged since its formation sixty-four years earlier to an Irish republic, and now headed by Collins, advised its members to make up their own minds. In the Dail the split became emotional and bitter as the debates went on. Collins argued the case for the Treaty on pragmatic grounds, that it gave freedom and security in the form of the Irish Free State. He also emphasized that the history of Ireland was not, as so many people had it, one of constant armed resistance, but of 'peaceful penetration . . . It has not been a struggle for the ideal of freedom for 750 years symbolized in the name Republic. It has been a story of slow, steady economic encroach by England . . . Nobody notices, but that is the thing that has destroyed our Gaelic civilization.' The Treaty, he was convinced, gave Ireland a unique opportunity to halt this penetration, and on these grounds urged its acceptance.

De Valera countered with an alternative Treaty of his own, 'Document No. 2'. In it he proposed 'External Association', whereby the King would be recognized only as head of the Commonwealth, with no oath of allegiance. Partition and the other substantive points of the Treaty were incorporated in de Valera's Document, which, however, was defeated in the Dail debates. He then argued that if the Treaty was accepted, the republic would be lost and Ireland would have only the freedom and security that Britain would allow. He gave a comparison from his own days in prison to make this point:

> *When I was in prison in solitary confinement our warders told us that we could go from our cells into the hall, which was about fifty feet by forty. We did go out from the cells to the hall, but we did not give our word to the British jailer that he had the right to detain us in prison because we got that privilege ... Rather than sign a document which would give Britain authority in Ireland, they should be ready to go into slavery until the Almighty had blotted out their tyrants.*

Hardly a word was said on either side about partition, and the arguments centred on the issue of the oath, the Crown and the republic.

On 7 January 1922 the Dail accepted the Treaty by a vote of sixty-four to fifty-seven. De Valera broke down in tears and resigned as President of the Irish Republic and head of the Dail Government. He was succeeded by Arthur Griffith. On 14 January, under the terms of the Treaty, a new government — the Provisional Government of Ireland — was formed with Collins as its Chairman to take over the British administration of Ireland until the Irish Free State could be constitutionally established. At this point, the positions of the various factions became complicated. The Dail, now led by Arthur Griffith, had decided to accept the Treaty. But the Treaty established the bi-cameral Parliament of Southern Ireland set up by the 1920 Government of Ireland Act as the sole legitimate parliament, and so the Dail was no longer a valid constitutional assembly as far as supporters of the Treaty were concerned. Despite a natural reluctance to admit this fact, Arthur Griffith accepted it and the Provisional Government and Dail Cabinet were so arranged that they consisted almost of the same people. The two governments ran side by side, sharing meetings and responsibilities and rarely clarifying the difference between them. Griffith became Collins' deputy in the Provisional Government (which was answerable only to Westminster), while remaining head of the Dail Government of the Irish Republic. For de Valera and opponents of the Treaty, the Dail Government was the only authority they recognized, and they subsequently refused to attend meetings of the Parliament of Southern Ireland, to obey decisions made in the name of the Provisional Government, or to take the oath of allegiance to the King.

Very few people who had been involved on the Irish side during the war with Britain regarded the Treaty as a victory. Michael Collins himself regarded the Treaty as a 'stepping stone', as a means of 'going forward to our ideal of a free independent Ireland'. Yet as the spectre of civil war began to loom large he wondered if it was worth it. Ever since 1920 there had been increasingly violent attacks by Orangemen on Catholics in Belfast, culminating in over 250 deaths in the first six months of 1922, and Collins became more and more frustrated by his inability to do anything about these killings, on one occasion declaring to a group of northern IRA officers that 'Lloyd George can have his bloody Treaty' unless the attacks stopped. Indeed, he went even further and arranged to send guns which his Provisional Government obtained from the British to the IRA in Dublin to replace their weapons being used by IRA men in the north: not the action of a committed supporter of the Treaty. To de Valera and the overwhelming majority of the IRA, the Treaty was a betrayal of the republic they had fought for. As the new Provisional Government began to recruit a new army, the National Army, of its own, often from ex-British army men, their attitude hardened.

As 1922 wore on, the IRA refused to accept the authority of their chief-of-staff, Mulcahy, who as Minister of Defence in both the Provisional and Dail cabinets tried to assert governmental control over them, citing the 1919 oath members of the Dail and the IRA had taken 'to defend the Irish Republic and the Government of the Irish Republic which is Dail Eireann'. Arguing that as far as the IRA were concerned the oath had ceased to operate once the Dail accepted the Treaty and thereby renounced the Irish republic; that they had not approved Mulcahy's appointment as their constitution entitled them to do, and that their loyalty was only to the Irish republic and to their own Executive, the IRA elected Liam Lynch to succeed Mulcahy. Lynch had organized and commanded what became the IRA's First Southern Division with headquarters in Cork. A tall, studious, shy man with a strong religious bent, Lynch now became the focus of attention as the IRA proceeded to repudiate their allegiance to the Dail on the grounds that it had ignored the oath to the republic, and declared once again that their own Executive was the only body whose authority they would recognize. As people waited to see if Lynch would start the fight for the republic once more, this time against Collins, a minority IRA group for whom Lynch was too cautious broke away and occupied the Four Courts in Dublin. There was sporadic fighting in Dublin and around the country. Finally, events came to a head.

On Thursday, 22 June, Sir Henry Wilson was murdered on the steps of his home in Eaton Square, London, by two IRA gunmen. While today we know that they probably acted at Collins' behest, implementing an order he had given to them possibly only weeks before, at the time it was thought that the Four Courts IRA were responsible. The following Monday one of the Four Courts men was arrested by soldiers of the Provisional Government, and in retaliation the IRA captured the deputy chief-of-staff of the National Army. At 4.07 am on the morning of 28 June, with 18-pounder guns borrowed from the British army earlier that night, Collins' men opened fire on the Four Courts and the civil war began in earnest.

During the previous weeks the IRA had occupied most of the provincial barracks evacuated by the British, and all over the country ill-disciplined bands had been holding up banks, raiding shops and behaving in a generally lawless manner. Frequent although unsuccessful attempts had been made to patch up the differences between the pro- and anti-Treaty sides, and Collins and de Valera even agreed to an electoral pact for the twenty-six county general elections to be held on 16 June, by which a panel of Sinn Fein candidates was divided between the two sides in such a

245

way as to preserve the *status quo*. Four days before the poll Collins, in the eyes of de Valera, broke this pact by asking the electors of Cork 'to vote for the candidate you think best of'. When the results came in there was a clear majority for the Treaty Party — fifty-eight seats to thirty-six — and the anti-Treaty share of votes and seats was nearly halved. With some justice, Collins and his supporters came to see themselves as defending democracy: but then, as republicans pointed out, no one had voted for the rising or the 1919–21 troubles which had produced the position Collins was now defending. Before the elected candidates could take their seats in whatever assembly they chose, the Dail or the Parliament, the fighting which had started in Dublin had spread to the rest of the country.

De Valera personally had been opposed to returning to the gun, but as he was no longer President of the Republic or even head of the Dail Government, his views no longer carried much weight with the IRA. All along he urged peaceful opposition to the Treaty, but events swept him aside. After the Four Courts attack, he re-enlisted as a private in the Third Battalion Dublin Brigade IRA, and Liam Lynch in Cork came to lead the republican side in the civil war. Six weeks later, Arthur Griffith died of a brain haemorrhage. After attending the funeral, Collins journeyed to Cork where, on 22 August during an ambush at a place called Beal na mBlath, on a misty evening, he was killed by a bullet in his head. He had apparently been trying to make contact with Lynch to try to put a stop to the war, but his death ended hope of an early peace. Thirty-six years later in his play *The Hostage*, Brendan Behan summed up perhaps best of all the mixture of emotions that surrounded Collins in life and in death:

> *'Twas on an August morning, all in the morning hours,*
> *I went to take the warming air all in the month of flowers,*
> *And there I saw a maiden and heard her mournful cry,*
> *Oh, what will mend my broken heart, I've lost my Laughing Boy.*
> *So strong, so wide, so brave he was, I'll mourn his loss too sore*
> *When thinking that we'll hear the laugh or springing step no more.*
>
> *Ah, curse the time, and sad the loss my heart to crucify,*
> *That an Irish son, with a rebel gun, shot down my Laughing Boy.*
> *Oh, had he died by Pearse's side, or in the GPO,*
> *Killed by an English bullet from the rifle of the foe,*
> *Or forcibly fed while Ashe lay dead in the dungeons of Mountjoy,*
> *I'd have cried with pride at the way he died, my own dear Laughing Boy.*

One maiden who was an abject admirer of Collins, Lady Lavery, the wife of the distinguished portrait painter Sir John Lavery, had had a premonition of her hero's death. Her husband remembered her saying:

> *'All day I have been seeing them carrying Michael covered with blood. Wherever I go I cannot get rid of the sight.' I got her to bed and sat with her until well into the night, and at last she went to sleep. At seven in the morning her very English maid came in with the tea. After she had put it down she said in a voice showing not the slightest trace of interest, 'They have shot Mr Collins, my Lady.'*

Within the next twelve months, seventy-seven IRA men were executed by the National Army firing squads, compared to the twenty-four executed by the British in 1919–21.

One of the first to be executed was Erskine Childers, who after 1918 became the most distinguished propagandist in the republican cause. Following his arrest, Childers had applied for an order of *habeas corpus* and appealed to the Dublin High Court. No judgement had been delivered when, at dawn on a November morning, he was shot on the authority of the Provisional Government. Three days later the IRA retaliated by announcing that the members of the Southern Parliament (which, confusingly, also referred to itself as the Dail) who had voted for the policy of executions might themselves be shot by the IRA. On 6 December, ten days after Childers' death, and the anniversary of the Treaty, the Irish Free State formally came into existence, replacing the Provisional Government. The following day, the Government of Northern Ireland exercised its Treaty option of contracting out of the new state and remaining separate. Also that day, Brigadier Sean Hales, a member of the Southern Parliament who had supported the execution policy, was shot down in a Dublin street. The next morning four leading Four Courts IRA men who had been imprisoned since June were taken out of their cells at Mountjoy Gaol and, without trial, shot 'as a reprisal for the assassination of Brigadier Hales'. More than any other event of the war, this seared the bitterness of fraternal strife upon the republican mind, providing future generations with reason enough to hate the new State and those who participated in it.

By now, the constitutional positions of the two sides in the civil war had become clarified. William Cosgrave, a founder-member of both Sinn Fein and the Irish Volunteers, had succeeded Collins in August 1922, becoming the first Prime Minister of the Irish Free State. He made it clear that as far as he and the pro-Treaty side was concerned, 'the functions of the Second Dail came to an end on June 30th ... The sovereign assembly of Ireland is now the Parliament elected in June last.' Technically, however, the Second Dail had never been suspended. On the republican side, the IRA Executive called upon de Valera to reform the Government of the Irish Republic which, since Griffith's death, had ceased to function in any form. De Valera was still urging the IRA to stop fighting, writing that the IRA and not himself or the politicians had to accept responsibility for the war: 'The Army Executive must publicly accept responsibility. There must be no doubt in the mind of anybody in this matter. This pretence from the pro-Treaty party that we are inciting the Army must be ended by a declaration from the Army itself that this is not so.' The IRA did not make such a statement, but instead reserved to itself the right to make final decisions. De Valera accepted this compromise and formed a new government with the republican members of the Second Dail, thus providing the republican side with a constitutional format. However, as the weeks went by the hopelessness of the republican cause became more and more apparent. Free State ruthlessness made it hard for the IRA men to find refuge and support, and the rapidly growing National Army with its modern equipment and ex-IRA leadership soon controlled most of the twenty-six counties. De Valera together with most of the IRA had to stay in hiding. Nevertheless, Liam Lynch was determined to fight on to the bitter end, even refusing de Valera permission to attend IRA Executive meetings on the grounds that he was preaching defeatism. On 10 April 1923, Lynch was killed in the hills near Clonmel in Cork; on 27 April de Valera and Frank Aiken, Lynch's successor as IRA chief-of-staff, published an order to stop fighting.

The IRA's unilateral cease-fire call was not acknowledged by the Free State government, and on 2 May two more IRA men were shot by a National Army firing squad. Three weeks later de Valera issued another message: 'Soldiers of the Republic, legion of the Rearguard: the Republic can no longer be defended successfully by your arms. Further sacrifice of life would now be in vain.' What was left of the IRA hid their guns and went home or emigrated. There was no formal end to the civil war, just as there had been no formal start. IRA men continued to be arrested and imprisoned without trial right into 1923, and in October, with over eleven thousand prisoners in gaols and camps, they started a mass hunger-strike in protest at their continuing detention. Forty-one days later, after several of their number had died, and after fierce hatred had divided those on strike from those who had given up or refused to strike, the fast was called off. Then, a few at a time, they began to be released. As the next decades were to show, many would accept their defeat, but many would also continue to fight for their republic.

The events of the seven years after 1916 were to dominate the political and cultural life of Ireland for the next fifty years. Hardly an Irish play or book would be written that did not look to this period for its inspiration. Politics in southern Ireland were to be dominated by two political parties with no doctrinal difference between them, but simply based on which side their supporters and, as time passed, their fathers, had taken in the civil war. Northern Ireland was to become the focus of IRA attack, and its society and politics increasingly began to reflect a siege mentality as the years wore on. Time and time again, the men and the myths of the Troubles were to be held out as justification for terror and violence, for votes and policies, and writers like Sean O'Casey, Sean O'Faolain and Frank O'Connor were left to develop a literature sadly reflecting on what had been and what might have been.

EPILOGUE

*'Desire some just war, that big house and hovel,
college and public house, civil servant — his Gaelic certificate
in his pocket — and international bridge-playing woman,
may know that they belong to one nation.'*

WILLIAM BUTLER YEATS, ON THE BOILER

The hopes of nationalists like Collins and de Valera for a reborn Gaelic Ireland were never realized. The civil war naturally prevented any immediate radical social or political changes after the Anglo-Irish Treaty was signed, and at the end of the civil war the Free State government and its supporters had clearly opted for conservatism. They wanted to govern Ireland in the British manner, with only the addition of Irish language requirements in education and the civil service. There was no attempt at social or economic reform. But the Free State leaders did succeed both in establishing their new state with popular, democratic support, and in forcing its acceptance on the anti-Free State politicians, many of whom had fought against it during the civil war.

In March 1926, de Valera split Sinn Fein for a second time by proposing that attendance at the Parliament of Southern Ireland should become 'a question not of principle, but of policy'. He left the Party, founding a new one — Fianna Fail ('a slightly constitutional Party' said Sean Lemass, one of its founders and forty years later de Valera's successor as Prime Minister), named after the same band of heroes the Fenians had chosen — and rapidly secured considerable electoral success, winning forty-four seats in the June 1927 general election while the Free State Party's representation slumped from sixty-three to forty-six seats. However, de Valera still could not bring himself to take the oath of allegiance to the King required by the Treaty, and in the midst of legalistic wrangling he and his supporters were turned away when they attempted to claim their seats. A fortnight later, on 10 July, Kevin O'Higgins, deputy leader of Cumann na nGaedheal (the Free State Party), Minister for Justice and acting Minister for External Affairs, was assassinated on his way to Mass.

Three ex-IRA men acting on their own initiative were responsible for the murder. They were never caught or officially identified. In the horrified reaction to O'Higgins' death, the government took strong action both to crack down on the IRA again and to compel Fianna Fail to enter the parliament or else to forfeit their places there. De Valera, already having recognized the Free State and seeing no way out, decided to take the oath and his seat. On 11 August he led his elected colleagues to Leinster House and, as far as the government and parliamentary officers were concerned, swore allegiance to King George V and his heirs and successors. Ever afterwards, de Valera and his supporters went to great lengths to insist that they had not, in fact, taken the oath, as Frank Aiken's description shows:

> Mr de Valera picked up the bible which was lying on the book containing the oath, carried it to the other end of the room, and placed it on the couch there. He then went back, signed his name on the line pointed out by the clerk, at the same time covering the writing above the line with some papers he held in his hand.

What was important was that Fianna Fail, representing much of the post-1916 Irish republican idealism, had at last brought most of the anti-Free State side into the Free State with, as de Valera was to demonstrate, Collins' stepping-stone approach to the Treaty as their policy. Cumann na nGaedheal after Collins' death had shown itself content to make the Treaty work as an end in itself, and so Fianna Fail had little competition. Five years later, in February 1932, Fianna Fail won the next general election with promises of removing the oath of allegiance to the King and ending the payment of land annuities agreed with Britain, whereby the Free State government was responsible for the payments to the British Exchequer required by the land reform legislation of the nineteenth and early twentieth centuries. Little attention was paid to the Cumann na nGaedheal's great achievement of re-establishing the rule of British-based law and administration at home. Nor was much thought given to the Irish Free State's leading role in channelling the development of the British Commonwealth into an association of free and equal partner-states, and in securing Dominion status for itself — the same status as Australia and Canada enjoy today.

In continuous power from 1932 until 1948, de Valera's Fianna Fail governments set about implementing the 'External Association' he had argued for during the Treaty debates of 1921–2. De Valera, mesmerized by the issues over which the civil war had been fought, was utterly determined to prove that the Irish Free State could be self-sufficient and completely independent of Britain. He downgraded the position of Governor General, the king's representative in Ireland. He removed the oath of allegiance from the constitution. He launched an 'economic war' with Britain by stopping the land annuities payment, forcing Irish farmers and industrialists to face retaliatory British import duties.

In 1937 de Valera unveiled a new constitution which, with amendments, has remained in force ever since. It changed the name of the twenty-six counties from the Irish Free State to Eire or Ireland (no mention was made of 'Republic'); provided for a President as Head of State (Douglas Hyde, the founder of the Gaelic League in 1893, was the first President); designated the Prime Minister 'Taoiseach'; declared the national territory to be 'the whole island of Ireland, its islands and the territorial seas' (much to Northern Irish unionist resentment, this clause has never been repealed), but, 'pending the re-integration of the national territory', the laws of the state would only apply to the twenty-six counties. A two-chamber parliament was restored (in 1936 de Valera had abolished the Senate because it had obstructed his anti-Blueshirt/IRA legislation), with a lower, proportionally elected house, the 'Dail', with full legislative power, and an upper, mostly appointed house, the 'Seanad', with only effective powers of delay. Article 44, which was to become the subject of controversy, recognized the 'special position' of the Roman Catholic Church as representing the religion of 'the great majority of the citizens', but at the same time guaranteed 'freedom of conscience and the free profession and practice of religion'. In a 1972 referendum, Eire voters overwhelmingly supported the removal of the section of Article 44 giving the church its 'special position'.

The results of de Valera's policies were mixed. The constitutional changes were calmly accepted by Britain, content to see Ireland remain within the Commonwealth. The economic war, on the other hand, not only helped make more permanent the border between British Northern Ireland and the south, but also had dire consequences for Eire. Unemployment soared as the Great Depression took hold worldwide and the British market (which until 1932 had accepted 85 per cent of Ireland's exports) became harder to penetrate. Between 1932 and 1938, industrial exports from the Free State fell by one-third, while agricultural exports were more than halved. In the same period, British exports to Ireland remained consistently higher than her Irish imports.

During the Second World War, although still a member of the Commonwealth, Eire remained neutral. Winston Churchill offered the possibility of a united Ireland after the war in return for Eire's participation, but de Valera adamantly refused, not convinced that Churchill could force unionists to agree to unity and seeing neutrality as the proof that he had secured effective independence for his twenty-six counties. In 1919 he had written that 'our whole struggle is to get Ireland out of the cage in which the selfish statecraft of England would confine her — to get Ireland back into the free world from which she was ravished — to get her recognized as an independent unit in a world league of nations'. So in 1939 he seized his chance to give effect to this view of Anglo-Irish relations. In 1945 he even went so far as to pay his condolences officially to the Nazi German Ambassador in Dublin upon the death of Hitler. 'So long as we retained our diplomatic relations with Germany,' he explained, 'to have failed to call upon the German representative would have been an act of unpardonable discourtesy to the German nation.'

Churchill, in his speech following the Allies' victory in Europe over Germany broadcast to the world by the BBC on 15 May 1945, insisted upon drawing attention to de Valera's policy of neutrality. He roundly declared that Britain could take pride in having 'left the de Valera Government to frolic with the German and later with the Japanese Representatives to their hearts' content' without laying 'a violent hand upon them, though at the time it would have been quite easy and quite natural'. Three days later de Valera gave a brilliant reply. While he probably enjoyed less than a tenth of Churchill's audience, the Irish leader touched his nation's consciousness, rebuking Churchill:

> *Could he not find in his heart the generosity to acknowledge that there is a small nation that stood alone not for one year or two, but for several hundred years against aggression; that endured spoliations, was clubbed many times into insensibility, but that each time on returning consciousness took up the fight anew; a small nation that could never be got to accept defeat and has never surrendered her soul?*

Three years later, Fine Gael (formed in 1933 as a successor to Cumann na nGaedheal), in coalition with the Labour Party and Clann na Poblachta, a new, ardently republican party, won the 1948 general election. The new government quickly showed that politics in Eire did not have to revolve around the civil war by tackling the social issues which de Valera, in his attempts to prove the strength of Irish sovereignty, had largely ignored. The great achievement of the coalition was its successful effort to eradicate tuberculosis, masterminded by the young and idealistic Clann na Poblachta Minister for Health, Dr Noel Browne. He mortgaged part of the future health-service revenue to raise the funds necessary to build, equip and staff the hospitals and clinics needed to fight the disease which regularly accounted for between three and four thousand deaths a year. Within a few years, tuberculosis had become a relatively infrequent illness, and had ceased to be the great killer-disease of Ireland.

The other major piece of health legislation that Dr Browne put forward, the Mother and Child Scheme, caused one of the most significant political controversies in Ireland. As part of his attempt to improve Irish health, Dr Browne determined to try and implement something approaching a national health service on the British welfare-state model. Being particularly concerned about the high level of infant mortality in Eire, he decided to introduce a scheme of free health care and education for mothers and children up to the age of sixteen. The Irish Medical Association opposed the scheme, arguing that it was 'socialist' and by introducing a state interest in patients would interfere with the doctor–patient relationship. As in Britain, where the medical profession employed the same arguments in opposing the National Health Service, these arguments could have been overcome. But Browne also faced the opposition of the Catholic hierarchy, who wrote to the Fine Gael Taoiseach John A. Costello that in their opinion the scheme threatened the sanctity of the family. In the view of the bishops, the scheme would be

> *in direct opposition to the rights of the family and of the individual and are liable to very great abuse ... If adoped in law they would constitute a ready-made instrument for future totalitarian aggression. The right to provide for the health of children belongs to parents, not the State. The State has the right to intervene only in a subsidiary capacity, to supplement, not to supplant.*

Browne strove to allay the bishops' fears, telling Costello, 'I should have thought it unnecessary to point out that from the beginning it has been my concern to see that the mother-and-child scheme contained nothing contrary to Catholic moral teaching,' but to no avail. He refused to compromise on the free nature of the scheme and, denied the support of the Cabinet and his own party, he resigned from the government in April 1951, releasing the correspondence on the affair to the press. A month later, as a direct result of defections from Clann na Poblachta in support of Browne, the coalition lost its majority in the Dail, and in the ensuing general election de Valera won a majority.

The whole affair demonstrated the clericalist and conservative nature of the State, convincing Northern Irish Protestants, for example, that a united Ireland would be a Catholic Ireland. In an editorial on Noel Browne's resignation, the *Irish Times* pointed out:

> *This is a sad day for Ireland. It is not so important that the mother-and-child scheme has been withdrawn to be replaced by an alternative project embodying a means test. What matters more is that an honest, far-sighted and energetic man has been driven out of active politics. The most serious revelation, however, is that the Roman Catholic Church would seem to be the effective government of this country.*

De Valera continued to dominate southern Irish politics. He led two more governments (1951–4, 1957–9), and was elected President of Eire from 1959 to 1973. He died in 1975, aged ninety-two, in old age a loved and respected statesman.

In Northern Ireland, sectarian differences had abated by 1951 and Unionist governments had proven effective in guarding unionist interests. In practical terms, the social and political development of the two states of Ireland since 1921 had taken place in isolation from one another. Apart from agreements about sharing electricity and cooperating over railways and postal and telecommunications services, Northern Ireland seemed happily unaware of its southern neighbour. But there was one other connection between the two states which was to have a decisive impact: the IRA.

For the IRA, defeat in the civil war was not taken as final. Always suspicious of de Valera, the IRA was not reconciled to the Free State by Fianna Fail, although the IRA's Army Council lent de Valera decisive support during his early election campaigns, helping Fianna Fail to develop one of the most effective and thorough political organizations in western Europe. As the 1930s progressed, however, a rift developed in the IRA between those who, especially after de Valera's 1937 constitution, believed that the best way to obtain a united independent Ireland was in cooperation with the Eire government, and a stronger group of those who believed that any Irish government (except one that the IRA would form) was a puppet of Britain and that the fight against Britain should continue until the IRA's objective of a thirty-two county Irish republic was established.

Despite his debt to the IRA, and his sympathy for their aims, de Valera after 1932 soon found that he could not tolerate a private, secret army with (since 1922) governmental claims of its own. Seizing the opportunity presented by the formation of the fascist-inspired Army Comrades Association ('Blueshirts'), de Valera cracked down on both them and the IRA, imprisoning many IRA men. When the IRA launched an abortive terrorist bombing campaign in England in 1939, de Valera took even stronger action, passing the Offences Against the State Act to ensure that, if the IRA tried an Irish campaign, they would be met with as much severity as the Free State had employed in 1922–3. During the 'Emergency' (as the period of the Second World War was called in Eire), de Valera's government executed six IRA men, allowed two more to die on hunger-strike in prison (another died in 1946, after the war), and shot three while they were attempting to escape or to avoid arrest. This harshness was justified by Fianna Fail on the grounds that unrestricted IRA activity against Britain, with Nazi German support, might compromise Irish neutrality and possibly even force Britain to invade Eire. To the IRA, however, these executions and deaths were the final proof that de Valera was a 'Free Stater', as willing to compromise the national ideal for the reins of power as W. T. Cosgrave and the Cumann na nGaedheal government of 1922–32 had been.

After 1945 the IRA slowly began to redefine its policy, clearly realizing that while its primary purpose was to concentrate upon forcing Northern Ireland into union with Eire, its secondary purpose was to develop a political philosophy for a united Ireland. In a misconceived attempt 'to take the gun out of politics', the Costello coalition government in 1949 unilaterally declared Ireland a Republic, outside the Commonwealth, hoping that the change of name would placate extreme nationalists. This action caught many Cabinet members by surprise: it was never fully discussed in Cabinet before it was announced by Costello at a press conference he held while visiting Canada. Thus the Irish Republic that exists today is really no more than the renamed Free State, its power and sovereignty having been fully obtained in the previous twenty-five years. The name change had no effect on the IRA, which continued to fight, and merely served to make more permanent the partition of Ireland. Before 1949, there was always the hope that within the British Commonwealth, Northern Ireland and Eire might one day unite peacefully. After 1949, when the connection with the Commonwealth was severed, Northern Irish unionists were even more estranged from Eire.

Northern Ireland was effectively a one-Party state, from its formation in 1921 right up to 1972, when Westminster closed down the Northern Irish parliament at Stormont and imposed direct rule in an attempt to control violence. Until then, the Unionist Party had provided uninterrupted government for fifty-one years. The sectarian rioting that had marred the first years of the new State died away as nationalists in Northern Ireland ignored the new Belfast government, believing it to be only a matter of time before Ireland would be united. Tension between Catholics and Protestants in the North relaxed to such an extent that in 1932 unemployed Protestants in Belfast demonstrated in support of unemployed Catholics who were attacked by the part-time 'B' Specials of the Royal Ulster Constabulary. The increased competition for jobs generated by the Great Depression (in 1933, for example, the Harland and Wolff shipyards did not launch a single ship), revived sectarian tensions once again, and in summer riots in 1935 eleven people were killed and six hundred injured.

During the war the Northern Irish economy, which in the nineteenth century had been one of the power-houses of the British Empire, once again expanded. The proud boast of Ulster unionists was, 'We find in Ulster the largest linen manufactory, the largest ship-building yard, the largest rope-making factory and the largest mineral water factory in the world.' By the end of the Second World War, Belfast ship-builders had launched more than 170 warships; Northern Irish farmers had doubled the area of land under cultivation and the government had provided training ground for 120,000 American troops. 'Without Northern Ireland,' said General Dwight D. Eisenhower, 'I do not see how the American forces could have been concentrated to begin the invasion of Europe.' Northern Ireland's participation in the war as part of the United Kingdom added another brick to the wall of partition.

After the war, the development of the British welfare state further strengthened the barriers between North and South. The National Health Service came into effect in Northern Ireland in 1948, providing free health care for the whole population, in contrast to the South. The same year saw the introduction of National Insurance in the North, providing greater social security benefits than existed in the South. But the most important legislation was the 1947 Northern Ireland Education Act, which for the first time provided grants and so threw open higher education to poor (and therefore Catholic) students. In the 1960s the first generation which benefited from these changes came to maturity and provided the impetus for the civil rights movement which culminated in the strife that has torn Northern Ireland apart. 'One man one vote' was the civil rights cry, as they protested in 1968 against the fact that in local government elections, apart from having a vote based on his residence, a man could have up to six more 'business' votes, depending on the number of firms he owned or held shares in.

Beneath this particular anomaly, however, the civil rights movement speedily became a vehicle for the expression of the simmering frustrations of the Catholic, nationalist minority in Northern Ireland. In obvious and hidden ways, Catholics in the North had been consistently discriminated against by unionists, who believed that they were all supporters of the IRA and all anxious to dismember the State of Northern Ireland together with Protestant, unionist rights, property and privileges.

In Londonderry, for example, while unionists were outnumbered two to one on the city council, they maintained a majority right up to 1968 by cleverly drawing constituency boundaries. In the Harland and Wolff shipyards in Belfast, without any obvious discrimination, hardly any Catholics had jobs. As one leading unionist declared in 1949, 'The Unionist Party should make it quite clear that it is loyalists who have the first choice of jobs. There is nothing wrong in this. Indeed, just the reverse; the Unionist Party was founded to further the objects of the loyalists.'

We can see now that the reforms that were instituted in Northern Ireland in the late 1960s and 1970s came too late. The result was horrendous violence, with the IRA reappearing with greater strength than at any time since 1921, and with Protestant paramilitary organizations sprouting up to protect — often by pre-emptive strikes — what they termed their 'Protestant way of life'.

The riots and demonstrations which began in 1968 were not inspired by the IRA, who, like the Northern Irish government, were taken by surprise. In 1956, the IRA had launched an abortive campaign against Northern Ireland. With men drawn almost completely from Eire, they tried to organize guerrilla columns in the six counties, but were quickly driven out by the combination of a broadly hostile civilian population and an efficient military and police force. In 1962 the IRA formally called off their campaign, and over the next six years its leaders decided that political rather than military activity offered the best hope of Irish reunification. During the same period, they also decided that the IRA would strive for a socialist republic.

When the violence flared up in the North, the more traditionally minded (and more numerous) members of the secret army, with the active encouragement and financial support of senior Ministers in the then Fianna Fail government in Dublin, broke away from the official IRA leadership in December 1969, forming the Provisional IRA. Its immediate purpose was to defend Northern Irish Catholics under attack in Belfast and Londonderry. The Provisionals' supporters believed that there would be a holocaust in the North unless they intervened. The Official IRA argued that by intervening the Provisionals would ensure that the conflict in Northern Ireland would become sectarian. They were right.

BIBLIOGRAPHY

The trouble with lists, I think, is that they are so often repetitive and, when long, offer a daunting prospect of further labour. So, while I have drawn on all the following books, I have not listed every book I have used. My comments are subjective, brief and intended to ease the burden of labour by referring to publications which are generally available and by attaching remarks which may facilitate choice. Sources which lend themselves primarily to research purposes are largely left out. Apart from the works of general survey with which I start, I have tried to group the rest in a chronological relationship to my chapters.

Very few books cover the whole range of Ireland's past. R. Dudley Edwards, *A New History of Ireland* (Dublin, 1975), is an informative and at times stimulating romp from the beginnings to the most recent troubles. His daughter, Ruth Dudley Edwards, has provided in the *Atlas of Irish History* (London, 1973) a most useful account of what has happened on the land of Ireland. Giovanni Costigan, *A History of Modern Ireland* (New York, 1969), provides a sketch of earlier times, is full of contentiousness and has a strong nationalistic bias. Brian de Breffny, *Heritage of Ireland* (London, 1968), covers the centuries up to the nineteenth with colourful detail.

De Breffny has written or had a hand in most of the books dealing with cultural history: *Castles of Ireland* (London and New York, 1977); *The Land of Ireland* (London and New York, 1979); as editor, *The Irish World* (London and New York, 1977); with R. ffolliott, *The Houses of Ireland* (London and New York, 1975), and with G. Mott, *The Churches and Abbeys of Ireland* (London and New York, 1976). Into this de Breffny fiefdom, few have entered, but Desmond Guinness and W. Ryan, *Irish Houses and Castles* (London, 1971), and J. Sheehy, *Discovering Ireland's Past, the Celtic Revival* (London, 1979), provide different illustrations and opinions of value.

The modern period is covered by some excellent general surveys, notably by F. S. L. Lyons, *Ireland since the Famine* (London, 1971), which is a miraculous combination of academic erudition and good writing. The pages flew by as I read Lyons, and I was amazed by the sheer volume of information he had piloted me through with apparently effortless ease. J. C. Beckett, *The Making of Modern Ireland, 1603–1923* (London, 1966), is a readable, objective and learned account of three hundred years, but it ends just a bit too soon, before the conflicts of the early 1920s are clearly resolved. E. R. Norman, *A History of Modern Ireland* (London, 1971), while controversial and madly unpopular with Irish nationalists (and, indeed, with many Irish historians), is in my opinion one of the best and most stimulating books on Ireland, full of provocative opinions firmly based in fact. Howard Smith, *Ireland, Some Episodes from Her Past* (London, 1974), is an excellent, factual and detailed voyage through the three centuries up to 1972. Oliver MacDonagh, *Ireland: the Union and its Aftermath* (London, 1977), is a brief but valuable essay covering the period since the Act of Union. All of these have contributed to the themes and arguments I have developed.

Prehistoric, Celtic and early Christian Ireland are well served by books in print. This is the period of Irish greatness. Accordingly, from the time of the Gaelic revival in the nineteenth century, the centuries involved have been covered in some detail. Michael Herity and George Eogan, in *Ireland in Prehistory* (Dublin, 1977), provide a detailed summary of the archaeological discoveries about early life in Ireland. E. R. Norman and J. K. S. St Joseph, *The Early Development of Irish Society* (Cambridge, 1969), and Peter Harbison, *The Archaeology of Ireland* (London, 1976), together provide a fully illustrated and interesting introduction to early Irish society. F. H. A. Aalen, *Man and the Landscape in Ireland* (London and New York, 1978), traces the relationship between the first and the most recent Irishmen through the geography of the country, linking past and present in an original way.

Myles Dillon, *Early Irish Literature* (Chicago, 1948), is a nice introduction to the study of Irish literature, but the best introduction to Gaelic literature is still Douglas Hyde, ed. Brian O'Cuiv, *A Literary History of Ireland* (London, 1980). Hyde, who liked to be called 'An Craoibhin Aoibhinn' ('The Delightful Little Branch'), was a gentle, moderate man who was one of the first to study Irish literature and brought to the subject a passion of love and discovery which still makes his writing and extensive quotation so useful and interesting. The literary quotations I have used come from Hyde, or from these three excellent anthologies of Irish writing: Brendan Kennelly, ed., *The Penguin Book of Irish Verse* (London, 1970); Kathleen Hoagland, ed., *1000 Years of Irish Poetry* (New York, 1947), and

BIBLIOGRAPHY

David H. Greene, ed., *An Anthology of Irish Literature* (New York, 1954). Padraic Colum, ed., *A Treasury of Irish Folklore* (New York, 1954), is full of interest and insight as well as valuable information about Irish life and legend. The art of the early period is well documented by Maire and Liam de Paor, *Early Christian Ireland* (London, 1958), and their book is also the classic survey of this period. Ludwig Bieler, *Ireland, Harbinger of the Middle Ages* (London, New York and Toronto, 1966), and A. T. Lucas, *Treasures of Ireland* (Dublin, 1973), are beautifully illustrated and informative.

The period between the first Norman invasion and the last Stuart king, James II, is a time which is attracting growing academic interest, but has not yet spawned many general works. Vol. III of *A New History of Ireland* (Oxford, 1976), edited by T. W. Moody, F. X. Martin and F. J. Byrne, deals with the period 1534–1691 with scholarly authority, and is the standard work on Tudor and Stuart Ireland. J. F. Lydon, *The Lordship of Ireland in the Middle Ages* (Dublin, 1972), is quite a racy account of the rise and fall of the Norman-Irish. John Watt, *The Church in Medieval Ireland* (Dublin, 1972), is full of unexpected details about the religious community and its adherents.

R. Dudley Edwards, *Ireland in the Age of the Tudors* (London, 1977), is a trail-blazing work which convincingly clarifies the turmoil of the time. Cyril Falls, *Elizabeth's Irish Wars* (London, 1950), and Grenfell Morton, *Elizabethan Ireland* (London, 1971), both provide sensitive accounts of the Queen's reign in Ireland, with useful reference to documents of the period. Edward MacLysaght, *Irish Life in the Seventeenth Century* (Cork, 1939), is still a standard social history. The Anglo-Scottish plantations have been studied in detail, with their consequences. A. T. Q. Steward, *The Narrow Ground: Aspects of Ulster, 1609–1969* (London, 1977), is a wonderful book, giving masterly treatment to the development of northern Irish Protestant society. T. W. Moody, *The Ulster Question, 1603–1973* (Dublin and Cork, 1974), while essentially an essay, is a stimulatingly detailed coverage of the years since 1920. My chapters dealing with this period have drawn from all of these authors.

Eighteenth-century Ireland has been studied in depth. Its wealth of art and architecture has provided excellent material for modern books, and the complexities of its politics and society have been covered in detail. The problem with Georgian Ireland, however, is that the story of non-Ascendancy people was never documented properly. R. B. McDowell, *Ireland in the Age of Imperialism and Revolution 1760–1801* (Oxford, 1979), is the most recent survey, concentrating on the reign of George III. It is a masterpiece. McDowell brilliantly deals with his chosen period in intimate and fascinating detail. It is with humility that I point out that the non-Ascendancy Irish world only rarely intrudes in his narrative, although in this McDowell reflects the lack of relevant documentation. My treatment of the 1798 Rising is heavily indebted to his book and to the enduring classic by W. E. A. Lecky, *History of Ireland in the Eighteenth Century* (London, 1892). J. C. Beckett, *Anglo-Irish Tradition* (London, 1976), and Terence de Vere White, *The Anglo-Irish* (London, 1972), are both lively and informative works which give a great deal of colour to the tempestuous Ascendancy. Hugh B. Staples, ed., *The Ireland of Sir Jonah Barrington (1832)* (London, 1967), is one of the most pungent Ascendancy memoirs. It was written by an extravagant, observant, witty and intelligent man of the time two years after both Houses of Parliament had forced him into exile as a result of his misappropriation of Admiralty court funds. G. C. Bolton, *The Passing of the Irish Act of Union* (Oxford, 1966), convincingly clears up many of the misconceptions surrounding the act. Daniel Corkery, *The Hidden Ireland* (Dublin, 1924), is still the best study of Gaelic culture and society in this period, and one that I have leaned upon.

The nineteenth century saw the coming of age of modern Irish nationalism, a subject as popular with historians, poets, writers, and dramatists as with Irish people themselves. Robert Kee, *The Green Flag* (London, 1972), is an excellent account of the journalistic coverage and the contemporary perceptions of Irish events, blended with a healthy scepticism for the myth-making which so frequently colours Ireland's story. Two books with the same title, Lawrence J. McCaffrey, *The Irish Question, 1800–1922* (Lexington, 1968), and Nicholas Mansergh, *The Irish Question, 1840–1921* (London, 1965), are both thoughtful and thought-provoking works. Whatever T. Desmond Williams writes is worth reading, and the series of essays edited by him, *Secret Societies in Ireland* (Dublin, 1973), pioneered proper historical interest in this vital area of recent Irish history. Gearoid O. Tuathaigh, *Ireland before the Famine, 1798–1848* (Dublin, 1974), and Joseph Lee, *The Modernisation of Irish Society, 1848–1918* (Dublin, 1973), are both excellent accounts of their periods, full of interesting observations. E. R. Norman, *The Catholic Church and Ireland in the Age of Rebellion, 1859–73* (London, 1965), provides much of the material I have used on the church in the nineteenth century. James Donnelly, *The Land and People of Nineteenth-Century Cork* (London, 1975), through the exhaustive study of one Irish county, illuminates life in the country as a whole. Two excellent books on the famine, T. Desmond Williams and R. Dudley Edwards, *The Great Famine* (Dublin, 1956), and Cecil Woodham-Smith, *The Great Hunger* (London, 1962), fully document and discuss the tragedy.

BIBLIOGRAPHY

T. W. Moody and J. C. Beckett, eds., *Ulster since 1800* (London, 1955 and 1957), cover the social and political development of that province's troubled history. William V. Shannon, *The American Irish* (New York, 1964), deals with its subject with insight, detail and refreshing straightforwardness. Malcolm Brown, *The Politics of Irish Literature* (London, 1972), is a much-needed revisionist work on Irish literary lions and is complemented by Richard Fallis, *The Irish Renaissance* (Dublin, 1978), a useful survey of the Gaelic revival. F. S. L. Lyons, *Charles Stewart Parnell* (London, 1977), and Roy Foster, *Charles Stewart Parnell, the Man and His Family* (Sussex and New Jersey, 1976), are both comprehensive, well-written, informative and scholarly works.

Our own century abounds with books of all descriptions on Ireland. John A. Murphy, *Ireland in the Twentieth Century* (Dublin, 1976), is the best single book on the politics of the period after 1918, with a deceptively simple presentation of developments in both Irish States. D. H. Akenson, *The United States and Ireland* (Cambridge, Mass., 1973), despite its title actually surveys modern Ireland with perception and in considerable detail. D. W. Harkness, *The Restless Dominion* (Dublin, 1969), is a fascinating study of the unexpected and central role of the Irish Free State in the development of the British Commonwealth. The Earl of Longford and Thomas P. O'Neill, *Eamon de Valera* (London and Dublin, 1970), is the approved biography of the man who will doubtless be regarded as having made modern Ireland. The book is basically a shorter version of the more detailed Irish-language *De Valera* (Dublin, 1968), by Tomas (Thomas P.) O'Neill and Padraig O. Fiannachta. Both treat their subject with reverence, as does Dorothy Macardle, *The Irish Republic* (London, 1937). Despite its obvious pro-de Valera republican approach, Macardle's book is an invaluable source of information about the 1917–24 period, and I have used it fully. But for much of the information in my last chapters I have depended upon my own research and unpublished material in public and private archive collections.

For those who would like more of the background to the present Northern Irish troubles, Paul Arthur, *Government and Politics of Northern Ireland* (London, 1980) gives an excellent account. J. Bowyer Bell's *The Secret Army: a History of the IRA 1916–79* (Dublin, 1979), is an authoritive study of this subject. Owen Dudley Edwards, *The Sins of Our Fathers: Roots of Conflict in Northern Ireland* (Dublin, 1970), is a provocative *cri de coeur*.

Finally, Henry Boylan, *A Dictionary of Irish Biography* (Dublin, 1978), is a source book of value and interest which I have relied upon for much biographical material.

INDEX

note: page numbers in italics refer to illustrations

ACKNOWLEDGEMENTS

Illustrations have been reproduced by kind permission of the following:

The Reverend Wm P. Allen, Christian Brothers, O'Connell School, Dublin 160, 228 (bottom), 229 (all), 233 (right), 237;
Anvil Press, Dublin 236 (both);
The Armagh County Museum (photo: The Allison Studio, Armagh) 143;
BBC Hulton Picture Library 11, 83 (right), 93, 105, 152, 155 (both), 158, 168, 183 (right), 195, 196 (left), 198 (Shaw, Wilde, Synge, O'Casey), 201, 206 (below), 238;
The Board of Trinity College, Dublin (photos: The Green Studio Ltd) 6, 51;
The British Library (photo: John Freeman Group) 102–3;
The British Library, Newspaper Library, Colindale 169, 170;
Cambridge University Collection (copyright reserved) 24;
J. Allan Cash Ltd 125;
J. Cashman 206, 245;
Central Press Photos 242 (left);
Commissioners of Public Works, Ireland 17, 20 (left), 21, 49, 55, 62 (bottom);
M.C. Connor, Killiney, Co. Dublin 210;
Dolmen Press, Dublin 46 (right);
The Franciscan Fathers, Dun Muire, Killiney, Co. Dublin 112;
Mary Evans Picture Library 135;
The Green Studio Ltd 70;
Imperial War Museum 208 (left);
Irish Tourist Board 15, 41, 54, 63;
Kelly Daly Ltd, Dublin 69;
Leeds City Art Gallery 138 (bottom);
Library of Congress, Washington, D.C. 172 (both);

Mansell Collection 182, 196 (right);
The Marquis of Tavistock and the Trustees of the Bedford Estates 85 (left);
George Mott 20 (right), 33, 72, 80, 83 (left), 114, 123, 124;
The National Gallery of Ireland 91, 94 (left), 110–11, 156 (bottom), 183 (left);
National Library of Ireland 64, 65, 85 (right), 137 (both), 179, 184, 187, 192, 194, 200, 215 (both), 216 (right), 228 (top), 230, 233, 242 (right);
National Museum of Ireland 16, 34 (both), 52 (both), 56, 58 (bottom), 61 (both), 82, 95, 119, 127 (left), 134, 147, 153, 164, 216 (left), 220 (bottom), 233, 239, 246;
National Museum of Ireland (Breandan O'Riordain) 58 (top);
The Trustees of the National Portrait Gallery, London 79, 127 (right), 198 (Joyce);
Pix Photos (photo: G.F. Allen) 2;
Press Association 221;
Public Records Office, London 87;
Royal Irish Academy (photo: The Green Studio Ltd) 46;
S & G Press Agency Ltd 220 (top right);
Source Photographic Archives 37, 220 (top left), 227 (right);
Colonel L.G. Stopford Sackville, Kettering (photo: Eileen Tweedy) 138 (top);
Major-General Joseph Sweeney, Dublin 225;
Tate Gallery (photo: Eileen Tweedy) 88;
Topix 235 (left);
Rod Tuach 43;
Ulster Museum, Belfast 156 (top), 161, 190, 191.

Quotations in the text:

Page 11 from *Song of Summer* and page 32 from *Voyage of Bran* translated by Kuno Meyer; page 98 'Woe to the Gael' from *The Flight of the Earls* translated by Robin Flower; page 129 from *Brightness of Brightness* and page 131 from *The Midnight Court* translated by Frank O'Connor; page 141 from *Getting Married*, page 165 from *Man and Superman* and page 197 from the introduction to *John Bull's Other Island* by George Bernard Shaw © The Society of Authors on behalf of the Bernard Shaw Estate; pages 41, 188, 199 and 250 from writings and speeches including *United Ireland* and *On The Boiler* by William Butler Yeats; pages 187 and 219 from *Portrait of the Artist as a Young Man* by James Joyce published by Jonathan Cape Ltd and in the U.S.A. by Viking Press, Inc., acknowledgement also due to the executors of the James Joyce Estate; page 217 from *Seventy Years Young* by the Countess of Fingall © Wm. Collins, Sons & Co. Ltd.; page 247 from *The Hostage* by Brendan Behan © Theatre Workshop, Stratford, London; page 247 from *Life of a Painter* by Sir John Lavery published by Cassells.